# SCOTTISH
# TRADITION

# SCOTTISH TRADITION

## A Collection of
## Scottish Folk Literature

Edited by

David Buchan

*Professor of Folklore*
*Memorial University of Newfoundland*

Routledge & Kegan Paul
London, Boston, Melbourne and Henley

First published in 1984
by Routledge & Kegan Paul plc

39 Store Street, London WC1E 7DD, England

9 Park Street, Boston, Mass. 02108, USA

464 St Kilda Road, Melbourne,
Victoria, 3004, Australia and

Broadway House, Newtown Road,
Henley-on-Thames, Oxon RG9 1EN, England

Set in 10/12 pt VIP Bembo by
Inforum Ltd, Portsmouth
and printed in Great Britain by
T.J. Press (Padstow) Ltd,
Padstow, Cornwall

Library of Congress Cataloging in Publication Data

Scottish tradition.
Bibliography: p.
Includes indexes.
1. Folk literature, Scottish.  2. Folk literature,
Scottish—History and criticism.   I. Buchan,
David, 1939–
GR144.S37  1984    398.2'09411      83–13754

British Library CIP available

ISBN 0-7100-9531-7

# CONTENTS

v

# FOLK LITERATURE

## INTRODUCTION

The term 'folk literature' poses certain problems, largely because of this word 'folk'. In popular usage the word tends to be applied to anything old, or earthy or couthy or even, in the Scottish context, vernacular. This batch of connotations casts a fine haze of imprecision over any attempt to employ it in a compound with pretensions to scholarly exactitude. Here, however, it is used in a precise sense as an adjective denoting 'of traditional culture'. Customarily one distinguishes three segments along the cultural spectrum: high culture, popular culture, and folk culture, three overlapping but distinct areas. Of these, folk or traditional culture is the culture maintained and transmitted by word of mouth and by customary practice rather than by written or printed document. Folk literature, therefore, is the literature of traditional culture, that is, the literature perhaps created by but certainly transmitted by word of mouth rather than written or printed document; it is the literature of tradition as distinct from the literature of print. (To differentiate between the two is, of course, in no way to ignore their various interrelations.)

Tradition, however, has two stages, what one might call the preliterate and the postliterate or the preindustrial and the postindustrial. In the first stage, the time of general nonliteracy before the Industrial Revolution, word of mouth tradition pervaded the life of all the people who could not read and write: it was, in a quite encompassing sense, their means of both 'instruction and delight'. In the second stage, the time of general literacy after the Industrial Revolution, word of mouth tradition had many of its functions gradually taken over by print, writing and 'official' education, but it continued adaptively within its contracted range, retaining older material and creating new, and becoming increasingly the carrier of

1

unofficial culture. Earlier antiquarians tended to search exclusively for relics of the preliterate stage as evidence of folk tradition, but modern folklorists take both stages as their province, considering both historical and contemporary phenomena or, in the current terminology, adopting both diachronic and synchronic perspectives. Folk literature, then, consists of the literary and linguistic products of both preliterate and postliterate tradition.

Folk literature, it is somewhat startling to realize, has been the literature of the bulk of the Scottish people. In standard usage the term 'literature' means the literature of high culture, but that was the literature of only a relatively small proportion of the population before the days of general literacy, a proportion made up of those who not only could read but also had both access to and interest in the material. For most of the population the literature was that of oral tradition. In Scotland, as in Europe generally, mass literacy came in the wake of the Industrial and Agrarian Revolutions,[1] and changing conditions exposed people to other kinds of literature and new forms of social activity, which both diminished folk literature's importance and altered its nature, but the old patterns of behaviour persisted, adapted to the new situation. As society changed, so did tradition and its literature. It was only after widespread education, in the nineteenth century, that there appeared many local books written by 'old residenters' about their communities and districts, and often expressly designed to record a past or passing way of life, which give some indication of the patterns of behaviour which fostered the perpetuation of folk literature. Here is a scatter of accounts, all from the nineteenth century, which indicate the prevalence and sketch in some of the contexts of folk literature:

> In winter, too, we beguiled the long evenings with story-telling, ballad-singing, tales of bogles and witches (in which all devoutly believed); and to these the wandering beggar and the pedlar, always welcome guests, added other varieties of entertainment.[2]

> In the long winter evenings in particular, when the whole household was assembled round the ingle-cheek, the song was very frequent: the young men, as well as the young maids, gave it alternately. They had sometimes a fiddle, but there was no dancing; that did not consist with the tasks of the maids, or the general thrift of the establishment, though they all liked to hear a spring. The herd-boy, too, took this opportune time, in the

winter evenings, of perfecting himself in his whistle. The other lads, in the interim, mended their own shoes, or the shoes of the maids. At other times they played at games – of *the dambrod*, or at *the tod and the lambs*: or they told queer stories to the lasses, or propounded guesses [riddles] to them, or to each other. Then, at times, they amused themselves with wads [forfeits], which never failed to produce great merriment. They had always some ploy or other in hand, that called forth 'The long, loud laugh, sincere' from the gloaming-time till about eight at night.[3]

On looking back, the first great falling off is in SONG. This, to me, is not only astonishing, but unaccountable. They have ten times more opportunities of learning songs, yet song-singing is at an end, or only kept up by a few migratory tailors. In my young days we had singing matches almost every night, and, if no other chance or opportunity offered, the young men attended at the ewe-bught or the cows milking, and listened and joined the girls in their melting lays. We had again our kirns at the end of harvest, and our lint-swinglings in almost every farm-house and cottage, which proved a weekly bout for the greater part of the winter. And then, with the exception of *Wads*, and a little kissing and toying in consequence, song, song alone, was the sole amusement.[4]

A large part of the amusements of the inhabitants in the last century consisted in the singing of old songs and the telling of many stories both old and traditional. At all their feasts and merry-makings they delighted in dancing strathspeys and reels. Their instruments of music were the violin and bagpipe, but commonly the latter.[5]

But on song-singing, story-telling, and 'speering guesses', there was laid no restriction; and round the fire, heaped with peats and sticks, peals of song and laughter rang through the sooty rafters, and round the clay brace, and up the 'muckle lum' of the Scottish farmer's kitchen at the 'haudin' the kirn', as well as all merry-makings of the kind enjoyed by the peasantry of Scotland in the olden times.[6]

Jean Barden was pre-eminently the story-teller of Sillerton . . . . The miller had only two strings to his bow – the miller word and the water kelpie; the blacksmith . . . dealt chiefly with feats

3

of manly strength that he had witnessed; while the tailor and his apprentice . . . retailed pretty much the gossip that they gathered during their wanderings throughout the country . . . little Sandy Simms, the cobbler . . . [related] stories that very graphically brought out the pawky character of Scottish humour. But Jean operated in another field altogether – the horrible in what was human, and the blood-curdling in what was supernatural, being the commodities in which she dealt. Nor was her stock of these by any means limited, as kelpies, goblins, fairies, brownies, elves, ghosts, wizards, witches, and sundry others of a kindred nature, were to her household words . . . . Then, in addition melancholy songs and ballads, all invariably of a lugubrious character, and covering a wide field of weird literature, her vivid imagination, and her peculiar faculty of finding suitable words to express her meaning, would alone have made her remarkable in any community . . . . Jean, along with her husband and family, occupied a small cottage in the village square . . . . I see that kitchen now, just as I used to see it fifty years ago. There is only an earthen floor, and apart from the dim light that is supplied by half a dozen smouldering peats, the only attempt at lighting the humble apartment is by a splinter of fir root stuck in the link of a crook or chain that hangs in the chimney, and as one of these primitive candles is consumed, another is lighted in its place.[7]

These comments include references to many of the genres and sub-genres of folk literature, which conventionally divides into the four large areas of narrative, poetry and song, language, and drama. These areas are discussed in the introductions to the individual sections.

The nineteenth century, we have observed, saw tradition undergo quite substantial alteration, and a major feature of this process was the devolution of traditional material and practice from adults to children. Folk drama customs, for example, moved down from men to youths to children; the traditional rhymes that once gave colour and fibre to discourse in the adult community came, after a similar shift, to be known as 'nursery rhymes'. The most complex of the narrative genres, the Märchen or wonder tales, became relegated to 'nursery tales' or, outside tradition, were prettified and rewritten into children's fairytales. All of this led to the view, one that still lingers on, that much traditional material belongs in some absolute sense to the juveniles, a misconception that ignores the shift in generations of the nineteenth century. The value of historical perspective in this instance underscores the usefulness of seeing tradition in its two stages, the preindustrial and postindustrial. The oral tradition of the preindustrial nonliterate culture performed a different range of functions from the verbal tradition of postindustrial literate culture, when competing media and new channels of transmission materialized, and folk culture interacted more extensively with popular and high culture. In response to the transformed conditions, the part played by different genres in traditional culture also altered. Some genres, like the wonder tale and the classical ballad, declined; some carried on, and prospered; some mutations, such as the riddle-joke, emerged; and some new genres, like the modern legend, came to prominence. The assumptions underlying much antiquarian writing, that tradition belongs only to the past, and that the material of tradition, having begun in a state of excellence, inevitably declines, have been rejected by modern folklorists, for tradition is always with us, evolving and adapting to changing circumstances. Certain genres may decline in usage, but others emerge, and the traditional processes continue. For clarity of view, however, it is necessary to maintain a historical perspective on the evolution of tradition from the preliterate period through the transformations of the nineteenth century to the present day, and to see the individual genres in relation to their different social and temporal contexts. The survival of the wonder tales and the muckle sangs among a distinct sub-culture, that of the travellers, should not blind us to the fact that these major genres of oral literature have now passed from the general traditional culture of Scotland, any more than that disappearance should blind us to the contemporary existence of other genres.

Folk literature possesses a number of characteristics which demarcate it from the literature of high culture, a major difference being folk literature's multiformity. What this means may become clear through concrete exemplification. Writers often refer to 'the ballad "Marie Hamilton" ' or 'the folktale "Rashie-coat" ', but what precisely do such phrases denote? When writers refer to 'the poem "The Holy Fair" ', there is no dubiety: there is a recognized text written by a specific author. But with 'Marie Hamilton' there is no such hard-and-fast-ness: there are over fifty versions recorded from different sources at different times and places, and these versions have certain constants but considerable variation. What we have, in short, is a ballad-story that is multiform: it manifests itself in many texts. To isolate one version from many and discuss it as 'the' text of 'Marie Hamilton' without reference to the others clearly distorts the subject since each text has a value as record, whatever aesthetic fluctuations may exist among the versions; they all have to come into consideration before any useful generalization about 'Marie Hamilton' can be made. The choice of example was deliberate, for ballad criticism has seen a fair share of writing that has failed to recognize the ambiguities of the phrase 'the ballad', and the consequent necessity for bearing constantly in mind the distinction between, *and* the relationship between, ballad-story and ballad-text. Multiformity, then, means that a work (or item or piece; there exists no one suitable term for the multi-generic referents) of folk literature has an 'idea' or, to adapt a phrase of W.P. Ker, a 'platonic essence' which achieves different textual realizations. The constant components of the essence constitute, in folkloristic terminology, a type, and the different realizations of the type, versions or variants. To illustrate the relationship of type to versions in short compass is difficult, but the following international versions of a proverb-type may provide some indication:

A birde in the hand is worth ten in the wood (English, 1562)
Better a bird in the hand than a thousand on the house (Romanian)
Better one bird in the cage than four in the arbour (Italian)
Better a sparrow in the hand than two flying (Portuguese)
Better one bird in the pot than ten in the wood (Finland-Swedish)
Better a sparrow in the hand than a crane on the roof (German)
A sparrow in the hand is worth a vulture flying (Spanish)
A finch in the hand is better than a thrush afar off (North Italian)
Better a bird in the hand than ten doves on the roof (Low German)
Better a hawk in the hand than two in flight (Icelandic)
Better a sparrow in the pan than a hundred chickens in the pastor's yard (North Italian)[8]

This basic conception of type and version has a practical utility across the genres of traditional culture, from literature to custom, belief, and material culture with, for example, its house-types and plough-types.

Multiformity means that the student of folk literature must have a flexible attitude to the dimensions of time and space. One cannot pin a piece of folk literature down as an early nineteenth-century sonnet written in the Lake District. The same song may appear in versions of the fourteenth century as a 'medieval lyric' and in the twentieth century recorded in the field as 'folksong'.[9] The same story or motif may appear in a seventh-century BC Homeric epic and in a nineteenth-century regional legend attached to an Aberdeenshire weaver;[10] or in the *Odyssey* and, in the twentieth century, as a Greek saints' legend, a tale among fishermen in Maine, and, as a cited legend, in a novel about Scottish West Coast fishermen.[11] The platonic essence of an item of folk literature may manifest itself in different texts over a long stretch of time – two and a half millennia – and also over considerable distance in space.

Folk literature possesses certain organizational features which originate in the processes particular to traditional transmission and produce those structural characteristics which by their density so often distinguish folk from high literature. The classic statement on these features as they occur in the narrative genres was made many decades ago by the Danish folklorist, Axel Olrik, who distinguished what can be seen as four sets of characteristics: unitary, binary, trinary, and general.[12] The first set includes the tendency to concentrate on a single plot strand, a leading character, and one or more striking scenes. The second set consists of the various manifestations of apposition and parallelism: the omnipresence of polarizing contrast, the starting movement from calm to excitement and the final movement from excitement to calm, the customary limit of two characters to a scene, and the habit of presenting in any list of persons the principal one first and the one who arouses our sympathy last. This last relationship Olrik expresses in nautical terms as 'the weight of the bow' (*das Toppgewicht*) and 'the weight of the stern' (*das Achtergewicht*), and he points out that the centre of gravity of the narrative always lies in the *Achtergewicht*, using as example the ubiquitous importance in the wonder tale of the last attempt of the youngest brother. He declares in fact that the principal characteristic of folk narrative is the combination of *Achtergewicht* with the next feature: folk literature's pervasive tendency to marshal its material – characters, ideas, events, plots – in threes. The general characteristics of the folk literature text include an internal logic, much patterning and repetition, and unity of plot. Olrik intended his generalizations to apply to those genres with narrative elements, but some, such as those on the appositional and triadic characteristics, apply also to

7

non-narrative genres like the proverb. By and large, the features occur in less marked fashion in postindustrial tradition, because they owe their genesis to the methods evolved by the nonliterate performer of preindustrial tradition to cope functionally with the business of literary creation. Many of these characteristics are exemplified by the schematic narrative structure of 'The Black Bull of Norroway', the first tale in the folk narrative section (where S = heroine, H = hero, $S^2$ = false heroine, and W = washerwife):

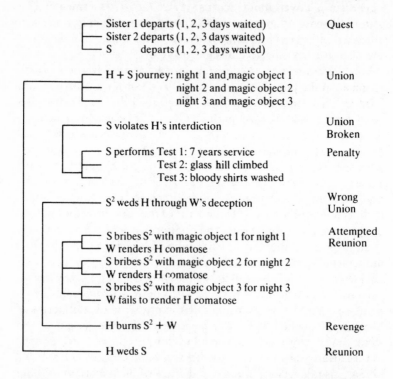

| | |
|---|---|
| Sister 1 departs (1, 2, 3 days waited) | Quest |
| Sister 2 departs (1, 2, 3 days waited) | |
| S          departs (1, 2, 3 days waited) | |
| H + S journey: night 1 and magic object 1 | Union |
| night 2 and magic object 2 | |
| night 3 and magic object 3 | |
| S violates H's interdiction | Union Broken |
| S performs Test 1: 7 years service | Penalty |
| Test 2: glass hill climbed | |
| Test 3: bloody shirts washed | |
| $S^2$ weds H through W's deception | Wrong Union |
| S bribes $S^2$ with magic object 1 for night 1 | Attempted Reunion |
| W renders H comatose | |
| S bribes $S^2$ with magic object 2 for night 2 | |
| W renders H comatose | |
| S bribes $S^2$ with magic object 3 for night 3 | |
| W fails to render H comatose | |
| H burns $S^2$ + W | Revenge |
| H weds S | Reunion |

The linguistic feature that first strikes the reader is likely to be the frequency of repetition, of words, of phrases, of sentences, and even of whole episodes. In folk literature there is no searching after linguistic diversity for its own sake, but instead an economical usage of the apt, the serviceable and the fitting, strictly subordinated to the main aim, the telling of a story, the capturing of an emotion, or the expression of a truism. Herein lies one of the main artistic differences between folk and high literature, for in the latter originality of expression ranks among the important virtues and repetitiveness or cliché among the grave defects. To stress the element of economical repetition in tradition is in no way to deny a delight in language itself, for that exists in full measure. The texts, of story, song, proverb or riddle, have a vigour, a directness, and a concrete vividness; they can be both precisely factual and soaringly fantastical, sometimes in the same sentence. They avoid linguistic superfluity but can dwell on the telling detail; they eschew psychological introspections but can embody in the narrative action or the proverb's phrase highly accurate perceptions of universal human behaviour. In the genres from preliterate tradition, the language may have the high stylization of the formulaic, in others it may have the lively jaggedness of heightened conversation. Even, however, after due allowance has been made for the differences in aesthetic canons between folk and high literature and for the way a good tune can transform an indifferent text, one has to admit that some texts are decidedly better than others, and inspire an interest more sociological and historical than artistic. But one should not be too ready to apply these judgments, for one has to bear in mind that folk literature, and indeed the individual genres, have their own aesthetic conventions that are not those of high literature.

Folk literature forms part of traditional culture and the study of traditional culture is the concern of a discipline well established by departments and research institutes throughout Europe and many universities in North America but largely disregarded in Britain. The variety of names that exist in English for the discipline reflects the fragmented nature of its British operations: (regional) ethnology, folklife studies, cultural tradition, folklore, and folkloristics. Empire-building countries like Britain and France preferred to study the primitive cultures of the empire rather than the indigenous traditional cultures, with the result that anthropology but not ethnology appeared in university curricula. In certain countries, in Scandinavia for example, one may find the discipline divided between two university subjects, one concerned with the material culture, the other with 'spiritual' culture. The subject has a particular value for small nations which have stood in a minority relationship to a larger and have been strongly affected by the language and mores of the majority culture, since in these cases it is often the folk tradition which has maintained the language and other distinctive expressions of the indigenous culture. Scotland is a case in point, twice over, for

Gaelic-speaking culture vis-à-vis Scottish, and Scottish vis-à-vis English.

The study of folk literature began with the early collectors of popular antiquities and accelerated in the nineteenth century with the pursual of field-collection, often inspired by the Grimms' activities, and the promulgation of some sweeping theories, often inspired by the Grimms' ideas. The end of the century saw in Britain some quite heated theoretical disputations in which the sanest voice belonged to Andrew Lang, the bellelettrist from the Borders.[13] Multiformity, we have seen, crucially differentiates the material of folk literature and print literature, and it involves problems of time and space, history and geography. It is, consequently, hardly surprising that the first widely accepted approach to folk literature focused on these factors: the historic-geographic method, also known as the Finnish method because its early practitioners were the Finnish folklorists. The aims of the historic-geographic method, when applied to a story, are these: to discover, through a study of all known texts, what best represents an archetype of the tale, the place of origin of the tale, and the routes by which it has been spread; as the scope is international, this is Comparative Literature with a vengeance. One aspect, then, of folk literature's multiformity is its internationality. Herein lies one of the most fascinating attractions of folk literature: it is both international and national at the same time, for while the platonic essence is international, the texts are national and regional. Careful comparative analysis of how different traditions realize the platonic essence can bring out and highlight the distinctive individualities of national and regional cultures.

While the historic-geographic approach is primarily a comparative method the more modern approaches, the structuralist and the contextualist, are primarily analytic and correlative. Structuralist works by writers such as Vladimir Propp and Claude Lévi-Strauss have shown illuminatingly how basic patterns of organization permeate not only texts but also genres.[14] There is a particular validity in structural studies of oral literature, for the structuring of oral texts holds the key to our understanding of them. It is readily understandable that a man who cannot read and write must organize a story in his mind so that he can remember it and control it in the telling. Structuring, then, has a specific function in the remembering of a story and composing of a text, and – as a direct extension of this – it affects pronouncedly the artistic character of the work.

The major approach of the past twenty-five years has been the contextualist, which emphasizes that a text must be seen in terms of the social group and the culture of that group. Recently a further emphasis has been added, an emphasis on the immediate context of performance, so that one studies a series of interactions between taleteller, audience and text, and observes how each is affected by the others. The sociologically oriented folklorists of the behavioural school hold, in fact, that the primary focus of study should be not the 'artefact' but the communicative process. Underlying the contextual approach is the premise that crucial to an understanding of a work and the values it transmits is its function or functions: its functions within the social group, the culture of the group, and the immediate event of performance. This concern with function, with the precise nature of the relationship between the literature and the society, is one of the hallmarks of modern scholarship in the subject.

The major approaches to folk literature embody two aims, aims that we can broadly call ethnographic and literary: that is, they are concerned with the relationship of the text to its culture and with the text *qua* literary text. In fact, the two aims are indissolubly linked since one cannot fruitfully consider a folk literature text as text without reference to its culture: the watchword of the discipline is 'text in context'.

By comparison with many countries in Europe, Scotland has rather neglected the serious study of the literature of tradition but the vineyard has not been empty. The earliest collectors, the writers of 'Colkelbie Sow' (an anonymous poem in the Bannatyne MS) and *The Complaynte of Scotland*, were collectors of titles, who provided lists, invaluable but tantalising, of songs, stories and dances. Of later field-collectors the literary figures and the ballad editors are quite well known, but largely unrecognized are such men as Thomas Wilkie, who recorded in the Borders, and Walter Gregor who collected in the Northeast and Galloway. The bibliographies indicate the major compilers and commentators in the different genres, but it would not be invidious to single out for praise the efforts of Robert Chambers who tried to furnish, although from a nineteenth-century antiquarian perspective, a multi-generic view of Scottish folk literature in his *Popular Rhymes of Scotland* from its first edition in 1826 to its revised fourth edition in 1870.

In Scotland there has been a long-running interaction of high and folk literatures; in fact, many of the best Scottish writers have been steeped in folk tradition. The medieval and early Renaissance writers show the kind of acquaintance with traditional material that one finds in other contemporary literatures, not surprisingly when one bears in mind that one of them, Sir David Lindsay, used to entertain his charge, the young James V, with the folktale of 'The Red Etin'. In later centuries, people reacted to a sense of encroachment upon the Scottish national identity by turning to the folk tradition, as did the antiquarian writers and editors of the eighteenth century, and Burns and Scott and Hogg, who both collected folk literature and utilized it extensively in the creation of their own work. Folk literature interacted with popular literature too, in a two-way interchange: the chapbooks and the broadsides derived material from tradition and they also sent material into traditional circulation. The interactions of folk with high and popular literatures offer fertile grounds for future research, as does folk literature itself, for not only are there still inedited manuscripts and the collectanea of the School of Scottish Studies, but there is also wide scope for field-collecting and for utilizing the conceptual advances of modern folkloristics.

This anthology does not include material from the Gaelic-speaking areas, which have, of course, a remarkably rich traditional culture of their own, so rich in fact that two-thirds of the holdings of the School of Scottish Studies derive from these areas.[15] This book is designed to provide a basic introduction to Scottish folk literature through exemplification of the various genres and sub-genres that have existed in tradition. Just as the genres should delineate what actually constitutes folk literature so the texts, representative of the genres, should illustrate the manifold relationships of the literature to the life; the intended result is an increased understanding of both the nature of folk literature and a substantial component of the Scottish cultural heritage. Supplementary aims have been to represent both preindustrial and postindustrial centuries and as many of the different regions as possible. The bibliographies and notes furnish ancillary information for those who wish to venture further in the subject.[16] Although the choice in certain sub-genres is relatively limited, the selection of texts generally has been guided by their intrinsic worth, their generic representativeness, their linguistic interest, and, because of the circumscriptions of space, by their being distinguished by brevity rather than length. The texts offer an intrinsic interest but also provide a focus for exploration of function and context, an understanding of which will, in turn, increase considerably an appreciation of both the work and its cultural matrix.

Folk literature affords both enjoyment and an insight into the imaginative sustenance of many generations. The study of folk literature, and folk tradition in general, has particular value in the Scottish context because, in quantitative terms, much of Scottish culture has been folk culture. For most of the people who lived in the preindustrial period, their culture was oral. With the Industrial and Agrarian Revolutions came the advent of general literacy, which is a traumatic event for any society but was for Scotland doubly so, because literacy arrived not in the native tongue but in English. Thereafter much – though not all – of that which was inherently Scottish in the native culture found uninhibited expression mainly in the postliterate folk tradition, because it was affected relatively slowly by the anglicizing effects of literacy. In short, in the preindustrial period Scotland's culture was transmitted for much of the population by preliterate folk tradition, and afterwards, Scotland's *Scottish* culture was to a considerable extent transmitted by postliterate folk tradition. The study of Scottish folk literature, then, can help crucially to further our understanding of the Scottish cultural identity, and further it, moreover, through a discipline that is at once national and international in its scope.

## Notes

1 Carlo M. Cipolla, *Literacy and Development in the West* (Harmondsworth, 1969).

2 An Old Farmer, 'Mode of Living among Scottish Farmers during the Early Part of Last Century' [signed Selkirkshire, June 25, 1818], *Scottish Journal of Topography, Antiquities, Traditions* (Edinburgh, 1848), II, 30.

3 George Robertson, *Rural Recollections* (1829), in *Scottish Diaries and Memoirs 1746—1843*, ed. J.G. Fyfe (Stirling, 1942), p. 281.

4 James Hogg, 'On the Changes in the Habits, Amusements, and Condition of the Scottish Peasantry', *Quarterly Journal of Agriculture*, 3 (1831-2), 256-7.

5 Robert Dinnie, *An Account of the Parish of Birse* (Aberdeen, 1865), p. 30.

6 Janet Hamilton, *Poems, Sketches, and Essays* (Glasgow: new ed., 1885), p. 362.

7 Duncan Anderson, *Scottish Folk-Lore* (New York, 1895), pp. 90-3.

8 Archer Taylor, *The Proverb and Index* (1931, 1934; Hatboro, Penn., 1962), pp. 22-4.

 9 A.E. Green, 'Folk-song and Dialect', *Trans. Yorkshire Dialect Society*, pt LXXII, vol. XIII, 27-35.

10 Hugh Gilzean Reid, *Lowland Legends* (Edinburgh, 1865), pp. 40-52.

11 Wm. F. Hansen, 'The Story of the Sailor who went Inland', *Folklore Today*, eds Linda Dégh *et al*. (Bloomington, 1976), pp. 221-30; Lillian Beckwith, *Green Hand* (London, 1967), pp. 48-9.

12 'Epic Laws of Folk Narrative' (1909), *The Study of Folklore*, ed. Alan Dundes (Englewood Cliffs, N.J., 1965), pp. 131-41.

13 Richard M. Dorson, *The British Folklorists* (London, 1968).

14 Vladimir Propp, *Morphology of the Folktale* (1928), 2nd ed. (Austin, 1968); Claude Lévi-Strauss, 'The Structural Study of Myth', *Structural Anthropology* (New York, 1967), pp. 202-28.

15 Alan Bruford, 'Oral History Material in the Archives of the School of Scottish Studies', *Scottish Oral History Group Newsletter*, no. 2 (October, 1979), p. 2.

16 For an encyclopaedia of the small narrative elements in international folk literature see Stith Thompson, *Motif-Index of Folk-Literature*, rev. ed., 6 vols (Copenhagen and Bloomington, 1955-8).

# 1

# FOLK NARRATIVE

## INTRODUCTION

Taletelling once occupied in Scottish life a position whose prominence may be difficult to comprehend in times when many media compete to provide entertainment and stimulation. It influenced both community life and family life:

> How stern and ample was the sway
> Of themes like these, when darkness fell,
> And gray-hair'd sires the tales would tell!
> When doors were barr'd, and eldron dame
> Plied at her task beside the flame,
> That through the smoke and gloom alone
> On dim and umber'd faces shone.[1]

What may strike us with particular force is the extent of the taletelling and the scope of the tale itself: 'My father could sit there, he could start at six o'clock in the [evening], he could finish at six in the morning . . . and he could tell one story to last that time.'[2] This is Andrew Stewart and Bella Higgins talking in 1955 about their father, John Stewart, and such a comment, made here about a Scottish travelling family which retained some of the habits of the old culture lost in the wake of education, literacy, and social change, can be parallelled from other traditional cultures.[3]

Folk narrative has been transmitted in Scotland for many centuries although, not surprisingly for a literature created through the medium of dramatic speech, documentation of its existence in earlier years does not abound, the most substantial evidence being the titles of traditional narratives in the list of tales to be found in the 1549 *Complaynte of Scotland*.[4] All the texts in the following section come from the last 200 years and, as will be readily apparent, they vary in

15

nature, for different kinds of recording techniques produce different kinds of text on the page. In the twentieth century the tape-recorded texts of the School of Scottish Studies provide word-for-word transcriptions of the actual tale told and also convey the flavour of the performance. The pen and paper method obligatory in the past can also furnish accurate transcriptions although the possibility of error is greater. Some of the older texts, like those supplied by Charles Kirkpatrick Sharpe from Nurse Jenny's repertoire, are recreated from memories of actual performance. Some make no attempt to recreate the spoken text but are in effect digests of the tale that seize on the narrative plotline. And in some texts the narrative essentials are reworked in a style and language deemed more acceptable for print. In the last two cases the procedure normally entails the narrative, if not necessarily the dialogue, being translated from Scots into English. The two versions (nos 3,4) of the same tale-type recorded in the Southwest at the beginning and end of the nineteenth century exemplify the difference between a text close to actual performance and a text containing a digest of the story. Infinitely desirable though it would be to have a selection composed entirely of meticulously transcribed spoken texts from this and earlier centuries, for a diachronic perspective on Scottish folk narrative one simply has to utilize the various kinds of texts that are extant.

How, the question may then arise, can one tell if a printed text actually belongs to folk narrative, if it has in fact been passed along by word of mouth? Frequently the context informs us of its traditional derivation, but often the indication is that the story belongs to the international body of folk narrative registered by the standard indexes. For the folktale the important international index is *The Types of the Folktale* first compiled by the Finnish scholar Antti Aarne in 1910 and twice revised and enlarged by the American Stith Thompson, most recently in 1961. This arranges the tale-types, summarizes their contents, allocates each a number and short title, and lists where each has been recorded and what has been written about it. The internationality of folk narrative material makes such a work indispensable; in place of lengthy plot summaries and swollen footnotes of parallels, folktale scholars need only refer to the number and short title in Aarne-Thompson. No.1 of this section, for example, 'The Black Bull of Norroway', is a version of AT 425 *The Search for the Lost Husband*. Area and national indexes supplement the international index, and that for Britain, excluding the Celtic material, is Ernest Baughman, *Type and Motif Index of the Folktales of England and North America*. Unfortunately the coverage of Scottish narrative in this book is less than satisfactory; of the twenty-four AT narratives in the following section which appeared in print before 1966 only two are listed by Baughman. A properly executed type-index of Scottish folktales is a great desideratum. For international legends Reidar Christiansen's *The Migratory Legends* provides, on the basis of the Norwegian material, a classification framework in which the numbering carries on from Aarne-Thompson, so that a scholar may refer to such a legend as the following no.45 from Burns's *Letters* as ML 3045 *Following the Witch*.

Folk narrative includes various kinds of tales which serve different purposes, demand different styles, and provide different enjoyments. The basic division distinguishes between folktale and legend, between fiction and ostensible non-fiction. The folktale category comprehends a number of genres, prominent amongst which is the Märchen or wonder tale, which is the kind of story most people are acquainted with in its rewritten and transformed guise of children's fairytale. The wonder tales involve a young hero or heroine undergoing a series of tests or tasks, often in a quest, that ends in a change of status: the young lad marries and gains land (he weds the princess and wins half the kingdom). These stories, with all their marvellous elements, enact in narrative form processes of psychic maturation for man and woman. The Märchen here (nos 1-7) include some of the earliest printed Scottish texts from the beginning of the nineteenth century, one from the late nineteenth century, and a long one recorded by field-workers of the School of Scottish Studies in 1976. In recent decades the School has recorded from members of the travelling folk many excellent Märchen whose length precludes a more substantial representation. The animal tale (nos 8-13) has not been found in any great numbers in lowland Scottish tradition and the religious tale (the term, like the former, is self-explanatory) even less so (no.14). Stray pieces of evidence, however, would suggest that the animal tale was at one time quite widespread. The novella (nos 15-16) is the realistic tale: 'the action occurs in a real world with definite time and place, and though marvels do appear, they are such as apparently call for a hearer's belief in a way that the Märchen does not'.[5] These stories generally concern themselves with cleverness, trickery, and the operations of a keen mind. After the novella in Aarne-Thompson comes a bridging section to the jocular tales

17

devoted to tales of the stupid ogre, represented here by a Galloway version of the Polyphemus story (no. 17).

Among the genres of the jocular tale is the numskull or noodle tale which deals in foolishnesses, often, as here in 'The Assynt Man's Mistakes' (no.18), ascribed to the people of a particular district or village. The 'most elaborate genre of humorous narrative' is the Schwank or merry tale which 'is a relatively long, well-structured, realistic narrative without fantastic or miraculous motifs. Its humour is obvious and easy to comprehend and the action is funny in itself without a punch line.'[6] The Schwänke here (nos 19-23) exemplify the description, though perhaps one should point out that while they do not contain the fantastic motifs found in Märchen their humour does often have an element of imaginative fantasy, seen here most particularly in the Angus tale (no.20). Along with the longer Schwänke is a compressed didactic tale from Orkney (no. 19) which occurs also in Scandinavia, France, Belgium, Hungary, Russia and the USA. Compression and reliance on the punchline characterize the joke (nos 24-28), a form which in tradition often derives its humour from the typifying attitude revealed by the climactic line. If succinctness characterizes the joke, exaggeration, together with a deadpan manner of telling, characterize the tall tale (nos 29-32). Although the tall tale may be thought of today as particularly American, once it existed widely and had firm habitation in Scotland. The formula tale usually contains a single idea or situation developed repetitively, and is represented by a relatively rare form, the dialogue story, in a tale from Edinburgh (no.33) noted by Aarne-Thompson as occurring only in Estonia and Romania, and by a cumulative tale from Aberdeenshire (no.34).

The legend is most conveniently defined as a prose narrative not told as direct fiction; or, to modify Stith Thompson's words, the legend purports to be an account of an unusual happening believed, by some people at some time, to have occurred. One cannot now-adays simply say the legend is a story told as true, for it can also be told within a frame of only partial belief or disbelief ('Well, that is what the old folks said, anyway . . .') though the teller feels some compulsion to repeat it. Broadly, there are six, often overlapping, categories of legend: aetiological (those dealing with the origins of things) (no.35), religious (no.36), supernatural (nos 37-48), historical (nos 49-57), personal (these are often anecdotes) (nos 58-59), and place (nos 60-62). Scotland is particularly rich in the supernatural and historical kinds. The modern legend (nos 63–65) is a story told as true circulating by word of mouth in contemporary society and exhibiting traditional variation. The tales normally deal with lucky or unlucky accidents, horrific or unusual events, and sometimes belong to the lore of a group such as students, but most móve widely through society.[7] These stories spread internationally in an astonishingly short time. It is the modern legend, the legend, the anecdote, and the joke which constitute the most active and hardy narrative genres of contemporary tradition.

It is possible to categorize the narratives of tradition from different perspectives when particular features of function, form, or content require to be stressed. The fable, for example, is a tale told with a conscious moral purpose: it frequently but not exclusively involves animals as characters (and just as not all fables are animal tales, not all animal tales are fables), and when it deals with human characters it is also called the moral tale. The cante-fable is a form where prose narration and singing intermingle (no.23). The hero tale is a term usually reserved, since so many tales have 'heroes', for one story in a cycle of stories that attach to a particularly outstanding and important character. The narrative categories should not of course be viewed as absolute watertight divisions, for considerable intermixing of the genres can occur: one story may be at the same time an animal tale, a fable, and an aetiological tale; no.50, for example, is both an international Schwank and a historical legend told about James V.

One genre whose absence may require a comment is myth. As Katherine Briggs has remarked, 'In Britain . . . Christianity has submerged the primitive mythical material so that it can often be discovered only in buried forms and by oblique hints. . . . The High Myths were swallowed by Christianity.'[8] Instead of the High Myths – 'sacred histories or expressions of symbolic truth', as she puts it – Britain has Secondary Myths, narratives with aetiological, cosmological, or eschatological elements which are often to be found in tales conventionally classified as aetiological legends, place legends, and Märchen; no.60 provides an instance.

What follows is a collection of texts of traditional material, and texts by themselves, however interesting, can afford only a partial reflection of tradition and its workings. But they furnish a focus for consideration of context and function, the taleteller and his audience, through which one can gain a deeper understanding of man and his culture.

## Notes

1 James Hogg, 'To Lady Anne Scott', *The Brownie of Bodsbeck*, ed. Douglas S. Mack (Edinburgh, 1976), p.174.
2 *Tocher*, no.21 (1976), 188.
3 See, for example, Linda Dégh, *Folktales and Society* (Bloomington, Ind., 1969), pp.82-4.
4 Ed. J.A.H. Murray (London, 1872), pp.63-4.
5 Stith Thompson, *The Folktale* (New York, 1946), p.8.
6 Linda Dégh, 'Folk Narrative', *Folklore and Folklife: an Introduction*, ed. Richard M. Dorson (Chicago, 1972), p.70.
7 For an extended discussion see David Buchan, 'The Modern Legend', in *Language, Culture and Tradition*, eds A.E. Green and J.D.A. Widdowson (Leeds and Sheffield, 1981), pp.1-15.
8 'Possible Mythological Motifs in English Folktales', *Folklore* 83(1972), 265-6.

## MÄRCHEN

## 1 The Black Bull of Norroway

In Norroway, langsyne, there lived a certain lady, and she had three dochters. The auldest o' them said to her mither: 'Mither, bake me a bannock, and roast me a collop, for I'm gaun awa' to spotch my fortune.' Her mither did sae; and the dochter gaed awa' to an auld witch washerwife and telled her purpose. The auld wife bade her stay that day, and gang and look out o' her back-door, and see what she could see. She saw nocht the first day. The second day she did the same, and saw nocht. On the third day she looked again, and saw a coach-and six coming alang the road. She ran in and telled the auld wife what she saw. 'Aweel,' quo' the auld wife, 'yon's for you.' Sae they took her into the coach, and galloped aff.

The second dochter next says to her mither: 'Mither, bake me a bannock, and roast me a collop, for I'm gaun awa' to spotch my fortune.' Her mither did sae; and awa she gaed to the auld wife, as her sister had dune. On the third day she looked out o' the back-door, and saw a coach-and-four coming alang the road. 'Aweel,' quo' the auld wife, 'yon's for you.' Sae they took her in, and aff they set.

The third dochter says to her mither: 'Mither, bake me a bannock, and roast me a collop, for I'm gaun awa' to spotch my fortune.' Her

mither did sae; and awa' she gaed to the auld witch wife. She bade her
look out o' her back-door, and see what she could see. She did sae;
and when she came back, said she saw nocht. The second day she did
the same, and saw nocht. The third day she looked again, and on
coming back, said to the auld wife she saw nocht but a muckle Black
Bull coming crooning alang the road. 'Aweel,' quo' the auld wife,
'yon's for you.' On hearing this she was next to distracted wi' grief
and terror; but she was lifted up and set on his back, and awa' they
went.

Aye they travelled, and on they travelled, till the lady grew faint
wi' hunger. 'Eat out o' my right lug,' says the Black Bull, 'and drink
out o' my left lug, and set by your leavings.' Sae she did as he said,
and was wonderfully refreshed. And lang they gaed, and sair they
rade, till they came in sight o' a very big and bonny castle. 'Yonder
we maun be this night,' quo' the bull; 'for my auld brither lives
yonder'; and presently they were at the place. They lifted her aff his
back, and took her in, and sent him away to a park for the night. In
the morning, when they brought the bull hame, they took the lady
into a fine shining parlour, and gave her a beautiful apple, telling her
no to break it till she was in the greatest strait ever mortal was in in
the world, and that wad bring her out o't. Again she was lifted on the
bull's back, and after she had ridden far, and farer than I can tell, they
came in sight o' a far bonnier castle, and far farther awa' than the last.
Says the bull till her: 'Yonder we maun be the night, for my second
brither lives yonder'; and they were at the place directly. They lifted
her down and took her in, and sent the bull to the field for the night.
In the morning they took the lady into a fine and rich room, and gave
her the finest pear she had ever seen, bidding her no to break it till she
was in the greatest strait ever mortal could be in, and that wad get her
out o't. Again she was lifted and set on his back, and awa' they went.
And lang they rade, and sair they rade, till they came in sight o' the
far biggest castle, and far farthest aff, they had yet seen. 'We maun be
yonder the night,' says the bull, 'for my young brither lives yonder';
and they were there directly. They lifted her down, took her in, and
sent the bull to the field for the night. In the morning they took her
into a room, the finest of a' and gied her a plum, telling her no to
break it till she was in the greatest strait mortal could be in, and that
wad get her out o't. Presently they brought hame the bull, set the
lady on his back, and awa' they went.

And aye they rade, and on they rade, till they came to a dark and ugsome glen, where they stopped, and the lady lighted down. Says the bull to her: 'Here ye maun stay till I gang and fight the deil. Ye maun seat yoursel' on that stane, and move neither hand nor fit till I come back, else I'll never find ye again. And if everything round about ye turns blue, I hae beaten the deil; but should a' things turn red, he'll hae conquered me.' She set hersel' down on the stane, and by-and-by a' round her turned blue. O'ercome wi' joy, she lifted the ae fit and crossed it owre the ither, sae glad was she that her companion was victorious. The bull returned and sought for, but never could find her.

Lang she sat, and aye she grat, till she wearied. At last she rase and gaed awa', she kendna whaur till. On she wandered, till she came to a great hill o' glass, that she tried a' she could to climb, but wasna able. Round the bottom o' the hill she gaed, sabbing and seeking a passage owre, till at last she came to a smith's house; and the smith promised, if she wad serve him seven years, he wad make her airn shoon, wherewi' she could climb owre the glassy hill. At seven years' end she got her her airn shoon, clamb the glassy hill, and chanced to come to the auld washerwife's habitation. There she was telled of a gallant young knight that had given in some bluidy sarks to wash, and whaever washed thae sarks was to be his wife. The auld wife had washed till she was tired, and then she set to her dochter, and baith washed, and they washed, and they better washed, in hopes of getting the young knight; but a' they could do, they couldna bring out a stain. At length they set the stranger damosel to wark; and whenever she began, the stains came out pure and clean, and the auld wife made the knight believe it was her dochter had washed the sarks. So the knight and the eldest dochter were to be married, and the stranger damosel was distracted at the thought of it, for she was deeply in love wi' him. So she bethought her of her apple, and breaking it, found it filled with gold and precious jewellery, the richest she had ever seen. 'All these', she said to the eldest dochter, 'I will give you, on condition that you put off your marriage for ae day, and allow me to go into his room alone at night.' So the lady consented; but meanwhile the auld wife had prepared a sleeping drink, and given it to the knight, wha drank it, and never wakened till next morning. The lee-lang night the damosel sabbed and sang:

> Seven lang years I served for thee,
> The glassy hill I clamb for thee,

The bluidy shirt I wrang for thee;
And wilt thou no wauken and turn to me?

Next day she kentna what to do for grief. She then brak the pear, and fan't filled wi' jewellery far richer than the contents o' the apple. Wi' thae jewels she bargained for permission to be a second night in the young knight's chamber; but the auld wife gied him anither sleeping drink, and he again sleepit till morning. A' night she kept sighing and singing as before:

Seven lang years I served for thee, &c.

Still he sleepit, and she nearly lost hope a'thegither. But that day, when he was out at the hunting, somebody asked him what noise and moaning was yon they heard all last night in his bedchamber. He said he heardna ony noise. But they assured him there was sae; and he resolved to keep waking that night to try what he could hear. That being the third night, and the damosel being between hope and despair, she brak her plum, and it held far the richest jewellery of the three. She bargained as before; and the auld wife, as before, took in the sleeping drink to the young knight's chamber; but he telled her he couldna drink it that night without sweetening. And when she gaed awa' for some honey to sweeten it wi', he poured out the drink, and sae made the auld wife think he had drunk it. They a' went to bed again, and the damosel began, as before, singing:

Seven lang years I served for thee,
The glassy hill I clamb for thee,
The bluidy shirt I wrang for thee;
And wilt thou no wauken and turn to me?

He heard, and turned to her. And she telled him a' that had befa'en her, and he telled her a' that had happened to him. And he caused the auld washerwife and her dochter to be burnt. And they were married, and he and she are living happy till this day, for aught I ken.

## 2   The Wal at the Warld's End

There was a king and a queen, and the king had a dochter, and the queen had a dochter. And the king's dochter was bonnie and guid-natured, and a'body liket her; and the queen's dochter was ugly and ill-natured, and naebody liket her. And the queen didna like the king's dochter, and she wanted her awa'. Sae she sent her to the wal at the warld's end, to get a bottle o'water, thinking she would never come back. Weel, she took her bottle, and she gaed and gaed or she cam to a pownie that was tethered, and the pownie said to her:

> Flit me, flit me, my bonnie May,
> For I haena been flitted this seven year and a day.

And the king's dochter said: 'Ay will I, my bonnie pownie, I'll flit ye.' Sae the pownie ga'e her a ride owre the muir o' hecklepins.

Weel, she gaed far and far and farer nor I can tell, or she cam to the wal at the warld's end; and when she cam to the wal, it was awfu' deep, and she couldna get her bottle dippit. And as she was lookin' doon, thinkin' hoo to do, there lookit up to her three scaud men's heads, and they said to her:

> Wash me, wash me, my bonnie May,
> And dry me wi' yer clean linen apron.

And she said: 'Ay will I; I'll wash ye'. Sae she washed the three scaud men's heads, and dried them wi' her clean linen apron; and syne they took and dippit her bottle for her.

And the scaud men's heads said the tane to the tither:

> Weird, brother, weird, what'll ye weird?

And the first ane said: 'I weird that if she was bonnie afore, she'll be ten times bonnier.' And the second ane said: 'I weird that ilka time she speaks, there'll a diamond and a ruby and a pearl drap oot o' her mouth'. And the third ane said: 'I weird that ilka time she kaims her head, she'll get a peck o' gould and a peck o' siller oot o' it.'

Weel, she cam hame to the king's coort again, and if she was bonnie afore, she was ten times bonnier; and ilka time she opened her lips to speak, there was a diamond and a ruby and a pearl drappit oot o' her mouth; and ilka time she kaimed her head, she gat a peck o' gould and a peck o' silver oot o't. And the queen was that vext, she didna ken what to do, but she thocht she wad send her ain dochter to see if she could fa' in wi' the same luck. Sae she ga'e her a bottle, and tell't her to gang awa' to the wal at the warld's end, and get a bottle o' water.

Weel, the queen's dochter gaed and gaed or she cam to the pownie, an' the pownie said:

Flit me, flit me, my bonnie May,
For I haena been flitted this seven year and a day.

And the queen's dochter said: 'Ou ye nasty beast, do ye think I'll flit ye? Do ye ken wha ye're speakin' till? I'm a queen's dochter.' Sae she wadna flit the pownie, and the pownie wadna gie her a ride owre the muir o' hecklepins. And she had to gang on her bare feet, and the hecklepins cuttit a' her feet, and she could hardly gang ava.

Weel, she gaed far and far and farer nor I can tell, or she cam to the wal at the warld's end. And the wal was deep, and she couldna get her bottle dippit; and as she was lookin' doon, thinkin' hoo to do, there lookit up to her three scaud men's heads, and they said till her:

Wash me, wash me, my bonnie May,
And dry me wi' yer clean linen apron.

And she said: 'Ou ye nasty dirty beasts, div ye think I'm gaunie wash ye? Div ye ken wha ye're speakin' till? I'm a queen's dochter'. Sae she wadna wash them, and they wadna dip her bottle for her.

And the scaud men's heads said the tane to the tither:

Weird, brother, weird, what'll ye weird?

And the first ane said: 'I weird that if she was ugly afore, she'll be ten times uglier.' And the second said: 'I weird that ilka time she speaks, there'll a puddock and a taid loup oot o' her mouth.' And the third ane said: 'And I weird that ilka time she kaims her head, she'll get a peck o' lice and a peck o' flechs oot o't.' Sae she gaed awa hame again, and if she was ugly afore, she was ten times uglier; and ilka time (&c.). Sae they had to send her awa' fra the king's coort. And there was a bonnie young prince cam and married the king's dochter; and the queen's dochter had to put up wi' an auld cobbler, and he lickit her ilka day wi' a leather strap. Sae ye see, bairns, &c.


# 3   Whuppity Stoorie

I ken ye're fond o' clashes aboot fairies, bairns; and a story anent a fairy and the guidwife o' Kittlerumpit has joost come into my mind; but I canna very weel tell ye noo whereabouts Kittlerumpit lies. I

25

think it's somewhere in amang the Debateable Grund; onygate I'se no pretend to mair than I ken, like a'body noo-a-days. I wuss they was mind the ballant we used to lilt langsyne:

> Mony ane sings the gerse, the gerse,
> And mony ane sings the corn;
> And mony ane clatters o' bold Robin Hood,
> Ne'er kent where he was born.

But hoosoever, about Kittlerumpit: the goodman was a vaguing sort o' a body; and he gaed to a fair ae day, and not only never came hame again, but never mair was heard o'. Some said he listed, and ither some that the wearifu' pressgang cleekit him up, though he was clothed wi' a wife and a wean forbye. Hech-how! that dulefu' pressgang! they gaed aboot the kintra like roaring lions, seeking whom they micht devoor. I mind weel, my auldest brither Sandy was a' but smoored in the meal ark hiding frae thae limmers. After they war gane, we pu'd him oot frae amang the meal, pechin' and greetin', and as white as ony corp. My mither had to pike the meal oot o' his mooth wi' the shank o' a horn spoon.

Aweel, when the goodman o' Kittlerumpit was gane, the goodwife was left wi' a sma' fendin. Little gear had she, and a sookin' lad bairn. A'body said they war sorry for her; but naebody helpit her, whilk's a common case, sirs. Howsomever, the goodwife had a soo, and that was her only consolation; for the soo was soon to farra, and she hopit for a good bairn-time.

But we a' weel ken hope's fallacious. Ae day the wife gaes to the sty to fill the soo's trough; and what does she find but the soo lying on her back, grunting and graning, and ready to gie up the ghost.

I trow this was a new stoond to the goodwife's heart; sae she sat doon on the knockin'-stane, wi' her bairn on her knee, and grat sairer than ever she did for the loss o' her ain goodman.

Noo, I premeese that the cot-hoose o' Kittlerumpit was biggit on a brae, wi' a muckle fir-wood behint it, o' whilk ye may hear mair or lang gae. So the goodwife, when she was dichtin' her een, chances to look down the brae, and what does she see but an auld woman, amaist like a leddy, coming slowly up the gaet. She was buskit in green, a' but a white short apron, and a black velvet hood, and a steeple-crowned beaver hat on her head. She had a lang walking-staff, as lang as hersel', in her hand – the sort of staff that auld men

26

and auld women helpit themselves wi' lang syne; I see nae sic staffs noo, sirs.

Aweel, when the goodwife saw the green gentlewoman near her, she rase and made a curchie; and 'Madam,' quo' she, greetin', 'I'm ane of the maist misfortunate women alive.' 'I dinna wish to hear pipers' news and fiddlers' tales, goodwife,' quo' the green woman. 'I ken ye've tint your goodman – we had waur losses at the Shirra Muir; and I ken that your soo's unco sick. Noo, what will ye gie me gin I cure her?' 'Onything your leddyship's madam likes,' quo' the witless goodwife, never guessin' wha she had to deal wi'. 'Let's wat thooms on that bargain,' quo' the green woman: sae thooms war wat, I'se warrant ye; and into the sty madam marches.

She looks at the soo wi' a lang glowr, and syne began to mutter to hersel' what the goodwife couldna weel understand; but she said it soundit like:

> Pitter patter,
> Haly watter.

Syne she took oot o' her pouch a wee bottle, wi' something like oil in't, and rubs the soo wi't abune the snoot, ahint the lugs, and on the tip o' the tail. 'Get up, beast,' quo' the green woman. Nae sooner said nor done – up bangs the soo wi' a grunt, and awa' to her trough for her breakfast.

The goodwife o' Kittlerumpit was a joyfu' goodwife noo, and wad hae kissed the very hem o' the green madam's gown-tail, but she wadna let her. 'I'm no sae fond o' fashions,' quo' she; 'but noo that I hae richtit your sick beast, let us end our sicker bargain. Ye'll no find me an unreasonable greedy body – I like aye to do a good turn for a sma' reward – a' I ask, and wull hae, is that lad bairn in your bosom.'

The goodwife o' Kittlerumpit, wha noo kent her customer, ga'e a skirl like a stickit gryse. The green woman was a fairy, nae doubt; sae she prays, and greets, and begs, and flytes; but a' wadna do. 'Ye may spare your din,' quo' the fairy, 'skirling as if I was as deaf as a door nail; but this I'll let ye to wut – I canna, by *the law we leeve on*, take your bairn till the third day after this day; and no then, if ye can tell me my right name'. Sae madam gaes awa' round the swine's-sty end, and the goodwife fa's doon in a swerf behint the knockin'-stane.

Aweel, the goodwife o' Kittlerumpit could sleep nane that nicht for greetin', and a' the next day the same, cuddlin' her bairn till she

27

near squeezed its breath out; but the second day she thinks o' taking a walk in the wood I tell't ye o'; and sae, wi' the bairn in her arms, she sets out, and gaes far in amang the trees, where was an old quarry-hole, grown owre wi' gerse, and a bonny spring well in the middle o't. Before she came very nigh, she hears the birring o' a lint-wheel, and a voice lilting a sang; sae the wife creeps quietly amang the bushes, and keeks owre the broo o' the quarry, and what does she see but the green fairy kemping at her wheel, and singing like ony precentor:

> Little kens our guid dame at hame
> That Whuppity Stoorie is my name!

'Ah, ha!' thinks the wife, 'I've gotten the mason's word at last; the deil gie them joy that tell't it!' Sae she gaed hame far lichter than she came out, as ye may weel guess, lauchin like a madcap wi' the thought o' begunkin' the auld green fairy.

Aweel, ye maun ken that this goodwife was a jokus woman, and aye merry when her heart wasna unco sair owreladen. Sae she thinks to hae some sport wi' the fairy; and at the appointit time she puts the bairn behint the knockin'-stane, and sits down on't hersel'. Syne she pu's her mutch ajee owre her left lug, crooks her mou on the tither side, as gin she war greetin', and a filthy face she made, ye may be sure. She hadna lang to wait, for up the brae mounts the green fairy, nowther lame nor lazy; and lang or she gat near the knockin'-stane, she skirls out: 'Goodwife o' Kittlerumpit, ye weel ken what I come for – stand and deliver!' The wife pretends to greet sairer than before, and wrings her nieves, and fa's on her knees, wi': 'Och, sweet madam mistress, spare my only bairn, and take the weary soo!' 'The deil take the soo for my share,' quo' the fairy; 'I come na here for swine's flesh. Dinna be contramawcious, hizzie, but gie me the gett instantly!'

'Ochon, dear leddy mine,' quo' the greetin' goodwife; 'for-bear my poor bairn, and take mysel'!'

'The deil's in the daft jad,' quo' the fairy, looking like the far-end o' a fiddle; 'I'll wad she's clean dementit. Wha in a' the earthly warld, wi' half an ee in their head, wad ever meddle wi' the likes o' thee?'

I trow this set up the wife o' Kittlerumpit's birse; for though she had twa bleert een, and a lang red neb forbye, she thought hersel' as bonny as the best o' them. Sae she bangs aff her knees, sets up her mutch-croon, and wi' her twa hands faulded afore her, she maks a

28

curchie down to the grund, and, 'In troth, fair madam,' quo' she, 'I might hae had the wit to ken that the likes o' me is na fit to tie the warst shoe-strings o' the heich and mighty princess, *Whuppity Stoorie!*' Gin a fluff o' gunpowder had come out o' the grund, it couldna hae gart the fairy loup heicher nor she did; syne down she came again, dump on her shoe-heels, and whurlin' round, she ran down the brae, scraichin' for rage, like a houlet chased wi' the witches.

The goodwife o' Kittlerumpit leugh till she was like to ryve; syne she takes up her bairn, and gaes into her hoose, singin' till't a' the gaet:

> A goo and a gitty, my bonny wee tyke,
> Ye'se noo hae your four-oories;
> Sin' we've gien Nick a bane to pyke,
> Wi' his wheels and his Whuppity Stoories.

## 4 Marget Totts

Once on a time a man was very hard towards his wife, and laid tasks on her no one could accomplish. He at one time gave her such a quantity of flax to spin within a fixed time that the work was beyond human power. As she was sitting in the house bemoaning herself, and thinking of what was to be done, a woman entered. Seeing her in great distress and perplexity, she asked her what was the matter with her. She told her of the task that has been laid on her by her husband. The stranger said to her: 'I'll tack awa' yir lint and spin't t' you, and bring't back t' you on such and such a day (naming the day), if ye can tell me my name.' The guidwife agreed at once, and gave the woman the lint. But she was now in as great straits as ever, and could in no way come to her apparent friend's name, and the day on which the lint was to be brought back was drawing near. As she was one day sitting at her wits' end in the house a man came in. He asked her what ailed her that she was looking so cast down and sad. She told him all her tale. Now near the house there was a small hill covered with thorn bushes and whins. The man told her to go to this hill and hide herself among the bushes near an open space on it, and she would hear something to help her. She did as she was told. She had not been long in her hiding-place till a lot of fairy women came with their spinning wheels and sat down on the open space not far from her. She saw her friend amongst them. As she span she went on saying, 'Little does the guidwife ken it my name's Marget Totts.' The woman withdrew without being seen by the fairies. The day fixed for bringing back the yarn came, and the woman appeared with it. 'Here's yir yarn, if ye can tell me what my name is.' 'Your name's Marget Totts,' said the guidwife. The spinner went up the lum in a blaze of fire, and left the yarn.

5

There was ance a gentleman that lived in a very grand house, and he married a young lady that had been delicately brought up. In her husband's house she found everything that was fine – fine tables and chairs, fine looking-glasses, and fine curtains; but then her husband expected her to be able to spin twelve hanks o' thread every day, besides attending to her house; and, to tell the even-down truth, the lady could not spin a bit. This made her husband glunchy with her, and before a month had passed, she found herself very unhappy.

One day the husband gaed away upon a journey, after telling her that he expected her, before his return, to have not only learned to spin, but to have spun a hundred hanks o' thread. Quite downcast, she took a walk along the hill-side, till she came to a big flat stane, and there she sat down and grat. By-and-by, she heard a strain o' fine sma' music, coming as it were frae aneath the stane, and on turning it up, she saw a cave below, where there were sitting six wee ladies in green gowns, ilk ane o' them spinning on a little wheel, and singing:

> Little kens my dame at hame
> That Whuppity Stoorie is my name.

The lady walked into the cave, and was kindly asked by the wee bodies to take a chair and sit down, while they still continued their spinning. She observed that ilk ane's mouth was thrawn away to ae side, but she didna venture to speer the reason. They asked why she looked so unhappy, and she telt them that it was because she was expected by her husband to be a good spinner, when the plain truth was, that she could not spin at all, and found herself quite unable for it, having been so delicately brought up; neither was there any need for it, as her husband was a rich man. 'Oh, is that a'?' said the little

30

wifies, speaking out at their cheeks like. [*Imitate a person with a wry mouth.*]

'Yes, and is it not a very good *a*' too?' said the lady, her heart like to burst wi' distress.

'We could easily quit ye o' that trouble', said the wee women. 'Just ask us a' to dinner for the day when your husband is to come back. We'll then let you see how we'll manage him.'

So the lady asked them all to dine with herself and her husband on the day when he was to come back.

When the goodman came hame, he found the house so occupied with preparations for dinner, that he had nae time to ask his wife about her thread; and before ever he had ance spoken to her on the subject, the company was announced at the hall door. The six little ladies all came in a coach-and-six, and were as fine as princesses, but still wore their gowns of green. The gentleman was very polite, and shewed them up the stair with a pair of wax candles in his hand. And so they all sat down to dinner, and conversation went on very pleasantly, till at length the husband, becoming familiar with them, said: 'Ladies, if it be not an uncivil question, I should like to know how it happens that all your mouths are turned away to one side?' 'Oh,' said ilk ane at ance, 'it's with our constant *spin-spin-spinning.*' [*Here speak with the mouth turned to one side, in imitation of the ladies.*]

'Is that the case?' cried the gentleman. 'Then, John, Tam, and Dick, fye, go haste and burn every rock, and reel, and spinning-wheel in the house, for I'll not have my wife to spoil her bonny face with *spin-spin-spinning.*' [*Imitate again.*]

And so the lady lived happily with her goodman all the rest of her days.


## 6  Rashie-coat


Rashie-coat was a king's daughter, and her father wanted her to be married; but she didna like the man. Her father said she bud tak him; and she didna ken what to do. Sae she gaed awa' to the hen-wife, to speer what she should do. And the hen-wife said: 'Say ye winna tak him unless they gie ye a coat o' the beaten gowd.' Weel, they ga'e her a coat o' the beaten gowd; but she didna want to tak him for a' that. Sae she gaed to the hen-wife again, and the hen-wife said: 'Say ye winna tak him unless they gie ye a coat made o' the feathers o' a' the

birds o' the air.' Sae the king sent a man wi' a great heap o' corn; and
the man cried to a' the birds o' the air: 'Ilka bird tak up a pea and put
down a feather; ilka bird tak up a pea and put down a feather.' Sae ilka
bird took up a pea and put down a feather; and they took a' the
feathers and made a coat o' them, and ga'e it to Rashie-coat; but she
didna want to tak him for a' that. Weel, she gaed to the hen-wife
again, and speered what she should do; and the hen-wife said: 'Say ye
winna tak him unless they gie ye a coat o' rashes and a pair o'
slippers.' Weel, they ga'e her a coat o' rashes and a pair o' slippers; but
she didna want to tak him for a' that. Sae she gaed to the hen-wife
again, and the hen-wife said she couldna help her ony mair.

Weel, she left her father's hoose, and gaed far, and far, and farer nor
I can tell; and she cam to a king's hoose, and she gaed in till't. And
they speered at her what she was seeking, and she said she was
seeking service; and they ga'e her service, and set her into the kitchen
to wash the dishes, and tak oot the ase, and a' that. And whan the
Sabbath-day cam, they a' gaed to the kirk, and left her at hame to
cook the dinner. And there was a fairy cam to her, and telt her to put
on her coat o' the beaten gowd, and gang to the kirk. And she said she
couldna gang, for she had to cook the dinner; and the fairy telt her to
gang, and she would cook the dinner for her. And she said:

> Ae peat gar anither peat burn,
> Ae spit gar anither spit turn,
> Ae pat gar anither pat play,
> Let Rashie-coat gang to the kirk the day.

Sae Rashie-coat put on her coat o' the beaten gowd, and gaed awa' to
the kirk. And the king's son fell in love wi' her; but she cam hame
afore the kirk scaled, and he couldna find oot wha she was. And
whan she cam hame she faund the dinner cookit, and naebody kent
she had been oot.

Weel, the next Sabbath-day, the fairy cam again, and telt her to put
on the coat o' feathers o' a' the birds o' the air, an' gang to the kirk,
and she would cook the dinner for her. Weel, she put on the coat o'
feathers, and gaed to the kirk. And she cam oot afore it scaled; and
when the king's son saw her gaun oot, he gaed oot too; but he
couldna find oot what she was. And she got hame, and took aff the
coat o' feathers, and faund the dinner cookit, and naebody kent she
had been oot.

An' the niest Sabbath-day, the fairy cam till her again, and telt her to put on the coat o' rashes and the pair o' slippers, and gang to the kirk again. Aweel, she did it a'; and this time the king's son sat near the door, and when he saw Rashie-coat slippin' oot afore the kirk scaled, he slippit oot too, and grippit her. And she got awa' frae him, and ran hame; but she lost ane o' her slippers, and he took it up. And he gared cry through a' the country, that onybody that could get the slipper on, he would marry them. Sae a' the leddies o' the coort tried to get the slipper on, and it wadna fit nane o' them. And the auld hen-wife cam and fush her dochter to try and get it on, and she nippit her fit, and clippit her fit, and got it on that way. Sae the king's son was gaun to marry her. And he was takin' her awa' to marry her, ridin' on a horse, an' her ahint him; and they cam to a wood, and there was a bird sittin' on a tree, and as they gaed by, the bird said:

> Nippit fit and clippit fit
>    Ahint the king's son rides;
> But bonny fit and pretty fit
>    Ahint the caudron hides.

And whan the king's son heard this, he flang aff the hen-wife's dochter, and cam hame again, and lookit ahint the caudron, and there he faund Rashie-coat greetin' for her slipper. And he tried her fit wi' the slipper, and it gaed on fine. Sae he married her.

> And they lived happy and happy,
> And never drank oot o' a dry cappy.

## 7   The Cat and the Hard Cheese

Well, this was an aald woman, you see, an she had two sons, and – nae money as usual, things were hard up, an one o her sons, he wid try an find work an dae this an that, but the ither one, they cried him Silly Jeck; he used tae jist lie – like me – in front o the fire aa the time, an half covered wi ashes an stour, an he wouldnae bother tae dae anything, an they never bothered him very much tae dae anything, because they jist cried him Silly Jeck. But anyway, everything wis jist comin tae a head an they were gonna be put oot o the hoose if they couldnae find the rates, an nae money, nae nothin. (The man lang dead, ye see.) So this other brother, John, he says, 'Ma, Ah'll have tae go an push ma fortune,' he says, 'an see if I can find anything tae keep the roof ower yir heid.' So he's away, hi tae the road an ho tae the road

an on an on an on an on an on – but before he left the hoose his
mother says, 'Well, ye'd better take somethin wi ye!' She says, 'Ah'll
mak ye a wee bannick an A'll fry ye a wee callop,' she says. She says,
'D'ye want the wee yin wi the blessin, or the big yin wi the curse?'

He says, 'Oh, A'll need plenty, ye'd better gie me the big yin.' So
she fried this callop tae him an she made a bonnick – ye ken, that's a
big oatcake – and she put it intae a hankie an away he goes. An he wis
getting weary fae walkin on an on an on an on an now he says, 'Och,
A'll sit doon here' – it wis the side o a wee stream, ye see? – 'an A'll
get a drink an eat ma bannock.' An he's sittin there, an he's sittin
eatin an this aal man come alang.

An this small man says, he says, 'That looks aafae good, that
bannock an that collop.'

'Ah weel,' he says, 'it may look good,' he says, 'but I need it masel,'
he says, 'fir it's aa A've got, an God knows when A'll get the next.'

An the aal man says, 'Oh, it's aa rycht, laddie,' he says, 'I suppose
ye're richt enough,' he says, 'ye're young an ye need yir bite.'

So away he went then, on again an on an on again, kept walkin an
walkin an walkin: nae razor wi him or nothin, ye ken, an his baerd
wis growin an his shoes were gettin holes in them – no, no: jist hid
tae keep goin. But eventually he come tae this gates o a big estate
and on the gates it says they were men wanted, ye see? So he went in
an he went up an this wis a great big castel he come tae. And he rang
the bell at the back door; he says, 'A see they're advertisin here fir
men.'

He says, 'Oh aye,' he says, 'but,' he says, 'I don't think ye'll ever
dae the work.'

'Well,' he says, 'there nae hairm in tryin.'

He says, 'No, there nae hairm in tryin,' he says, 'but if ye fail,' he
says, 'ye see aa they heids stickin on the gate doon there?' he says:
'yours'll be the next.'

'Ah well,' he says, 'A cannae help it,' he says, 'I'd be as weel deid
onyway as goin on like this.' So they took him in tae the kitchen
anyway an they fed him well an gave him a bed and says, 'You'll be
aa right.' An the next night he says, 'Ye've tae start yir duties.'

So he wis brought before the king an the king says, 'Well,' he says,
'it's three tasks ye have tae do.' He says, 'If you can do this three
tasks,' he says, 'as naebody his done yet,' he says, 'ye'll no only get
money,' he says, 'but ye'll get the princess to marry, and,' he says, 'a
place o yir own, and this kingdom when I die.'

So he says, 'Well, what have A got tae do?'

'Well,' he says, 'do you see that big bog down there?' He says, 'I want that oot o there before mornin.' He says, 'That's whit ye have tae dae, ye've tae clear it aa before mornin.' He says, 'There ye go,' so he gien him a mutchkin o whisky, and he gave him sandwiches an meat awaa wi him an he says, 'Awaa ye go.'

So away he went doon, an he says, 'There's a baler an a shuffel an everything tae ye.' So he goes doon an he starts balin this water, an balin an balin an balin. But it was just rinnin back in as fast as he could bale 't oot. 'Oh no, no,' he says, 'nae use. Na', he says, 'I ken what A'm gaunnae do,' he says, 'A'm clearin oot.' So he tried tae run away, but the king's men got him an brought him back, an he's head was stuck on the gates.

So this aald woman's aye waitin for any news o this laddie, ye see, an she waited an waited an waited an waited, but na, na. And, 'Oh,' she says, 'I doot, laddie,' she says, 'there something's happened tae John,' she says; 'he's no comin back.' She says, 'You'll hae tae try an dae something, Jeck,' she says, 'would ye rise oot o there,' she says, 'an try an dae somethin?'

He says, 'What am A gaunnae dae?'

She says, 'I don' know, but ye could go an look fir yir brother, at least,' she says. 'A'm no able to traivel or nothing.'

'Aa richt,' he says. So he got up an he gien he's sel a shake, an there was mair – as much stoor aff him as would ha' blin't ye, an ashes an things. But anyway he got up, an he says, 'Well, A'll go, Ma,' he says, 'an A'll see if I can find him an see if I can find any money or anything tae keep the roof abeen yir heid.' He says, 'Mak me a wee bannick an fry me a wee callop,' he says, 'afore I go tae tak the road.'

She says, 'Dae ye want the big yin wi the curse or the wee yin wi the blessin?'

He says, 'Ach, the wee yin 'll dae fine,' he says.

So she baked him this wee bannick an she fried this wee callop tae him, an she tied it up in a hankie, an he's away, an he's hi tae the road and ho tae the road, through sheep's parks an bullocks' parks an all the high an the low mountains o Yarrow; and there was no rest for poor Jeck, till the birds were makin nests in his heid an the stones were makin holes in his feet . . . no rest fir him. But he came tae a stream – A don't know if it wis the same stream his brither wis at or no, but he thought he would hae a drink an eat his bannick, ye see. An he sat doon, an he's eatin this bannick and takin a drink ae the water,

35

when this same wee aald man comes up tae him. And he's standin lookin at him like that, an he says, 'That smells good,' he says, 'that scallop [sic] an that bannick.'

He says, 'Are ye hungry, aald man?' He says, 'Ye're nae to be hungry,' he says. 'Here, you tak that bit,' he says, 'or tak the half.'

'No, no, Jack,' he says, 'ye'll need it.'

'Ah,' he says, 'A'm a young man,' he says, 'different fae you. Come on,' he says, 'you tak it.' An he gave it tae him.

The aald man says, 'We'll share it.' So they sat an shared it, an they sat an drunk the water, an they sat an newsed fir a while, an Jack says, 'A'll have tae go, though,' he says. 'A'm lookin fir ma brither,' he says. 'Ma mither's worried aboot him; an A'm lookin for work o any kind tae.'

So this auld man pit his hand in his pocket, but . . . an he says, 'A've nothin now, Jack,' he says, 'but there's a wee box' – an it was just a wee tin box like an Oxo box, ye ken? – He says, 'If ye tak that,' he says, 'mycht haud yir tobacca or onything,' he says, 'pit it in yir pocket.'

So he took it an put it in his pocket. An he gets up an he's away on an on an on an on again, till he came tae this place – well, somebody directed him tae it, says, 'There's a place on there,' he says, 'they're advertisin fir men tae work,' he says. 'If ye go there ye'll maybe get something.' [Change of tape] Well, he saw this notice on the gate anyway and he went tae the castel, an they took him in an they fed him well and says, 'Ye'll see the king in the mornin and he'll tell ye whit ye have tae dae.'

So in the mornin the king saw him, an he says, 'Well,' he says, 'ye've three tasks tae dae,' he says. 'Naebody's ever been able tae dae them, but if you can dae them,' he says, 'you'll get my daughter, the princess, fir a wife, an my kingdom when I die.'

'Ah,' he says, 'I can only try.'

'Well,' he says, 'tonight,' he says, 'ye'll go doon – ye see that bog doon there?' he says. 'I want that cleared.'

'Ah me,' he says, 'wha could dae that?'

'Well,' he says, 'ye wanted a job, an that's the job, an that's what ye have tae dae.'

So anyway they gave him a muskin o whisky, an they gave him meat wi him, tied up ye ken, an away he goes too. An he went doon an he says, 'Ach,' he says, 'there's nae sense in tryin tae dae that,' he says, 'a waste o time. A'm just as weel tae drink ma whisky an lie doon, an,' he says, 'if he kills me,' he says, 'it's jist too bad,' he says, 'A'll jist hae tae dae.' So he's sittin an he says, 'Ach, A could dae wi a smoke.' So he took out his wee cley pipe, an he says. 'A wonder would there be ony tobaccae,' he says, 'intae that wee box?' He opens up the box, an when he opens up this box, here there wis a wee man in the box. An he says, 'Wha're you?'

He says, 'I am the noble Jack o Clubs, an whit's your will, master?'

He says, 'Whit?'

He says, 'I'm the noble Jack o Clubs, an whit's yir will?'

'Will?'

He says, 'Whit dae ye want?'

'Whit dae A want?' he says, 'tell ye whit A want.' He says, 'A want that –' he says, 'Well, I dinnae want, but the king wants that shifted before mornin,' he says. 'That's whit's wanted.'

'Oh well,' he says, 'jist you lie doon an drink yir whisky.' So he lay doon an drunk his whisky: he couldna ha' cared less, he'd jist reached that stage. But in the morning, when he woke up, this bog was gone: it was jist like a green lawn . . . when he looks.

And he gets up, an he gies he's sel a shake, an . . . he's runnin up tae the castel, and he gave this bell a pull – it was one o yon bells that ye pull oot, ye ken? – he pulls it tae it rattled through aa the castel. An they cam oot – 'Whit's aa this noise?'

He says, 'Well,' he says, 'A've come back: that's yir job done.'

They took him in, an the keeng's come oot, an he came doon, and he looked – 'Aye,' he says, 'Jack,' he says, 'ye're a clever man,' he says, 'but . . . no so clever as yir learnin maister, whoever he wis!'

He says, 'Naebody!'

'But,' he says, 'ye're no finished yet, ye've two ither tasks tae dae. So', he says, 'come in'; but oh, he was treated tae the best then, ye ken, he wis given aa good meat, everything, as much as he could drink, a lovely bed an everything: he says, 'Now you go an hae a sleep; then A'll tell you whit yir next task is.' So the next night he says, 'Dae ye see that aald ruin o a castel doon there?' he says: 'it's half o it's doon an half o it's up: well,' he says, 'it's h'unted wi a giant, and,' he says, 'you've tae go doon there the nicht an kill the giant,' he says. 'That's yir next task!'

'Oh,' he says, 'that, A'll shuin dae that.' So he's away doon, wi his whisky an that again, an he went in . . . in this great big damp dungeon o a place, ye ken, an aal castel. He's sittin, an he heard the thump, thump, thump, thump, and . . . this aald ruins was jist shakin wi the noise o this giant's feet. An he looks up, an this wis a giant right enough, three heids on him. 'Ohhh!' he says. So he oots wi his wee box, pulls it open quick. He says, 'Are ye still there?'

He says, 'Aye, A'm still here! Whit's yir will, master?'

* An the giant's getting closer, ye see, an he says, 'Do ye think ye could dae onything wi him?'

'Ah, dinnae worry aboot that, Jeck,' he says. So he grabbed this sword off the castle wall: he says, 'Take a ha'd o it now, Jeck.'

And Jeck says, 'I cannae dae nothin wi a sword!'

He says, 'Go an try.'

So he gets the sword: but this sword was jist goin itsel, ye see, – first one head . . . skidded to the one side o the castel, an anither heid went skiddin, till the three heads were aff the giant, an Jack sut – he fell doon, he didnae sit doon, he fell doon, an he says, 'My God!' So he says, 'If I go back,' he says, 'they'll no believe me that I've killed this giant,' so he went an he cut the three tongues oot o the giant's heids, because he'd tried tae cairry the heids wi him, but they were too heavy. So he cut the tongues oot an put them intae a bag, and he flew back tae the castel;* and he near tore the bell oot o the socket this mornin, with ringin it tae let the king see this three tongues!

'Ah ha,' the king says, 'ye're really a clever man, Jeck,' he says, 'but I wish I kent your learnin mester.' So he says, 'Well, my next task,' he says, 'is a task,' he says, 'that you'll no dae, Jeck,' he says, 'that naebody'll dae.'

He says, 'Whit is it?'

He says, 'It's a very simple one,' he says, 'but you'll no dae it!'

He says, 'Whit is it?'

He says, 'I want you to tell me,' he says, 'how many stars there is in the sky.' So he says, 'That's all there is tae it, an if you can tell me that, Jack,' he says, 'my kingdom's yours an my daughter. So,' he says, 'there's your whisky, ye can sit an coont them!'

So he goes oot, an he's sittin: he says, 'Ah . . . are ye still there?'

He says, 'Aye, A'm here,' the wee man says, 'A'm here', he says, 'an A'm the noble Jack o Clubs. Noo whit's yir will, master?'

He says, 'Could you tell me how many stars there is in the sky – that's what the king wants tae know.'

He says, 'No, A couldnae tell ye, but jist go in,' he says, 'an tell him, "There are three thousand million, seven hundred an one, an",' he says, ' "if ye dinnae believe me, coont them fir yirsel!" ' So . . . he says, 'Aye,' he says, 'jist dae that,' he says, 'an . . . it'll be a lang, lang time before he can mak ye a leear.'

So . . . he near took the bell clean oot this next mornin . . . . So the king says, 'Did ye find oot?'

'Aye,' he says, 'seven hundred million . . .' an he telt him onywey.

An he says, 'Are ye su –'

'Yes, that's the dead number,' he says, 'an if ye dinnae believe me,' he says, 'ye jist coont them fir yirsel.'

So the king realised, ye see, that he couldnae dae nothin aboot this, an he says, 'Well,' he says, 'Jeck,' he says, 'you've won,' he says. 'You have definitely earned', he says, 'whit ye're gaen tae get.' He says, 'Now A won't go back on my word,' he says: 'there's my daughter the princess. Ye can marry, an,' he says, 'A'm no deid yet, but I have a castel,' he says, 'jist doon the wey a bit, an yeze can have that till I dee.'

\* An he went an telt the princess that she hid tae mairry Jeck. She says, 'A'm no mairryin that,' she says, 'not me, wi aa this whiskers an dirt an baerd an the smell aff o'm,' she says, 'not me, A'm no mairryin that man,' she says. 'Faither, A jist couldnae dae it!'

He says, 'I've gien my word an you'll jist hae tae dae it!' He says, 'Now, ye ken that.' So she wisnae very pleased aboot this at aa: 'Na, na,' she says – she wis tryin tae get oot o it . . . but she kent she would have tae dae what her father said.

So the weddin come roond an everything: but in the mean time, ye see, they had taken Jeck an shaved him an cut he's hair an bathed him an cleaned him all up an put a beautiful suit on him. An when she was standin there greetin an thinkin aboot rinnin awa, they come in, and she looked roon like this. She says, 'A've never seen that man before,' an she's waitin for Jeck comin in! An her father says, 'Well, here's yir husband!' An she couldnae believe her eyes, he wis sich a handsome man efter he wis aa cleaned up an sorted an dressed up.

So they got mairriet, an they went to live in this castel, and they're happy in this castel – he's fine an pleased, but he says, 'There's one thing A'll hae tae dae,' he says, 'A'll hae tae go back tae ma mither: she'll be winderin whit's keepin me.'

'Oh,' she says, 'that's all right,' she says, 'we'll both go back.' (She spoke kinda p'lite, ye see?) So they got their carriage ready an away they go back this road tae whar his mother lived. An she wis there sittin in the hoose, an she heard the horses' feet on the road jist outside the door, an she went tae the windae an keeked oot. 'Oh,' she says, 'my God, gentry,' she says, 'A wonder what they can be wantin: they've surely lost their road!' An he cam oot o the carriage an he cam ower tae the door: she says, 'He's comin in here onywey!' An she went oot tae the door tae see if she could help them – thought they were lost or something.

And he spoke tae her and she says – she wis bendin an curtseyin an almost grovellin at his feet, ye ken – he says, 'Mither, whit's adae wi ye, wumman?'

She looked up an she says – she couldnae believe her eyes, she says, 'That's no you, Jeck, is it?'

'Aye, it's me, mither,' an he grabbed her in his airms: he says, 'Come on, ye're no bidin here nae langer, ye're comin wi me!' So he took his mother back tae the castel an she led the life o a lady from that on until she died. An in the meantime Jack an his wife had hed twa bonnie bairns.*

But he was learnin aa the gentry's cairry-on now, he's horses an away huntin an shootin an all this cairry-on. An he was away shootin one day up in the mountain an he came back. Now when he came back there was nothing but twa'r three stones – jist . . . waa stanes.

'Oh my God,' he says, 'what's happened? Nae castel, nae nothin, jist a rubble o stones. Oh my God,' he says, 'what's happened here?' An he sat doon; he says, 'I dinnae ken whit's happened!'

An he's sittin thinkin an thinkin tae hissel, an this wee black cat come, an it wis rubbin itsel up against his legs, an rubbin up against his legs, an rubbin up against his legs, ye see? An he says, 'Oh, pussy, pussy,' he says, 'if only you could speak, ye could tell me!' an he's clappin this wee cat . . .

'Speak?' she says. 'I *can* speak!' She says, 'Naebody ever asked me tae speak.'

'Well,' he says, 'could you tell me whit happened?'

'Ah, fine that,' she says, 'I can tell ye whit happened.' She says, 'Ye forgot aboot the wee Jack o Clubs, didn't ye, intae the box?' She says, 'Well', she says, * 'it wis the cook an the butler.' She says, 'The butler found yir aald jaiket that ye kept in the closet wi the wee box in it,* an opened it, and so that's whit's happened, an your wife's gone.'

'Have ye any idea whar –'

'No, I couldnae tell ye,' she says, 'whar they are or whar they went, but that's whit happen't,' she says, 'he found the box.'

'Oh well,' he says, 'A'll jist hae tae get – A'll hae tae find them,' he says, 'A'll hae tae find ma wife.' So . . . 'Will ye come wi me pussy?'

'Aye,' she says, 'A'll come wi ye,' she says, 'if I can be ony help tae ye, but A've nae idea whar they went!' So they're on an on an on an on ower this moors an mountains an everything, ye see, tearin aa wey (?)

He says, 'It's aafae cauld the nycht, hiv ye any idea where we could sleep, an . . .' he says, 'A'm stairvin! Have ye nae idea whar we could get onything tae eat?'

'Well,' she says, 'doon there at that fairm there's a barn,' she says, 'an there's a great big kebbick o cheese,' she says. 'It's hard richt enough, but it would be aa richt, we could eat it. A fine big kebbick o cheese,' she says, 'it would dae me an you's haert good,' she says, 'an we could go doon there.'

An he says, 'Oh, come on!'

'But,' she says, 'it's hauntit!'

'What is it haunted wi?' he says.

She says, 'It's haunted wi a huge rat.'

'Oh,' he says, 'surely you, a big cat like you wouldnae be feared o a rat, wid ye?'

She says, 'Ah, A dinnae ken,' she says, 'this is nae ordinary rat.'

An he says, 'A cannae help it,' he says, 'I cannae help it, the hunger's gettin the better o me, A'll hae tae gang doon fir a bit of this hard cheese.' So they go doon tae this fairm, intae the barn, an there wis some strae, ye ken, in the barn.

An she says, 'Noo, we've got this cheese right enough,' an it wis aa richt, apart from bein hard, ye ken, so they sat an they gorged theirsel wi this cheese. Then she says, 'Now,' she says, 'you'd better go in among that strae,' she says; 'cover yirsel up wi the strae an bide richt in the corner, an don't move – don't breathe,' she says, 'when this thing comes.'

So he got in the corner an she scratched the strae up ower him an he happed he's sel up wi the strae. *So in the deid saelins o the nycht the rat came. *An he's lyin there an he's peepin through, ye see, an he seen this rat comin in right enough, but it wis just an ordinary-sized rat. An it come in, and the cat got its back up, ye ken, like this, an 'Chhh! Pffph!' [spitting noises] an the rat's 'Tschch!' and the two o them are at each ither. And they're fightin an tearin an fightin an tearin, an this rat, it's gettin bigger an bigger, an the cat, it's getting bigger an bigger! An the rat gets bigger an the cat's getting bigger, an the rat's getting bigger an the cat's getting bigger, till Jack's cooried in the corner like this, on his knees, right intae the corner wi the strae

41

ower him an he says, 'Oh, me, me!'

*But she kept her back tae this corner whar Jack wis so that he wouldnae get crushed, ye see, the cat did. An they fought an fought an fought an fought fir aboot three strucking 'oors, an all the time he's gettin bigger an she's gettin bigger till the barn wis almost packed wi them, an it wis takin her aa her time fir tae keep Jeck safe in this corner under the strae.*

But this cat, she says, 'When ye see that A'm as good as whit you are, will ye no leave me alane?'

An the rat says, 'When ye see that A'm as good as whit you are, will you no leave *me* alane?' An he says, 'Well, will we hae a truce an jist say one's as good's the ither, an we'll jist leave it at that?'

An the cat says, 'Aye; but there's something A would like tae ask ye.'

An he says, 'Whit's that?'

She says, 'Hev you any hailt or hair o a strange castel aboot this airts?'

'No, no,' he says, 'no; but,' he says, 'A tell ye whit A can dae,' he says. 'I can gie ye the power tae call all the beasts an ask them.'

She says, 'Well, you gie me that,' she says, 'an A'll leave ye alane' – because she near had the eyes oot o this –

So she [sic] says, 'Well leave me alane then, an A'll tell you,' he says . . . 'A'll . . . put the power on ye, an,' he says, 'you can call on all the beasts in the land tae see.' So – whew – the rat disappears, an this cat she shrunk back tae her normal size, an she says, 'Are ye there, Jeck?'

'Aye, A'm here,' he says, 'A'm here – whit's left of me's here,' he says. 'A'm near aa shrunk awa wi the fricht wi (?) me.'

She says, 'Come oot, it's aa richt,' she says. 'A've got something that'll help us.'

So the next day she went oot, and she called this words that the rat had given her, an all the animals startit comin. An they came an they came, an every one wis asked the same question, did they hear any hairt or hair o this castel.

'Na.' 'No.' 'No.' 'No, no.' Always no, no, no.

'Ah,' Jeck says, 'it's nae use,' he says, 'nae use at aa. Well, if she disnae come,' he says, 'A'm goin tae throw masel in the wa –'

'Ah, shut up,' she says, 'what are ya gaein tae throw yirsel in the water fir? We'll get her yet.'

So at the last he wis jist giein up when he seen this wee moose comin: it wis aa half-drookit, an it seemed – it was aa thon drookit

42

wey, ye ken, like a half-droon't moose. An here it comes up. An he says, 'Ahh,' he says, 'we neednae ask you.'

'Whit is it?' she says.

'Did ye hear any hilt or hair on a strange castel or a strange –'

'A'm jist new awa fae it!' she says.

'Are ye sure?'

'Aye!' she says. 'A'm sure. A'm jist newly awa fae it,' she says, 'across the border there,' she says, 'and a beautiful young –'

And she says, 'Whar –'

'Oh,' she says, 'she's aa richt rycht enough, but she'll no hae nothing tae dae wi this cook: he hes her locked up until she will hae something tae dae wi him.'

And he says, 'Well,' he says, 'moose, A tell ye whit A want ye tae dae,' he says. 'You go back across,' he says, 'an look, an ye'll see an aald jaiket, and there's a wee roostie box in it,' he says. 'If you could get that box tae me,' he says, 'A'll gie ye the bonniest wee locket fir yir neck that ever ye seen in yir life.'

'Ah, Jeck,' she says, 'you're good at promisin, but A bet ye ye're no sae good at giein.'

He says, 'As sure as God,' he says, 'if you go back there,' he says, 'you'll get it.'

'But,' she says, 'hoo am I gaan tae get back across that water?' (This wis a big moat, ye see, ootside thon aa (?).)

The cat says, 'Wait, I ken whar tae get across the water. Come doon here.' So they come doon tae the water's edge, and she says, 'Jack, you lift that stone.' So Jack took this great big stone an he lifted it, an this wis a great big toad under the stone . . . . It was either a puddick or a toad, but A think it wis a puddick.

And he says, 'Wghgh [growl], whit are ye disturbin folk like this fir, noo, a little bit (?) Whit are ye disturbin me fir?'

He says, 'A want ye tae dae somethin fir me.'

'God, God,' he says, 'could ye no leave folk at peace nae time? whit dae ye want?'

He says, 'A want ye tae take this young woman across the water.'

'Whit wumman?'

He says, 'This wee moose here,' he says, 'an if you dae that,' he says, 'ye're all right fir the rest o yir life,' he says, 'ye'll get everything ye want.'

'Ah,' he says, 'ye're good at promisin, but ye're no sae good at –'

He says, 'Honest tae God,' he says, 'as sure as God, you dae this fir me –'

43

So this puddick he says, 'Get on ma back, then, moose.' So the moose got on the puddick's back, an across the water, intae the castel, an up tae whar this aald jeckit wis hingin, ye see? And she dis get this wee box, but she couldnae get it oot. So she gnawed a hole in the bottom o that until if fell doon on the floor, an she pu'd an pu'd an pu'd it till she got it oot . . . . An the puddick says, 'Hoo am I gaun tae get this across the water?' An he says, 'Aa richt'. So he lay on his back, an he says; 'Noo, you sit on ma belly – pit the box on there an you sit on the tap o it an hadd it on my belly, an A'll go backie-weys across the water.' And he went across the water like this tae whar Jack wis, an gave –

'Oh,' Jack says [to the wee man], 'are ye there?'

'Aye, A'm here.'

He says, 'Is ma wi – '

'Aye, she's all right,' he says.

'Well,' he says. 'A wish she wis back. An,' he says, 'A wish the cook and this butler, the two o them,' he says, 'tae be tarred an feathered an pit a match tae.' And nae suiner said than the deed wis done, and they were burnt in izel [cinders] and he wis back wi his wife in his ain castel an everything, an that's the end o ma story. And the last time A wis there,

> A got brogues o butter an clippins o gless,
> An A come slidin doon the brae on ma – . . .

ANIMAL TALE

# 8   Why the Wolf is Stumpy Tailed

One day the wolf and the fox were out together, and they stole a dish of crowdie. Now the wolf was the biggest beast of the two, and he had a long tail like a greyhound, and great teeth. The fox was afraid of him, and did not dare to say a word when the wolf ate the most of the crowdie, and left only a little in the bottom of the dish for him. But he determined to punish him for it: so, the next night, when they were out together, the fox said, 'I smell a very nice cheese, and' (pointing to the moonshine on the ice) 'there it is, too!' 'And how will you get it?' said the wolf. 'Well! stop you here till I see if the farmer is asleep, and if you keep your tail on it, or put it through the ice, nobody will see you, or know that it is there: keep it steady, though I may be some time of getting back.' So the wolf lay down, and laid his tail on the moonshine in the ice; and there he kept it for an hour, till it was fast. Then the fox, who had been watching him, ran in to the farmer and said, – 'The wolf is there, he will eat up the children – the wolf, the wolf!' Then the farmer and his wife came out with sticks to kill the wolf, but the wolf ran off, leaving his tail behind him: and that is why the wolf is stumpy, and the fox has a long brush.

## 9  The Fox and the Goose

One day the fox succeeded in catching a fine, fat goose, asleep, by the side of a loch. He held her by the wing, and making a joke of her cackling, hissing, and fears, he said: 'Now, if you had me in your mouth, as I have you, tell me what you would do?' 'Why,' said the goose, 'that is an easy question. I would fold my hands, shut my eyes, say a grace, and then eat you.' 'Just what I mean to do,' said Rory, and folding his hands, and looking very demure, he said a pious grace, with his eyes shut. But, alack! while he did this, the goose had spread her wings, and was now half-way over the loch: so the fox was left to lick his lips for supper. 'I will make a rule of this,' he exclaimed, in disgust, 'never, in all my life, to say a grace again till after I feel the meat warm in my belly.'

## 10  The Fox and the Wrens

A fox had noticed for some days a family of wrens, off which he much wished to dine. He *might* have been satisfied with one, but he determined to have the whole lot – father and eighteen sons; and all so like, he could not tell the one from the other, or the father from his children. 'It is of no use to kill one son, because the old cock will take warning and fly away with seventeen: I wish I knew which was the old gentleman.' He set his wits to work to find out, and one day, seeing them all threshing in a barn, he sat down to watch them. Still he could not be sure. 'Now I have it,' he said. 'Well done, the old man's stroke, he hits true,' he cried. 'Ah!' replied the one he often suspected of being the head of the family, 'if you had seen my grandfather's strokes you might have said so.' The sly fox pounced on the cock, ate him up in a trice, and then soon caught and disposed of the eighteen sons, all flying in terror about the barn.

## 11   The Fox and the Cock and Hen

One day the fox chanced to see a fine cock and a fat hen, off whom he would much have liked to dine, but at his approach they flew up into a tree. He did not lose heart, however, and soon began to make talk with them, inviting them at last to go a little way with him. There was no danger, he said, no fear of his hunting them, for there was peace now between men and beasts, and among all animals.

At last, after much parleying, the cock said to the hen, 'My dear, do you not see a couple of hounds coming across the field?' 'Yes,' said the hen, 'and they will soon be here.' 'If that is the case, it is time I should be off', said the fox, 'for I am afraid these stupid hounds may not have heard of the peace,' and with that he took to his heels, and never drew breath till he reached his den.

## 12   The Three Wee Pigs

There was once a pigs' house where they were getting thick on the ground. The old sow had a younger family, so one day she sent out Dennis and Biddy and Rex to find their fortunes for themselves. They wandered on and on, till they got up by the Devil's Elbow and Glenshee, and the wind was blowing, and it was snowing and raining at once, and oh! but their trotters were sore! So they sat down by the roadside, under the shelter of a wood. They sat for an hour. They had but one pipe and one match between them, and Dennis lent his pipe to Rex, and Rex dried the match in his hair, for it was soaked, and he sat and smoked the wee cuttie pipe. Presently they heard a cart coming along, and it was loaded with straw. Biddy thought she'd build herself a house, if the man would give her some straw. And the man was very kind and obliging, for he was sorry for them, turned out of their Mother's house on such an awful day, just because Dennis had trod on one of the wee piglets by mistake.

So he gave them the straw, and some matches too, and Biddy built herself a cosy wee house. The other two were sitting a bittie longer, when they heard a cart coming up with slats of wood on it, and who should be driving it but Jimmie McLauchlan, who was at school with Dennis. So Dennis asked him for some slats of wood, to build himself a wee wooden housie. And Jimmie gave it him and welcome. Well, Dennis had hardly set to work when a lorry from Fife came up the road, with a load of bricks on it. Rex cried to the man, and he stopped, and threw out as many bricks as Rex needed to build himself a brick house. And there they were all settled for the night. But as Biddy was sitting in her cosy wee house, she heard someone knocking. 'Is that you, Dennis?' she said, 'Oh, no it's an old friend,' said a voice that she knew well. 'Just let me in and have a news with you.' 'Oh, no, I'll not let you in,' said Biddy, for she knew the wolf's voice when she heard it. 'Then I'll puff, and I'll blow, and I'll blow your house in,' said the wolf, and he blew so hard that all the straw scattered. But just as he got in at the front door, Biddy ran out at the back, and went to Dennis's house. 'He'll not blow this down,' said Dennis. And that moment they heard the wolf at the door. 'Let me in, I've a great piece of news for you.' 'No, we'll not let you in,' they said. 'Then I'll puff and I'll blow, and I'll blow your house in.' And he blew so hard that he blew all the slats apart, and Biddy and Dennis had only time to get out of the back door, and scamper to Rex's house before the wolf was in at the front.

He raced on after them to Rex's house, but though he puffed and he blew, he couldn't blow it down. So he crept up on to the roof to jump down the lum. But Biddy had given Rex some straw to make a bed, and when they heard the wolf on the roof he threw all the straw on the fire, and it blazed up, and burnt him to death. So they hooked him down the chimney, and cut him up into collops, and roasted him for their supper. But there are no houses up in the wood now, for the pigs were all taken to the old people's houses, and there they died.

## 13   The Cushie Doos and the Peeseweeps

Langsyne the cushie doos built their nests on the ground, and the peeseweeps built their nests on trees. The cushies were greatly annoyed by cattle, horses, and sheep trampling their nests and otherwise disturbing them. To get rid of this annoyance a great gathering of cushies was convened, when, after much serious deliberation, the suggestion of an 'auld-farrant doo', that they should try to induce the peeseweeps to exchange nests with them, was adopted. In this endeavour, after a good deal of 'fleeching', they were successful, and immediately took possession of their new quarters. On getting fairly settled down, the cushies were so pleased with the change that they gave voice to their triumph by crying. 'Coo-come-noo-coo-oo – comenoo-come noo'; while the peeseweeps, on discovering how they had been victimised, broke out into that wild melancholy wail heard upon our moors, pee-ee-weep, pee-ee-we-weep.

## RELIGIOUS TALE

## 14

On another night the same Saint [Serf] was at Alva, being entertained by a certain poor peasant who had no substance, except one pig, which he killed that night for the holy man, and when he rose on the morrow, he found it alive in his yard. At another time there was a man in Aitheren who had a sheep which he loved and nourished in his house. But a thief coming stealthily stole it away from him. Now the ram was sought through the whole parish, and was not found, and lo! when the thief was brought into the presence of the blessed man and interrogated by the Saint whether he was guilty of the crime laid to his charge, he affirmed on oath that he was not. And beginning again to swear by the staff of the holy man, the wether bleated in his bowels. And the wretch confessed his sin, and asked and received pardon from S. Servanus.

## NOVELLA

## 15   The King and the Miller

A'm tellin ye a little story about a miller an his daughter: he hed one o the nicest daughters could be seen in the country, an everybody hed a fancy of her. And the keeng – the young king was livin not very far from her an he had a notion of her, an he didnae know what way for tae gain this girl. An he went doon tae the mill one day, and he said, 'A'm goin to gie ye three questions,' he says, 'miller, and ye know,' he says, 'the keeng's word's never broke. And if ye don't answer me that three questions,' he says, 'your head will go on my gate.'

'Well,' says the miller, 'if A can answer them A'll try ma best.'

He says, 'Ye know,' he says, 'that I can do what I like,' he says, 'I'm keeng o this country, an my word'll stand.'

'Very well,' says the miller, he says, 'what is it?'

'Well,' he says, 'you must tell me,' he says, 'the weight o the moon. That's wan. You must tell me,' he says, 'hoo many stars is in the heavens. That's two. An you must – third one,' he says, 'you must tell me what A'm thinkin on.'

'Oh, well,' says the miller, he says, 'A doot my heid'll go on yir gates.'

An he says, 'Gin this time a year an a day,' he says, 'A'll be doon,' he says, 'an ask ye the questions. An if ye're not right,' he says, 'yir head comes off.'

So this poor miller now, he's gaun up an doon, thinkin tae himsel what could he say or what could he do. An there's a young shepherd lad not very far away, and he was helpin him at the hairvest, takin in the hairvest. An . . . the shepherd chap says tae him, 'Gosh bless me, miller,' he says, 'what's ado wi ye? Ye're aa(?) awfae dour be when I cam here first.'

'Yes,' he says, 'laddie, A'm dour. An if you kent,' he says, 'what I ken,' he said, 'you would be dour too.'

He says, 'What is it?'

So he told the shepherd what he wis told be the keeng. An he says, 'You know the keeng's word,' he says, 'goes far.'

'Oh well,' he says, 'A'll tell you one thing,' he says, 'miller,' he says: 'if you promise me tae get your daughter,' he says, 'as a wife,' he says. 'A'll clear ye o that.'

'Well,' he says, 'A can't give her,' he says, 'unless she's willin.' An he goes in tae his daughter an he asks her a question; he says, 'My daughter,' he says, 'ye know,' he says, 'what I've tae suffer.'

She said, 'Yes.'

He says, 'Would you get my life saved,' he says, 'fir tae mairry a man?'

She says, 'A wid mairry,' she says, 'the day, if it wid save yir life.'

'Well,' he says, 'there a man'll save my life if ye marry him.'

49

'Who is he?' she says.

He says, 'So and so's shepherd.'

'Well,' she says, 'he'ss as good as what I am. A'll marry him if he'll save yir life, but not, faither, till yir life's saved.'

'A'll bet yez (?) he'll save my life – I think.'

So the shepherd an them agreed that he would save his life. So that day year – it's a Hogmanay night – he was up the side o the dam an who did he meet but his young keeng.

'Good evenin, shepherd' – A'm going wrong wi ma story now . . . Just a minute . . . . A should have said that the shepherd dressed himsel up with a white baerd an put on the miller's suit o clothes on him, and he's away up beside the dam fir tae meet the keeng: this was the night he wis tae meet him an answer his questions. So –

'Good evenin, Miller.'

'Good evenin, my noble keeng,' he said.

'Did you answer my questions?'

'Oh well,' he says, 'so far as I think,' he says, 'A hiv.'

He says, 'What weight is the moon?'

He says, 'The moon'll be a hundredweight. There's four quaarters in the moon,' he says, 'an there four quarters in a hundredweight.'

He says, 'That's very good! Can ye tell me hoo mony stars,' he says, 'as shines in the heavens?'

'Oh, there'll be aboot seven million, five hundred and fifty-five, and if ye dinnae believe me ye can coont them yirsel.'

'A cannae – I cannae coont them,' . . . says the keeng. He says, 'Ye cannae tell me,' he says, 'what . . . A'm thinkin on. This one'll . . . puzzle ye,' he says.

'Yes,' he says, 'A can. You think,' he says, 'ye're speakin tae the auld miller, but ye'll fin' it's his son-in-laa ye're talkin to!'

So the young fella got the auld man saved an married the girl. So that's the end o ma story.


# 16   The Professor of Signs

It is said to have taken place in the reign of James VI of Scotland, and shortly after he had removed to London. . . . The Spanish ambassador, a man of great learning, but, like many others, 'wi' a bee in his bonnet', had the idea that in every university there should be a Professor of Signs, whose duty should be the making men of various countries understand each other by signs, thus doing away with the tedious and laborious process of learning different languages . . . One day he was lamenting to the king this great and important deficiency in our university education, declaring that he could not understand how it should have been so long overlooked. The king, who was as fond of a joke as he was of *cock-a-leekie*, said that he laboured under a very great mistake in supposing that this important branch of education had been entirely forgotten in this country, for in the most northerly of all his universities there was a Professor of Signs, whose fame was very great.

'And where may that be?' inquired the ambassador.

'At Aberdeen, some six hundred miles off, and too far for you to travel.'

'Though it were ten thousand leagues off I'll go and see him, and prove the truth of his fame. Such a man is not to be found every day, and I will at once set out for this place, however remote it may be.'

The king, seeing he had 'put his foot in it', and finding he could not very well back out, wrote to the principal of our university an account of the matter, advising him of his coming, and desiring the professors to put him off the best way they could. The ambassador arrived almost at the same time as the letter, and presented himself at the university before they had concocted any plan . . . .

There was a 'souter', some say a butcher, named Geordie, who lived in the old town, blind of an eye, noted for his waggery and quickness of repartee. One of the professors meeting him explained the dilemma in which they were placed, and said that they did not know what to do. Geordie, ready for any sort of fun, declared that if they would entrust the matter to him, he would undertake to send the ambassador away pleased with his visit, and brimful of information, to his native country.

At their wits' end, and glad of any opportunity of sending their guest away, they granted Geordie's request, particularly enjoining him not to *speak*, as that would be sure to spoil the whole matter. Dressed in professional robes and a flowing wig, Geordie was placed in a chair of state in one of the rooms of the college, adjoining which was the reception-room, into which the ambassador was ushered . . . . The professors informed him that the Professor of Signs was in the adjoining room waiting his appearance. The ambassador entering, walked up and took a keen survey of Geordie's features, which he bore with the greatest equanimity. Suddenly he shoved one of his

51

hands into his pocket, and producing an orange held it up to the bright eye of Geordie; the 'souter', nothing daunted, thrust his hand into the pocket of his coat, and produced a piece of oaten cake, which he held up to the surprised and delighted ambassador. While they were thus gazing at each other, the ambassador replacing the orange in his pocket, held up one finger, on which Geordie held up two. The ambassador then held up three, on which Geordie clenched his hand and held it sternly in the air. On seeing this the ambassador smiled in a most gratified manner, bowed most profoundly, and left the presence of the pretended professor.

On entering the room where the professors were anxiously awaiting his return, he held up his hands and declared that their Professor of Signs was a perfect miracle, and worthy of having come much further to see. 'When I entered the room,' said he, 'and looked carefully at him, I drew from my pocket an orange and held it up before him, signifying the richness of the country from which I came. He promptly put his hand into his pocket and drew forth a piece of oaten cake, showing me that his country was better than mine, for it produced bread, the staff of life. I then held up one finger, meaning that there was only one God. He held up two, showing that there were two persons in the Godhead. I held up three, meaning that there were three persons in the Godhead. He clenched his hand to show that the three were one.'

On the departure of the ambassador, delighted with his interview, Geordie was called in to give his version of the story. 'The scamp,' said Geordie, very indignantly, 'what do you think did he dee? He cam forret and stared in my face as gin I had been a forren loon like himsel. After this piece o impudence he shoved his hand into his pouch, and pullin' out an orange held it up afore me, as much as to say, "Your peer country canna produce that!" I shoved my hand into my pouch, and pulled out a whang o' oaten cake and held it up, darin' him to show ony thing like that. Then fut do ye think did the rascal dee? He held up aye finger, meanin' that I had only aye e'e. I held up twa, meanin' that he had only twa. He held up three, meanin' that there was only three between us. I then clenched my hand, and was in sic a rage that gin he hidna gane out o' the room pretty quick I wid hae knocket out baith his blinkers.'

52

# 17

A giant and his wife lived in a cave now called the Giant's Cave at Aldequhat. One day the giant fell asleep in his cave whilst a big kettle of fish was cooking. A man that was fishing in the loch went into the cave, found the giant asleep and his wife away. He overturned the boiling kettle over the giant's face, and blinded him. He jumped up in his pain and tried to catch the author of his misery. It was in vain. He could not see him. He asked his name in hopes that he might in after times have an opportunity of exacting justice from him. 'I mysel' is my name,' was the answer. After chasing the man to no purpose he roared: 'A' burnt, a' burnt.' The roar was heard by his wife, and she called back: 'Quha did it? Quha did it?' He answered: 'I mysel' did it.' Her reply was: 'I thysel' can blaw thysel.' The man, dreading the wife's return, meantime made his escape from the cave with all speed, mounted his horse and fled, as the wife was coming to the cave. When she found out what had taken place, she set out in pursuit of the man that had done the evil deed. It was a hard race, but she overtook him. She seized the horse by the tail. The man turned round in the saddle and struck out with his sword and cut off her arm, and so escaped.

## JOCULAR TALE: (1) NUMSKULL TALE

## 18 The Assynt Man's Mistakes

The Assynt man's wife once asked him to take her spinning-wheel to be mended. The wind catching the wheel set it turning, so he threw it down, and said, 'Go home, then, and welcome!' He then struck across the hill, and on arriving asked his wife if her wheel had got home yet? 'No,' she replied. 'Well, I thought not, for I took care to take the short cut. It will be here presently.'

A traveller stopping one day at his house asked the hour. The Assyindach, lifting a large sun-dial from its stand, put it in the stranger's lap that he might see for himself.

Seeing a four-wheeled carriage, he exclaimed, 'Well done the little wheels! the two big ones won't overtake them today.'

He took his child to be baptised. The minister, who knew him, said he doubted if he were fit to hold the child for baptism. 'Oh, to be sure I am, tho' he is as heavy as a stirk.' This answer showing but little wit, the minister then asked him how many commandments there were? The Assynt man boldly replied twenty. 'Oh, that will never do. Go home first, and learn your questions' (catechism). On his way back the Assynt man fell in with a neighbour. 'But how many commandments are there? There must be a great many, for the minister would not be content with twenty.' When set right on this point he went back to the minister, and to keep the baby warm he slipped it into his coat-sleeve, tying up the mouth of the sleeve with a string. But as he walked the string came off, the baby fell out, and slipped into a snow-wreath. Not till he was in church did the Assynt man discover his mistake. 'I am very sorry,' he said 'but not a bit of Kenneth have I got now.' – (N.B. No wise person names an unbaptised infant; it is unlucky, and this infant died in the snow.)

The Assynt man once went as far as Tain to buy meal. A man overtaking him asked him what o'clock it was. 'Well, last time it was twelve; but if it is striking still it must be nearly twenty.'

He carried two bags full of cheese to market one day. One bag broke, and the cheese rolling fast down hill testified to a power of locomotion on their part which he was sorry not to have found out sooner, as they were very heavy. He, therefore, opened the second bag, and sent its contents after the first ones, walking on himself to market. He was surprised, as he said, not to find his cheeses. He waited all day, and then consulted his mother, who advised him to look for them at the bottom of the hill. There, to his great joy, he found them all.

On seeing a hare for the first time he took it for a witch, and while repeating the Lord's Prayer he backed from it. Unluckily he backed into a pond, and there, but for his wife's help, he must have been drowned.

## JOCULAR TALE: (2) SCHWANK

## 19

There's a fine story about a man that was lookin for a wife wance, and he watched how she ate cheese. So win woman cut a great chunk of this skin and throwed it away: so he thought she was too extra-vagant, he wouldn't have anything to do with her. And then the second one ate it all: so he thought there was something wrong with her, she was too mean, she ate the skin and all. So the third one gave the skin a bit scrape, you see and then she ate it: and he married her. Shö was the most successful wife, he thought.

## 20   Master Above All Masters

Once upon a time there was a tailor who had got on in the world. He had made so much money, he could now afford to keep a man-servant. He kept on living in the same house, but now that he had grown so rich and grand he thought he'd need to change the name of everything in his household.

One day, as he was sitting in the garden, he called the man-servant to him and asked, 'What do you call me?'

'I call you "Master",' replied the man-servant.

'Call me no more "Master",' said the tailor. 'Call me "Master above all Masters".'

The man-servant nodded his head.

'What do you call these?' asked the Master above all Masters, touching his trousers.

'I call them "trousers",' replied the man-servant.

'Call them no more "trousers",' said the tailor. 'Call them "stunti-fiers".'

The man-servant nodded his head.

'What do you call my wife?' next asked the Master above all Masters.

'I call her "the Master's Wife",' replied the man-servant.

'Call her no more that,' said the tailor. 'Call her "Madame for the Dame".'

The man-servant nodded his head.

'What do you call my son?' asked the Master above all Masters.

'I call him "The Master's Son",' replied the man-servant.

'Call him no more that,' said the tailor. 'Call him "Sir John the Greater".'

The man-servant nodded his head.

'And what do you call my cat?' wondered the Master above all Masters.

'I call him "The Master's Cat",' replied the man-servant.

'Call him no more that,' said the tailor. 'Call him "Old Killie-craffus".'

'And what do you call that?' asked the Master above all Masters, pointing with his stick to the chimney.

'I call that "The Master's Lum",' replied the man-servant.

'Call it no more that,' said the tailor. 'Call it "The Top of Montaigo".'

The man-servant nodded his head.

'What do you call that?' enquired the Master above all Masters, pointing to the well.

'I call that "The Master's Well",' replied the man-servant.

'Call it no more that,' said the tailor. 'Call it the "Well of Strath-fountain".'

The man-servant nodded his head.

'And what do you call my house?' asked the Master above all Masters.

'I call it "The Master's House",' replied the man-servant.

'Call it no more that,' said the tailor. 'Call it "The Castle of Kilmundy".'

The man-servant nodded his head.

One night, some time after this, the house went on fire. The man-servant ran upstairs and called –

> 'Arise, Master above all Masters,
> Put on thy Stuntifiers,
> Waken Madame for the Dame
> And Sir John the Greater,
> For Old Killiecraffus
> Has gone to the top of Montaigo,
> And if you don't apply to the Well of Strathfountain
> The whole Castle of Kilmundy
> Will be burned in twa minutes.'

By the time the man-servant had finished this long rigmarole, the whole place was in a blaze, and they escaped with the skin of their teeth.

## 21   The Robbers and the Auld Woman

There was oncet an aul' wummin, she lived hersel in a little wee hoosie in the country, oh, in the back of beyont, but she was turnin very very aul'. She was awa aboot echty or echty-odds, and of course she was getting a bittie dottled, kind of things, speakin til hersel and one thing and another. Bit she was supposed to hae a lot of money, ye see, hidden in this hoose – a *lot* of money (she was real miserly-kind, ye know) and there was three men cam to rob her that nicht – three men. And one of this men wantit ae ee, but the three of them was gaun to help each ither and get the money – steal the money and murder the aul' wummin and get awa wi'd ye see, 'cos 'twas in a lonely place. One of this men wantit ae ee.

But it happent to be, oniewey or anither, that that nicht this puir aul' cratur she had the brander (you know the brander she used to keep in her fire, and some of them has them yet in the country, real auld-fashiont they used to roast the kippers and things upon the branders, ye see). And she was – wi this auld-fashioned brander on – she was roastin this kippers for her supper. But she was speakin away to the kippers as if they were human beings, ye see, as dottled folk does, cos I've sat and watched them, ye see. She's speakin away to this kippers, rockin hersel back and forth, ye see, in an aul' chair, owre this aul'-fashiont fire, ye see, roastin this kippers and turnin them, ye see.

But she didnae ken there was three men come to murder her and rob her 'at night. But one was comin doon the lum (that was the wey that he was gaun to enter, ye see, because the hoose was aa lockit up, and he was gaun to enter – coming doon the lum). But she's this wee bittie o a fire on, ye see, nae very much, twa-three sticks, and she's roastin this kipper. The first kipper, and she says, 'Ha ha,' she says, 'there's three o yese, and there's one of yese,' she says, 'gaun awa', she says, 'soon,' she says, 'for I'll roast you and I'll toast ye,' she says, 'and I'll eat ye for ma supper.' Ye see.

Now, a lot o them aye said, not only wis she a miser, but a lot o them said that she was an aul witch, ye see – well, they believed it in that days, onieway – whether they were or no, they'd only to say it.

But this – there was a story oot, oh, years afore, that this aul woman was an aul witch, ye see. An this man at this time, was the

first yin wis comin doon the lum when she was roastin the first
kipper, and she's speakin to the kipper, and she's not speakin tae him
at all. She didnae ken aboot a man comin doon the lum, so that's whit
she said.

'Ha ha,' she says, 'there's three o yese and there's one of yese gaun
awa,' she says, 'but I'll roast ye,' she says, 'and I'll toast ye and I'll eat
ye for my supper.'

He says, 'God bliss us!' he says, 'she kens I'm comin doon.' He
says. 'She's gaun to roast me and toast me and eat me for her supper.'

So he's up the lum an oot 'n it. 'Naw, naw,' he says to the ither
yins, he says: 'Praise God!' he says, 'I'm nae gaun to rob her,' he says,
'or kill her – she kens,' he says, 'that I wis comin doon her lum – she
kent,' he says, 'we're here. She said there wis three o us and that I wis
– ye know – was gaun awa and she wis gaun tae eat me – roast me and
eat me, ye see,' so he says: 'No, no,' he says – 'I'm nae taen nothing to
dae.' He's off and away. He got feared.

Ach, doon the second yin goes. He says, 'He's too yella,' ye see.
'She's nae a witch,' and aa this and the next thing, bit he gaes doon the
lum. Now she's roastin the second kipper by this time. And she says,
'Ha ha, there's one o yese away,' she says, 'an this is the second yin to
come,' she says. 'But I'll rost ye and I'll tost ye,' she says, 'and I'll eat
ye for my supper.'

But he took a hert-fricht tae, ye see, and he's up the lum – he
wondert whit wey she kent – cos naebody seed them gaen near this
place, ye see. An he's up the lum and he tells the ither yin – 'No, no,'
he says, 'that's a witch richt enough,' he says. 'She kent,' he says, 'at I
was comin, and she was preparin for to rost me and tost me and eat
me for her supper. So,' he says, 'no no,' he says, 'I'm nae g' t' hae
nothing to dae wi her,' so he's away too, runs away too. Noo the last
yin to come wantit ae eye. Bit is jist happent to be that her last kipper
didnae hae an ee either – it wantit an ee. Well, we wadnae pay onie
notice whether the kipper had an ee or no, bit an aul dottled bodie
like this sees queer kinna wee ferlies; they staund oot to them. So she
pits the kipper on and she's roastin it and turnin it, ye know, and
doon comes this man wantin the ee, and he's more desperater, and
he's the yin that was gaun to murder her. An he's comin doon quite
desperate for to kill her and get her money.

'Ha ha!' she says, 'come oan,' she says, 'come awa, A'm jist waitin
fur ye! she says. (But it was her kipper she was speakin til.) She says,
'Jist come awa,' she says, 'hurry up and come,' she says, 'I'm waitin

upon you,' she says. 'Ye're the third yin to come,' she says, 'and ye want a ee.'

Noo this made it mair convincin to him when he heard her sayin this. 'An,' she says, 'the third yin wants a ee,' she says. 'Ye're the third. But,' she says, 'I'll rost ye,' she says, 'and I'll tost ye, and I'll *eat* ye for my supper.' (She beginnin to get high kind noo, ye see, wi this kipper wantin the ee.)

So when he hears this he says, 'God bliss us! It's richt enough.' He says, 'she even kens I want a ee.' So he's up the lum and away. So it was only the puir aul dottled wumman speakin till her three kippers, that saved her ain life.

## 22   Biddable Jock

Jock was an ill laddie, and no' very biddable, but ae day he was sent to buy Livers and Lichts, and was tell't to gang straight there, come straight back, and no' gang near the water.

Weel, Jock gaed a' richt and got the Livers and Lichts, but he gaed oot by the water instead o' comin' hame as he was tell't, and the Livers and Lichts fell into the water. Jock ran alang, roarin' and greetin', and aye crying:

Livers and Lichts and a' come up,
Livers and Lichts and a' come up.

Noo Jock met a man that had been drinkin', and the man was bockin' and spewin', and Jock cries oot, richt fornent him:

Livers and Lichts and a' come up.

Sae the man juist took him and threshed him, and said: 'Ye maunna say that ony mair.'

'What maun I say, than?' quo' Jock.

Ye maun say, 'I wuss they may never come up,' quo' the man, and Jock promised.

He gaed on till he cam' to a man sawin' corn, and Jock says to him: 'I wuss they may never come up.'

'What's that ye say, sir?' quo' the man; and he cam' owre the dyke, and threshed Jock, and gar'd him say: 'Ane be the year, a hunner be the next.'

Jock gaed on till he met a funeral, and he said – 'Ane be the year, a hunner be the next.'

Sae ane o' the murners took him into the roadside and gied him a sair talkin' to, and tell't him to say: 'God rest her sowl', for it was a woman they were buryin'.

Jock gaed on a bit till he met twa men wi' a big wild-lookin' dowg on a raip, and Jock at ance says: 'God rest her sowl.'

The men thocht Jock was tryin' to mak' fun o' them, but they gied him a cuff or twa and tell't him it was only – 'Twa men takin' a mad bitch to be hanged.'

Jock gaed on till he met a waddin' pairty, and he cried oot – 'Twa men takin' a mad bitch to be hanged.'

Some o' them were angry, and some o' them snirted and leuch, but they tell't him he wasna to say that.

'What maun I say, than?' quo' Jock.

Say, 'I wuss ye guid luck to lie thegither.'

Jock gaed on till he cam' to a man and his horse lyin' in a ditch.

Quo' Jock, 'I wuss ye guid luck to lie thegither.'

'Here,' quo' the man; 'help me oot o' this.'

Sae Jock gied him his han', and the man tell't him no' to say that, but to say: 'The tane's oot, and I wuss hoo sune the ither may be oot.'

Jock next met a man wi' ae ee, and he says till him: 'Ane's oot, and I wuss hoo sune the ither may be oot.'

Sae the man gied him a guid wallopin', and gar'd him say – 'I wuss it may never gae oot.'

Wi' this Jock was back at the end o' the village, and there he saw the mill on fire; and the miller was stampin' and ragin' in the middle o' the road, and Jock gangs up till him, and he says – 'I wuss it may never gae oot.'

Sae the miller juist took Jock by the cuff o' the neck and the erse o' the breeks and flang him intil the bleeze.


## 23   The Parson's Sheep

Away back in the old days in Orkney there were some gey pitiful times. Jimmock o' Tissiebist, wi' a scrythe o' peerie bairns, were warse off than maist: wi' the sheep a' deein', and the tatties a failure, things at Tissiebist wisna lookin' ower bright for Christmas. Whatever wyes or no, one blashie dark night, Jimmock was away a while, and twa-three days efter, an uncan yowe was seen aboot the hoose. Some of the bairns surely kent the yowe, for one day when ane of them was oot herdin' the kye, he was singin' to himsel' aboot it, something like this:

> Me father's stol'n the parson's sheep
> An' we'll hae mutton an' puddin's tae eat,
> An' a mirry Christmas we will keep,
> But we'll say nethin' aboot it.

> For if the parson gets tae know,
> It's ower the seas we'll have tae go,
> And there we'll suffer grief an' woe
> Because we stole fae the parson.

Well, up jumps the parson fae the other side o' a faelie dyke, and he says tae the boy: 'Boy, look here, if you'll come to the church on the Sabbath and sing that same song, I'll gie thee a suit o' claes and half a croon.'

So, on the Sunday mornin' service, efter the minister had read a psalm and said a prayer, he stood up and he said in an a'ful lood voice: 'I hev the following intimation to make. Stand up, boy, and sing that same song as I heard you singin', herdin' the kye.'

But the peerie boy hed mair wit than that. This is what he sang:

> As I was walkin' oot one day
> I spied the parson very gay:
> He was tossin' Molly in the hay –
> He turned her upside down, sir.

> A suit o' claes and half a croon
> Was given tae me be Parson Broon
> Tae tell the neighbours all aroon'
> What he hed done tae Molly!'

## JOCULAR TALE: (3) JOKE

### 24

'Eh, Dauvit, gin I wad slip awa', hoo sune wad ye hae anither? Ye wadna hae time to gae through as mony as the decent man wha's third spouse speired at him whilk o' them a he likit best. He claw'd his pow; wi' a wink o' his e'e, quo he, "Ye're fond o' news. Gin ye maun ken, the first wis the love o' my youth, the second wis the mither o' my bairns, an' as for you, it's jist hoo ye behave yersel".'

### 25

A well-known individual in the west of Scotland, named Jock, occasionally came from Airth, with the great canal passage boat, and generally managed to escape passage free. A gentleman who knew he had not paid any thing one day, accosted him, 'Weel, Jock, did you pay your fare to-day?' 'Deed, sir,' said Jock, 'I looked roun' me, an' I saw this ane payin' an' that ane payin', an' I just thocht it was surely needless for every body to be payin'.'

### 26

A neighbouring laird in the estate of Kinneston . . . on one occasion called out to one of his young lads, who was passing somewhat smartly, 'Whaur noo, Jock?' 'Od maister, I'm gaun to my supper; it's sax o'clock isn't?' 'Maybe it is, Jock,' says the laird, 'but what hae ye been daein' the day?' 'O,' says Jock, 'I was helpin' Tam Broon.' 'Just so,' says the laird, 'but what was Tam Broon daein'?' 'Weel,' says Jock . . . 'he was daein' naething.' . . . It is to this day a proverb in the district to say of anyone who is lazy and doing little, that he has been 'helpin' Tam Broon'.

### 27

There was a farm in Dumfriesshire which had the reputation of working its men pretty hard, and one man went there to work and after a while met a friend who asked what it was like on the farm, to which he replied 'Oh, it's just like heaven.' 'Just like heaven?' replied the friend, taken aback. 'Aye,' he said, 'there's nae night there either.'

## 28

A teacher wis affa made up at a pupil 'at wis aye missin fae school. Every time she asked him he said he wis helpin his mither 'at the washin'. Ae weet day he wis absent an after school she met the lad an said, 'Now, William, why were you absent today?'

'I wis helpin my mither.'

'But she wasn't washing today.'

'No, she wis makin jam.'

'But she doesn't need you to make jam.'

'Oh bit aye. Aa day she's hid me rinnin up an doon ti the kirk-yaird for the jeely jars.'

## JOCULAR TALE: (4) TALL TALE

## 29

[William Smeaton] often told of a daring encounter he had with a large dog which attacked him one time when he was fishing at Lochearn. Seeing that there was no escape from it, he quickly rolled his handkerchief round his right hand, and when the infuriated animal had its mouth wide for attack, William with a tremendous effort sent his hand down its throat and through its body, and catching its tail firmly, drew back his hand and turned the animal inside out.

## 30

[Bilzy Young] said he knew there were two large hares in a park near by, and he determined to have them both. Arriving at the gate, with his dog, early in the morning, he fixed his large gully-knife in the passage, in such a way as he thought would secure the death of one of the hares, while he knew his dog would be certain to catch the other. Having done this, he sent his dog through the park to start the game, which was speedily done, and the dog in full cry after the two hares direct for the gate. But he said he miscalculated the proper position for erecting his gully betwixt the gateposts, for one hare passed by one side of it, and the other the other side, while his dog, after running straight against the knife, severing himself exactly in two *perpendicularly*, caught both hares in an adjacent park, the several halves of the dog turning to the right and left of the *gully*, pursuing each its own hare, and killing it.

## 31

Dan was bragging of some fine sport he had one day shooting gulls in the Brandy Cove. 'Ye ken naething about shootin',' cried the Deacon. 'I min' aince on a time o' firin' at a covey o' partricks, oot gaed my shot, it killed three hunner o' th' brutes, an' my ramrod gaed aff wi' the shot, gaed two mile i' th' cluds, and stringed seven wild geese, a' sailin' in a troop, by th' een, the shot wis sae strang, the gun puttit me, ower I gaed, an' killed a fat hare i' the seat, an' as I wis tryin' tae get up I put my taes i' the yird and I kicked twenty pints o' honey oot o' a foggy bees' byke – that wis a shot tae blaw o'.'

## 32

One of the farmers of Kirkbride, near Creetown, was a great man for bees, of which he kept many 'skeps'. He used to tell a story about a swarm that had hived one warm summer day. He observed them making off in a westerly direction towards Wigtown; and bethinking himself that his gun was loaded with 'small hail', he ran into the house for it, intending to do some execution on the receding bees. He fired right amongst the hive, and killed every one of them except seventeen, (so he said), which seventeen turned out to be the best skep of bees he ever had. A short time after this splendid and wonderful 'deed of arms', the hero was met by the minister of the Parish – the Rev. J. Sibbald, who had heard the story with great good humour, as he could relish a joke of the kind exceedingly. He was anxious to hear the story genuine from the fountainhead. The farmer gave the minister the whole tale, and the latter asked 'whether none of the seventeen were wounded'. He was assured that none of the seventeen had suffered the slightest injury.

## FORMULA TALE: (1) DIALOGUE STORY

### 33

A.   Good morning, good fellow.
B.   I'm not a good fellow; I'm a new married man.
A.   Oh man, that's gude!
B.   Not sae gude as ye trow.
A.   What then, lad?
B.   I've gotten an ill-willy wife.
A.   Oh man, that's bad!
B.   Not sae bad as ye trow.
A.   What then lad?
B.   She brought me a gude tocher and a well-plenished house.
A.   Oh man, that's gude!
B.   Not sae gude as ye trow.
A.   What then, lad?
B.   The house took a-fire, and brunt baith house and plenishing and gear.
A.   Oh man, that's bad!
B.   Not sae bad as ye trow.
A.   What then, lad?
B.   *The ill-willy wife was burnt in the middle o't!* &c.

## FORMULA TALE: (2) CUMULATIVE TALE

### 34   The Mousie and the Rotten

A mousie and a rotten were to try a race to America. The mousie fell and broke its hinch, and gaed to the souter to get it shewed.

'Souter, souter, shew my hinch unto my pinch, and lat me win my wasie.'

65

'Na, awyte no,' says the souter, 'I winna shew your hinch unless ye gang to the soo for birse to me.'

'Soo, soo, birse me that I may birse the souter, the souter shew my hinch unto my pinch and lat me win my wasie.'

'Na, awyte no,' says the soo, 'I winna birse ye unless ye gang to the brewster wife for bran to me.'

'Brewster wife, brewster wife, bran me that I may bran the soo, and soo, soo, birse me that I may birse the souter, the souter shew my hinch unto my pinch and lat me win my wasie.'

'Na, awyte no,' says the brewster wife, 'unless ye gang to the coo for milk to me.'

'Coo, coo, milk me that I may milk the brewster wife; brewster wife bran me that I may bran the soo; the soo birse me that I may birse the souter; the souter shew my hinch unto my pinch and lat me win my wasie.'

'Na, awyte no,' says the coo, 'unless ye gang to the barn-man for strae to me.'

'Barn-man, barn-man, strae me, that I may strae the coo; and coo, coo, milk me that I may milk the brewster wife; brewster wife bran me that I may bran the soo; soo, soo, birse me that I may birse the souter; souter, souter, shew my hinch unto my pinch and lat me win my wasie.'

The coo got the strae, the brewster wife got milk, the soo got the bran, the mousie got the birse, and the souter shewed its hinch, and the mousie was first in America.

## LEGEND: (1) AETIOLOGICAL

## 35

But the Steeple's the glory o' oor toon. Maister Hogg prents it on his sugar-pocks, an' says date 1200. But it's far aulder than that; it gaes back tae the misty ages. It wis nae Pict that biggit it; as they telt me at the skule, it was the pixies. They stood in a row ae nicht fae Dunnin' tae the Lomond Hills an' passed the stanes as quick as thocht. At dawn it wis near the copin' whan a wiffie looked oot an' jist got a glint o' the wee men afore they vanished, laein' ithers tae finish their wark.

## LEGEND: (2) RELIGIOUS

## 36

Strathtay tradition has it that St Columba himself travelled adown the Tay to Dunkeld. Below St Colmes, in Dowally, the Saint grew tired, rested, took off his sandals, and found that his heels were badly blistered; however, near the spot where he rested he found a soft oily mould, and applied it to his heels, which were instantaneously made whole. Even till very recent times this earth was considered efficacious for cuts and sores. It was called in Gaelic 'Uir Chalum Chille' – St Columba's Mould.

## LEGEND: (3) SUPERNATURAL

## 37

Eh, but it's won'erfu' the brownies, fairies, and witches we've had in an' about Dunnin'. There's Brownie's Knowe, to be seen to this verra day up the burn. Puir chield! In a quiet day i' back end, ye may hear him fellin' trees an' breakin' sticks for his Yule fire. My granny's telt me, whan the guidwife o' Bawhandie wis in sair grip, an' naebody tae rin for the midwife, brownie saddled the mare, rade doon tae Dunnin', syne brocht her up the hill. Whan she cam' tae the door she said – 'I'm fleyed tae gang in for brownie.' 'Ye needna be that,' said he, as he raxed her doon; 'ye've ridden ahint him a' the road.' Gude keep's! it's awfu' tae think o't! hoo they wad com i' dead o' nicht an' spin the 'oo, and twine the hesp, an' ravel the yarn i' their cantrips, an' no lae a tick o' creesh i' the cruisie whan they gaed aff at skraigh o' day. Whan we war lasses we aye tuk the millband aff our spinnin' wheels afore we creepit, drummelt wi' sleep, intae the box-beds. The wey tae get quat o'brownie an' stop his middlin' wis tae gie him claes.

> Gie brownie a coat, gie brownie a sark,
> Ye'll get nae mair o' brownie's wark.

Hech, sirs! but thae brownies warna to prat wi'! They played gey
pliskies whiles, an' did muckle mischeef. My man, he's telt me – (ye
met auld Dauvid daunderin' doon the bank enoo; he has an unco
hoast, an' he's gey bou'd wi' the rumatics an' muckle sair wark.
Aince he wis a strappin', weel-faured chiel when first he gaed to see
the lasses. Losh, that's lang-syne) – that at the first ploy o' that kind
he wis black-fit tae Jock Ramsay, wha hed a tryst wi' twa braw
hizzies at Gilmertoun. Whan they got near the hoose, they war fain
to see licht. There wis nae mune, an' 'twis as dark as pick. They
dichtit the glaur aff their shoon on a pickle strae, snoddit theirsels,
joukit round the grozit bush, an' keekit in at the windie. Preserve us
a'! sic ongauns! Lads an' lasses loupin' an' dancin'; steamin' jougs
o'toddy an' succer-bread on a buffit-stool, an' a wee broun mannie
fiddlin' like mad on the dresser. Jock glower'd, turned blae, an' maist
dwained awa'. Syne his birse got up. 'Dod, that's queer usage; she'll
no' mak' a fule o' me again,' said he, banged roon', an' spak nae mair
till he cam' tae the Brig o' Kinkell – puir Dauvit, hirplin' alangside,
fley'd tae cheep. Jock wis a gude man, soor'd an' spilt for the rest o'
his life; he ne'er coorted anither lass, but lived an' dee'd a crabbit auld
carle, aye railin' at women. An', wad ye believe it, 'twis a brownie's
wark! The lasses, puir dawties, war sitting i' ben-end, courin' i' dark,
waitin' for a tirl at the pane to lift the sneck an' let the lads in. They
war gey sair daunted whan the 'oors gaed by an' nae lads cam' wi'
couthie crack to wile awa the nicht, ae hand in her's an' th' tither
roon' her waist. Jess mairit anither Joe, for she wis ane o' the kind that
aye keeps the halter fu'.

## 38

An honest miller once dwalt in Menstrie. He had a very bonnie wife,
and the fairies takin a notion o' her, carried her awa'. The puir man
was much cast doon at the loss o' his wife, mair especially as he heard
her, every morning, chanting aboon his head (but he could na see
her):

> O! Alva woods are bonnie,
>   Tillicoultry hills are fair;
> But when I think on the braes o' Menstrie,
>   It maks my heart aye sair.

Riddlin caff (chaff) ae day at the mooth o' his mill door, he chanced to stand upon ae fit, as the hens do in rainy weather – the enchantment which bound his wife was immediately broken, and lo! she stood beside him. The Miller o' Menstrie had a brither in misfortune – the drucken *Sautman* o'Tullibody. His wife was continually flyting upon him for his misconduct, but a' she said fell like rain in a desert, and produced nae effect. Seeing she could na be happy wi him, she prayed that the fairies might tak' her awa'. The fairies took hold of her in a twinklin', and up the lum they flew singin' –

> Deedle linkum dodie,
> We're aff wi' drucken Davie's wife,
> The *Sautman* o' Tullibody.

They carried her to Cauldhame – the palace o' the faries – whaur she lived like a queen. 'Blude,' they say, 'is aye thicker than water,' and the wife asked permission to live wi' her husband again. This was granted, and as she left the fairies, one of them presented her wi' a sma' stick, saying, 'as lang as ye keep this, your gudeman will drink nae mair.' The charm was successful. Davie becam' a sober man, and the gudewife never forgot the kindness o' the fairies.

## 39

Geordie More wis the gudeman o' Bagour; his wife wis at the doun-lyin', an' the fairies needed a nurse. Whin her babe wis born the fairies carried her aff an' pat a deid woman in her place. A' the gowd glitter o' Fairyland cudna content her; her hert wis aye wi' her babe, an' mony a time she cam' in the dead o' nicht an' kaimed her bairnie's hair. Aince Geordie waukened up an' saw her. 'Wha are ye, an' what are ye dain' there?' said he. 'I'm yer ain wife, an' sair grieved tae bide fae ye.' 'Ye leein' limmer, my wife's deid an' buried.' 'Atweel she's no' that! I jist stappit atower the door yon bonnie munelicht nicht; I hedna been kirked or the bairn kristened, so the fairies had power owre me an' carried me awa. 'Gae awa wi' yer nonsense,' said Geordie; 'ye dinna expect ony reasonable mortal tae believe the like o' that.' 'Ye'll believ't an' see't baith gin ye'll pit ye're fit on a firm stane whan the mune shines on Clocky Mill Dam. Let the first troop o' fairies gae by, ye'll grip me in the second.' 'Gin the deil hed power

tae tak ye, he can keep ye,' grumphed Geordie, wha had anither lass
coorted tae pit in her place.

# 40

Its mony years since an awfu' drooth happened in this kintra, which
turned a' oor bonnie green fields and hills as broon as a docken, and
as dry as poother. Everything was quite withered, and really the
thing appeared sae judgmentlike, that some fasted, some prayed, and
ithers were thrown into a state bordering on despair. The vera
streams and wells were nearly a' dried up. This drouth continued for
twa months, in which time a great mony fine kye dee'd, and likewise
sheep; and by the loss, sma' farmers were reduced to a state o' perfect
poverty. The fairies, puir bodies, did a' in their poor to assist the
distressed, and it was strange that their rings and hillocks never
suffered in the least frae the heat, but on the contrary, remained fresh
and green as ever.

In this sad time, there was a man o' the name o' Crawfurd, wha
had obleeged the fairies on several occasions; and weel can thae folk
repay a benefit, and weel can they revenge an injury. He was the best
man (I have heard it said) that ever lived, for he could never bear to
see his fellow creatures want, and as lang as he had a bawbee to spare
he never held in his hand. His three kye had perished, and they being
the principal thing he depended upon for the support o' his wife and
family, it was no wonder that he became sae dooncast. As he was
sitting ae night by the side o' the fire, after a' the family had ben
bedded, planning a thousand schemes, nae doot, how he might be
enabled to keep in his ain life and the lives o' them that were
depending upon him, a 'hugger' cam doon the lum and fell at his feet.
He lifted it up, and finding it very heavy, opened it. His astonishment
was great when he fand it fu' o' goud pieces, and at the bottom was a
sma' bit o' paper, wi' the inscription –

> Tak' the goud and buy a koo,
> You minded us, we've minded you.

Next morning, Crawfurd trudged away, without tellin' his wife ony
thing about it, to a rich farmer about Kinross, whaur he laid out part
o' his siller in buying twa fine kye, which he brocht hame. But in
buyin' them, he hadna considered hoo they were to be kept, and he

fand himsel' as far back as ever. But the fairies sune settled that matter, for they tauld him to drive them here – which at that time was a' covered wi' rashes, whins, and briers. Crawfurd kent the place fu' weel, and was gaun to laugh at the proposal, but hafflins afraid lest he should offend those wha has been sae gude to him, he drave his two kye awa to the Dell. If he was surprised at his present o' goud, he was quite dumfoondered at the changed appearance o' the place. Every bush and weed had disappeared, and in their stead sprung up a beautiful crop o' the richest and finest grass. The two kye gaed here, week after week, and month after month, and still there was nae sign o' the grass either withering or growing bare. Each o' the kye yielded atween saxteen and auchteen pints o' milk a day, and the butter made frae it surpassed ony thing o' its kind. The fame o't spread far and wide, and folk cam frae a' airts to get it. The neighbours began to grow jealous o' Sandy, and in a short time he had mony enemies, wha, thinking they wou'd get on as weel as him, turned their kye into the Dell. But what did it matter? Not a single koo but Sandy's ga'e a drap o' milk! The drooth, hooever, ended, and show'rs again fell in great abundance, sae that the kintra began to recover what it had lost. Sandy gaed on prosperously in th warl', never fa'en back a-day, and after layin' up a gude wheen bawbees, and leavin' his family in easy circumstances, he was gathered to his fathers, and lamented by a' wha had tasted o' his gudeness. His wife sune followed him, and the bairns were left weel provided for. As for the Gowan Dell, it has jist the self and same appearance enoo as it had that morning on which the twa kye o' Sandy's first set fit within it!

## 41

Two men were ploughing down in Closeburn parish, when they both felt a strong smell of burning cake; one of them said in an off-hand kind o' way, 'Yere cake's burnin'.' 'Make us a spurtle tae turn it wi', then,' said a voice apparently close at hand. The man good naturedly did as directed, and laid the article down on the ground. On returning to the spot he found the spurtle taken away, and bread and cheese left in its place. He partook of both, and likewise gave some to his horses, but his companion would neither taste himself nor allow his horses to taste. An affront of this kind could not be overlooked, and he had not gone many steps until he dropped down dead in the furrow.

## 42

Dae ye speir, my dawtie, what like the mermaids war? They war queer lookin' craters; the doon half like a fish, so that they cud soom; the head an' shouthers like a body's. I've speir'd at sailors gin they hed ever seen ony. They've telt me they had seen dug-fish an' beast-fish, but ne'er a marmaid. For a' that, there wis ance ane baid in Pairnie Burn. She whiles cam' oot o't an sat on a muckle stane, liltin awa' as she kaim'd her yellow hair an' makin e'en at a' the lads that gaed by. The gudeman o' Pairnie thocht, whan a spate cam', the stane sent the watter owre his ley, forbye bein' deav'd wi her skirlin' an' skeer'd wi' her muckle e'en; sae he brack it up an' biggit it intae dykes. The mermaid gaed wud wi' anger, an' sluthered intae the hoose when the woman war a' in the byre milkin' the kye. She whumml'd the cradle, smoor'd the bairn, an' as she plunked intae the burn, sang –

> Ye may look to your toom cradle, an' sae may
>    I to my broken stane;
> We'll maybe meet again, but we'll ne'er be at ane.

## 43

I dinna ken what awfu' wark the witches war aboot that twa should be brunt in Dunnin' parish. Ane wis brunt at Kinklady, an' the Witch-Tree lang stood there stuntit an' thrawn. Uncle Sandy minds o' the bairns gatherin' ashes an' banes near't whan he wis a bit callant. The tither witch has a braw monument o' grey stane wi' a bit cross on the tap o't. Markit oot wi' white pent is this inscription – 'Maggie Walls, burnt here as a witch, 1657'. Auld my Lord got it biggit whan her Leddyship wis frae hame, an' the cook wis telt tae hae a muckle haggis ready tae treat the masons. Some fouks say the witches war jist guid auld wives wha kent mair than the parish meenister, an' that's the wey the meenister had sic a spite at them. Others say they war ill-hearted, ill-gaeted hempies, stickin' preens in wax images to gar fouks dwine an' dee. Our forbears wad outwit them an' a' their magic, by tying a bit o' boutree to the byre-door whan the kye wadna let doon the milk, an' by pittin' a rag i' the kirn, or at warst jumpin' through a ring wantin' the sark whin the butter wadna come. There wis a wheen witches aboot Tirnawie, wha scoored the kintra in divers shapes. The guidman i' Ford o' Rossie wis sair teended by a hare aye loup, loupin' through his bere. He fired his gun mony a time, but neither scaithed nor daunted her. Ae nicht he loaded his gun, pat in a siller saxpence, let bang an' ran forrit. There wis nae hare there, but a woman lyin' dead wi' a saxpence in her e'e.

Tibbie Marshall's faither, wha farmed the Crafts, wis pleughin' wi' oxen, as wis the fashion in thae days. Without warnin' they drappit doon. He ran hame for help in an unco hurry. They telt him the witch-wife had been at the door, an' gane awa' angry at bein' refused. He gaed tae the head o' the toon, whaur he faund her in her ain hoose roastin' flesh on the coals. He reipit his pouch for a knife, but faund only a roosty nail, an' wi' that he scored her abune the breath till bluid cam'. Whin he gaed back his oxen war standin' in the pleugh weel eneugh. A neebor's coo wis bewitched by the same wife, an' de'd. They tuk' oot its heart, stuck it fu' o' preens, an' boiled it. The same nicht she cam' greetin' to their window sayin' her heart wis sae sair she wis like tae dee.

## 44

Auld Jean D — , whose mother and grandmother afore her were baith witches, cam' in ae morning afore a Moniaive fair day tae ask me tae help an' stack hay at Craigdarroch in her place, as she wanted tae gang tae the oo-rowin' at Glencrosh. My mither said 'Het! she's far ower young'; and I said 'I'm doost no gaun,' for, ye see, I had made up my min' tae gang tae the fair. Jean gaed oot o' the door gie ill-pleased like, and my mither said 'She's an ill body, and ye should maybe hae gaen'; but I doost gaed a lauch, an' thocht nae mair aboot it. Well, next morning, believe me or no as ye like, I couldna lift my heid, an' I had gaen tae my bed as weel as I ever felt in my life. My mither said 'Oo, lassie, I think she was bewitched ye'; an' tae tell the truth, I thocht sae mysel', for I never felt the same aither afore or since. I was doost ill wi' a queerness, but for the life o' me couldna tell what was wrang. Next day I was a' richt again, but by that time, of coorse, I had missed the fair.

## 45

On a summer's evening, about the time that Nature puts on her sables to mourn the expiry of the chearful day, a shepherd boy belonging to a farmer in the immediate neighbourhood of Aloway Kirk, had just folded his charge, and was returning home. As he passed the Kirk, in the adjoining field, he fell in with a crew of men and women, who were busy pulling stems of the plant ragwort. He observed that as each person pulled a ragwort, he or she got astride of it, and called out, 'Up horsie!' on which the ragwort flew off, like Pegasus, through the air with its rider. The foolish boy likewise pulled his ragwort, and cried, with the rest, 'Up horsie!' and, strange to tell, away he flew with the company. The first stage at which the cavalcade stopt, was a merchant's wine cellar in Bourdeaux, where, without saying, by your leave, they quaffed away at the best the cellar could afford, until the morning, foe to the imps and works of darkness, threatened to throw light on the matter, and frightened them from their carousals.

The poor shepherd lad, being equally a stranger to the scene and the liquor, heedlessly got himself drunk; and when the rest took horse, he fell asleep and was found so next day by some of the people belonging to the merchant. Somebody that understood Scotch, asking him what he was, he said he was such-a-one's herd in Aloway, and by some means or other getting home again, he lived long to tell the world the wondrous tale.

## 46

Fin I wis fee't wi' Roy o Waterton I wis a gey roch, haveless-livin' breet o' a chiel, and ae Setterday nicht that I wis awa' on the rig it wis into Sabbath afore I cam' hame, an' jist as I wis gyaun up the chaumer stair to ma bed, there wis Sawtan, in the shape o' a muckle black cauf, stan'in' glowerin' at me wi' the twa muckle een o' him burnin' like can'les in's heid, and I can tell ye the sicht gar't the caul sweat come oot o' me, and I've been a cheenged man ever sin' syne.

## 47

Mrs G —— on going out one afternoon to call upon a neighbour, who resided about half a mile distant across the moor, saw her friend evidently coming on the same errand. She therefore retraced her steps, and entering the house, awaited her friend's arrival. Her expected visitor not making her appearance, Mrs G —— went to the door to see what had detained her, but although she gazed in every direction there was no one to be seen. As the afternoon was now far advanced, she decided it would be better to defer her visit until the following day. Walking across on the morrow, she remarked, in the course of conversation, 'I saw you on the way to see me yesterday; what made you turn half-road?' 'Me coming to see you!' exclaimed her friend. 'I can assure you I wasna that, for I was scarce frae my ain fireside the hale day.' Both were positive, however, and it was agreed for the time being to avoid all further reference to the matter. A week later Mrs G ——'s neighbour died, and her corpse was carried to the churchyard over the very track upon which her wraith had been seen by Mrs G —— on the afternoon of her intended call.

## 48

Geordie Tamson, who lived near Jollybrands on the south turnpike, not far from the toll-bar, lay sick. After weeks of treatment by the doctor, Geordie lay ill, without the least token of improvement. A 'skeely woman' from the Dounies, a village not far off, was called in. She at once prescribed a supper of 'nettle kail', and added that the dish must be made of 'unspoken nettles', gathered at midnight. That very night by eleven o'clock three young men, friends of Geordie's from Cairngrassie, were on their way to the Red Kirkyard of Portlethen, where there was a fine bed of nettles. It was bright moonlight. It happened that during the previous week Jamie Leipar, from the Skatera, had been laid beside his fathers in the Red Kirkyard, and his body was being watched by his brothers, lest the body-snatchers, or 'resurrectionists', should carry it off for dissecting purposes. When the three yong men were nearing the kirkyard yitt, they heard whisperings inside the wall. Up to this time they had met no one, had been spoken to by no one. Now, if they were challenged, before they reached the nettles in the corner of the yard next the sea, and filled their basket, their labour was lost, and the herb was useless as medicine. Calling to mind who the whisperers were, and trusting that they and their errand were known, they cried: 'Dinna spyke, dinna spyke. Ye're watchin Jamie Leipar. We're nae resurrection fouk; we're fae Cairngrasie, come tae gaither 'unspoken nettles' tae mak Geordie Tamson better. Dinna spyke then: for God's sake, dinna spyke, or ye'll spilt a'.' In a moment the whispering ceased, not a word was spoken. To the sound of the waves breaking on the rocks behind the kirk the nettles were gathered, carefully taken to the sick man, cooked of course, and given him. A complete and speedy recovery followed.

## LEGEND: (4) HISTORICAL

### 49

The Muckle Stane stands in the Ailley amon' the yellow corn. There's been a hantle changes sin the Abbot o' Dunkeld pat on his helmet, buckled on his gude braid-sword, an grippit his shield tae follow the Thane o' Athole to fecht Duff for the Scots Crown at Duncrub. The Kirk wis then fu o' fechtin' priests, no like oor cannie billies fley'd tae kill a mawkin or toom a mutchkin. It was militant ense militaire; – I'm no sure o' thae langnebbed words. The only standard in my young days wis 'The Standard on the Braes o' Mar'. Thae auld priests wer' aye meddlin', and hed a muckle hand in ilka pie. Duff's men wan; they felled the Abbot at the Muckle Stane. Some years syne they howket beside it an' got a stane cist – naething in't but dust; sae maybe they tuk him back tae Dunkeld an' buried him in holy yird wi' bell, book, and canel. The route gaed by oor wey. Twa year syne, whin Uncle Sandy gaed doon tae the solid rock pittin' in poles for the claesraips, he fand the henchbane o' a man, nae doot ane o' thae auld Murrays. Two miles south Duff cam' up wi' Athole an dirket him at the Stanin' Stane on Knows farm. They ca't Thanesland tae this verra day.

# 50   The Guidman of Ballengeich and the Woodman

In days long gone by, when the greater part of Strathearn was a
forest, parties occasionally graced by Royalty frequently resorted
hither to enjoy its balmy breezes, redolent of the perfumes of the
mountain, and to pursue the bracing exercise of 'chasing the wild
deer and hunting the roe'. These excursions were always attended by
numerous merrymakers, so as to cause the time of the courtiers to
pass pleasantly away; but all the denizens of the forest did not
heartily enjoy the mirth. One poor woodman, whose sons had been
forced from home to join the army, and never returned, always felt
forebodings of evil when the season of these visits came round. On
one occasion he was far up among the hills, gathering a particular
kind of heather with which to make ropes and small besoms or
ranges. King James, who was out with a hunting party, had left his
comrades to have a quiet stroll, and observing the solitary man
among the moss, went along to where he was. The King, seeing that
the woodman did not recognise him, entered into a long conversation on various topics, and latterly landed on the severe toil of the
working man. The woodman gave his opinion freely, and laid the
whole blame on the eating of the apple by Adam, rating his great
progenitor severely for his delinquency in yielding to the solicit-
ations of his jade of a wife. The King defended Adam, and remarked
that many a man since Adam's time had done as foolish things for the
sake of a quiet life. The woodman would not allow any extenuating
circumstances in Adam's favour. He should not have taken the fruit
when he was forbidden; and if Eve was not content to live with him,
she should have been allowed to take up her bundles and tramp, as
many of her daughters have had to do since. Had he been there he
would have acted differently. The King, on leaving, arranged with
him to deliver several bundles of the heather at Scone Palace on a
certain day, and to ask for the 'Guidman of Ballengeich', who would
take them, and pay the account of both heather and carriage. At the
time specified, the woodman presented himself at the gates, and on
announcing his message was shown into a room, and took a seat. He
had not waited long ere his acquaintance of the hills entered and took
delivery of the heather, and paid accounts. On rising to leave, the
'guidman' invited him to take dinner, of which he was not loth to
accept, after such a long journey. The King, for such was the
'guidman', showed him all the dishes, etc., on the table, but told him

not upon any account to touch a particular covered dish on the corner. After the King retired, the woodman feasted in right earnest, and as he gradually lost his appetite his curiosity regarding the covered dish increased. He thought it must be something very grand, and surely worth seeing, at least, if not worth tasting. His curiosity became so powerful that it induced him to consider that there could be no great harm in merely lifting the lid, and he accordingly moved nearer the mystic dish. After satisfying himself that no one was watching, he trembling lifted the corner, when out popped a muse, which went out of sight in an instant. The woodman considered that the 'guidman' had placed the dish there by mistake. After wrapping himself in his plaid, he was preparing to leave, when the King entered, and expressed a hope that the woodman had enjoyed himself, and not touched the corner dish. As the woodman was returning thanks for the kindness shown, the King lifted the dish cover. 'What!' said the King, 'after all the fine things you have had, how dared you touch the dish?' The woodman tried to excuse himself, 'that he just wanted to see what was beneath it'. 'But', said the King, 'did I not strictly forbid you to touch it?' 'Yes, you did; but I could not resist the temptation to open it.' 'Well,' said the King, 'you remember of our conversation on the hill regarding Adam eating the apple, and how you condemned him severely for so doing?' 'Yes, I do,' answered the woodman, 'but I now think that Adam was not such a bad man after all, for had I been there and got the chance, most likely I would have taken a bite myself.'

## 51

While writing upon this subject I will record an incident in the life of one of my paternal ancestors who suffered much for conscience' sake during the days of Episcopal tyranny in Scotland. He had been under hiding for some time, and so strict was the search made for him that he dared not visit his home, although his wife lay upon her death-bed, pining and praying for her husband's presence. She died without that consolation; when a woman who had attended her in her last moments undertook to inform him of his bereavement, warning him at the same time that advantage would be taken of his expected presence at the funeral to apprehend him. Hearing this, he contrived to come under cloud of night to a neighbouring moor from whence he saw the mournful procession issuing from the door. As it approached, not daring to stand upright, he lay down, and dragging himself like a reptile through the long heather, as near to the road as he could with safety, wept that farewell to the cold clay as it was carried past, which could not be spoken by the bedside of the dying wife.

## 52   Anecdotes of the Battle of Sheriff-Muir

1st. – On the day of this memorable battle almost every Highlander bore a 'wallet' of oatmeal on his back for subsistence. The meal-bags of those that were slain being collected after the battle, they were emptied on a carpeting of tartan plaids, spread for the purpose, and tradition records that the whole amounted to many bolls – such was the number of the hardy sons of the north who were this day sacrificed.

2d. – Some shepherds, who witnessed the battle from one of the Ochils, ('Little-Hunt-Hill',) observed a considerable party of 'red-coats' cut off, and surrounded by a strong body of Clans. The 'red-coats' appeared to them at first, in the centre of the Clans, in the form of a 'red diamond', which gradually diminished in size, until it became totally extinct – not a man being spared by those merciless wielders of the dreadful claymore.

3d. – An old woman, then residing at the farm-house of Linns, in the immediate vicinity of the scene, used to tell that she saw eleven 'red-coats' killed on her own 'midden' – the poor fellows defending themselves to the last, – the Highland party then entering the house with their bloody swords still unsheathed, carried off every thing which they found valuable, or which they deemed of use to them – some of them declaring that they fought neither for 'King Shordy nor King Hamish, but for King *Spulzie*'.

4th. – During the dispersion of the left wing of the Royal Army, one Highlander, with a large uncovered curly head, having his plaid wrapt round his arm to ward off the bayonets, is said to have cut down nine individuals before he was over-powered; and, on the other hand, a single dragoon is related to have been chased through the bogs, to a stone dyke at Wharrie-burn, by a dozen of Highlanders, where he defended himself so well that no fewer than ten men fell under his arm before he was discomfited and slain.

## 53

Grannie, to use her own expression, was a 'lassock o' nine or ten year aul' when the Hielan'men cam' thro' in 1745'. She remembered going with her father through a field adjoining the high road from Edinburgh to see the Highland host pass by. She said her father being aware of the reiving propensities of that motley army, had put on his old clothes and shoes. Not so Dannie Brown, who went with him. He dressed himself and put on, said Grannie, 'his kirk shoon wi' the big siller buckles', and stood in a gap of the hedge. The buckles caught the eye of a clansman who wore a pair of old brogues, with his toes looking through the holes. With a half-humorous expression on his face he stopped before the astonished Dannie, saying – 'She'll juist pe changing a progue wi' her', at the same time glancing first at Dannie's feet and then at his own. The young man took the hint and quickly took off his shoes; the Celt picked them up, and casting his brogues at the young farmer, resumed his march.

## 54

No sooner, however, had he [the Duke of Cumberland] mounted his charger, and advanced about fifty yards, than an incident happened, which, had the design been fully accomplished, the cold-blooded, cruel, and barbarous massacres which followed the battle of Culloden, had, in all probability, never occurred. His Grace, with his officers and guard, while passing an ancient building, now uninhabited and in a dilapidated state, then the property of Lord Strathallan, and yet well known in Dunblane by the appellation of 'My Lord's House', very narrowly escaped being scalded to death by a pail of boiling oil, which was poured from an attic window of this house, directly over him. So near was the burning liquid of having the intended effect, that the whole fell right on the haunches of the Duke's horse, which suddenly starting from the excessive pain, darted in a moment from below his rider, and left him weltering in the mud.

During the confusion occasioned by this circumstance, the girl who had been instigated to commit this daring action, from 'love to the righteous cause', and hatred to 'the usurper', found means to escape from the house, and secreted herself in a tunnel which conveyed the filth of the town below ground to the brink of the river. This was the same girl who had shown so much devotion to the cause of Prince Charles at Balhaldie House, when presenting him with clean boots some four or five months previous. The most diligent search was made for her in and about the mansion, but in vain.

## 55

My grandparents, though not reduced to such extremities in their own condition, used to speak with deep feeling of some scenes which they had witnessed. They had seen, when the fearfully cold and long-delayed spring began to burst the bud and unfold the leaves, bands of haggard and emaciated women, and pale, skeleton-like children creeping slowly among the trees, stripping the branches of the beech of their tender leaves, returning to pick them day by day. These they carried home, and boiled them in water with a little salt – this mess supplying, in many instances, the only meal they could obtain.

My grandmother . . . would often relate incidents of the famine which had come under her own observation, which brought tears into the eyes of the little varlets, and moistened her own in the recital . . . .

One day my relative, on looking out at the door, saw what she took for a heap of dirty rags lying on the dunghill; going near she found it to be a small, famished-looking child, half naked, about five years of age, apparently dead. At the bidding of her mistress she lifted the child and brought him into the house, laid him before the fire, and poured some drops of warm milk into his mouth. The child, who had only fainted from want, began to revive, and after making a hearty meal of porridge and milk, he became quite happy and familiar with his kind friends, and, to their surprise and amusement, he sung in his weak, quavering voice, two lines of an old Scottish ditty; these are the words:

I maun ha'e my brose made in the nine-pint luggie,
A pund o' butter meltit in them, and wow but I'll be vogie.

I did not hear what became of this child afterwards, but it is likely he was taken care of by some one or other, his parents being dead.

# 56   A Story of the Black Officer

Among the many stories connected with Captain Macpherson of Ballachroan, the 'Black Officer', there is none that portrays the character of the man in a better way than the following:

There is still a right-of-way through Gaick Forest to Blair Atholl which, though seldom used now, was once much frequented by pedestrians, and more especially by pack merchants. One summer evening the 'Black Officer' was in Gaick Forest and espied two young men entering the glen from Blair Atholl side. He always had a number of sheep and cattle in the forest, and he hurried on to the bothy where his shepherd stayed. On this particular evening, however, the shepherd was away from the glen and would not be back till the following day. Disguising himself in the shepherd's clothes, the Captain waited at the bothy door for the weary and hungry travellers who, on their arrival, begged for a night's shelter and food.

The Captain said, 'You are quite welcome to the shelter of the bothy, a good peat fire and a heather bed, but I have not a bite of anything to eat in the place.'

His visitors thanked him for his hospitality, but were greatly disconcerted about the want of food, for they were very hungry, and consulted with one another as to what they should do.

'If you promise me you will not tell my master,' said the Captain, 'we will kill a sheep and you can have a good feast.'

The promise was readily given and the sheep was killed and cut up. Soon a pot of mutton was simmering on a good fire, and everything promised well, when the Captain remarked that he would have to leave them for the night as he had to watch foxes that were killing the lambs. He bade them make themselves comfortable, and he would see them again in the morning.

So he left his weary guests, caught his horse, which was grazing in a hollow near by, and galloped home to Ballachroan, where he dressed himself as became his station. By break of day he was back at the bothy, accompanied by the shepherd. The wayfarers failed to recognise their transformed host, and being caught red-handed sheep-stealing, were in a fearful state. The penalty for the crime in those days was the gallows; but the Captain gave them the choice of that or enlisting in the Army. They, of course, chose the latter alternative.

## 57

My great-granny, a woman Kirsty Banks frae Stroma – she wesna supposed to be very clever, but faith! she hed aal her wits aboot her. They used to dae a bit o distillin in that time, on their own of coorse, and wan time they hed a browst ready, fan they heird 'at 'e excisemen were comin. Noo she'd hedden a stillborn bairn no long afore 'at, an 'e excisemen kent 'at. And they'd no time til hide 'e malt. So she telt 'e bairns til make up a bed til her in 'e kitchen, and til put 'e malt in 'e bed, and she wes lyin on 'at fan 'e excisemen came in. And she telt them 'at she'd hedden a stillborn bairn no long afore 'at, and she wisna feelin very weil, but 'e bairns wanted her in 'e kitchen, til guide them and tell them fat til do. And 'e excisemen kent that was true, they kent she'd hedden a bairn. So they searched 'e rest o the hoose, but they didna touch 'e bed, and they got off wi it.

## LEGEND: (5) PERSONAL

## 58

One evening when Burns and Bacon were sitting in a room of the inn a man from Leadhills entered. In a little Burns rose and went out, and the man inquired who he was. Bacon answered that he was the poet, and the man remarked that he was but a clown, which doubtless Burns overhead. Thereupon Bacon bet a bottle of wine with him that Burns would make a poem on him when he came in. Accordingly on Burns's return he was asked to make a poem. Burns asked his name, and was answered Andrew Horner, and also when he was born, and was told 1739. Then said Burns:

> In the year seventeen hundred and thirty-nine,
> The deil got stuff to make a swine,
> And threw it into a corner,
> And called it Andrew Horner.

## 59

My host, Daniel Swankie, was one day being catechised by Mr

Aitken, the minister of St Vigeans, on the rather obscure doctrine of effectual calling, &c. Dan was fairly puzzled; in fact quite ramfeezl'd; could not give anything like a satisfactory reply. At last, in perfect desperation, he turned on the minister and asked him – 'Weel, sir, cud you tell me noo hoo mony hooks it wid tak' tae bait a fifteen-score haddock line?' The minister was completely routed. It was Daniel's son, Tam, who was up at the Manse 'gaen forrit', a colloquialism for joining the kirk by partaking of the Sacrament for the first time. The minister, among other questions, asked Tam, how many commandments there were? 'Aiblins, sir,' replied Tam, 'there micht be twenty.' 'Run away, Thomas, my man,' said Mr Aitken, 'and do not come back until you have mastered this simple question.' Tam Swankie left the manse, still pondering deeply on his way home on the vexed question to him of the number of the commandments. He met his cousin, Jock Cargill, also going up to the manse. 'I say, Jock,' said Tam, 'ye'll no ken hoo mony commandments th'll be?' 'There's ten, Tam.' 'Ah, Jock,' cried Tam gleefully, 'ye needna gae ony farrer, for I offered him twenty, and he widna ha'e them.'

## LEGEND: (6) PLACE

### 60

According to tradition, Bennachie was of old guarded by a giant, known by the name of Jock o' Bennachie. Jock's dimensions were somewhat enormous, as may be understood from the extent of ground which he required for his bed. The bed is still shown, and is known as 'Little John's Length' . . . . The spot where John dried his 'sark' is also pointed out on the north-west of Craig Shannoch . . . . It has a general resemblance to the garment named, being produced by the heather and turf having been at one time cut away from a bit of the hill face.

Jock seems to have required all his huge proportions to combat with his foes, who were both powerful and numerous, his principal opponent being Jock o' Noth. Noth is a well-known hill in the parish of Rhynie and district of Strathbogie, some thirteen miles to the north-west of Bennachie. That distance did not prevent a pretty frequent exchange of compliments, in the shape of hugh boulders,

between the two. On Tap o' Noth (it is said!) may yet be seen a stone
with the mark of five gigantic fingers thereon, which, according to
popular tradition, was thrown by Jock o' Bennachie from Oxen
Craig at Jock o' Noth. The latter, on this particular occasion,
retaliated by raising a huge mass of rock with the view of hurling it to
the mountain of the Garioch, when Jock o' Bennachie put out his
foot, just touching the mass. The result was that it never left Tap o'
Noth, and, indeed, if you care to look, you will find the mark of
Jock's toe thereon! . . . .

He, while he succeeded in defending himself against his visible
foes, had ultimately to succumb to enchantment, and is buried in a
cave, somewhere on the mountain that he was wont to guard. But let
it be understood Jock is not dead – he is merely under a spell, secured
by lock and key. Of course the key is lost, but as one version of a
prophecy . . . says:

> A wife's ae sin wi' ae e'e
> Sall fin' the kyey o' Bennachie,

and then the giant will be freed.

# 61

Whin I wis at the schule, auld Marg'et Niven telt me o' three
wonders in Dunnin' that her mither saw wi' her ain een – a waddin'
withoot a bride, a burial withoot a corp, an ordination withoot a
meenister. The ordination wis to be in the Head of the Toon Kirk,
but the lad didna come forrit, sae they keepit a diet o' worship in the
kirk, syne ate the dinner, forbye toomin a gallon o' Drummond's
best fae the Hosh. I'm thinkin that wad be aboot the time that they
hangit puir Charlie Hardie, the paerish meenister, owre the brig by
his heels, an' gae him sic a flig that he took a scunner at Dunnin', an'
sune efter dwined oot o life athegither. The burial – waes me, we a'
little ken the day we'll dee – wis the coffin o' a Hieland lass that wis
here at service and dee'd wi' the pox. Her ain fouk cam doon fae
Glenturret wi' a cairt an' a coffin, an' tuk the body hame. The coffin
made in Dunnin' wisna needed. They didna ken wha it micht fit;
they didna like to keep claes in't, sae they pat stanes in't, and buried it
at the steeple root in the auld kirkyaird. Gin it was resurrected by the
beadle an' hacket tae spunks tae kenel his fire wis onbekent. The

waddin dang a'. The bride was a lively queen that tuk a scunner at the man her fouk trysted her tae. Sae she ran aff wi' her ain jo, a pleughman. Nae doot she wis a glaiket jaud, a ram-stam randy, wha said she wad mairry nae grainin' gutcher to hae him aye stoiterin' roond the doors or flyting at the cheek o' the fire. They held the waddin in the Kirkstyle Inn wantin' the bride. It wis a penny waddin', an' ilka lad peyed his ain score. There were reels an' strathspeys, wi' plenty of loupin and heughin', an' country dances, Princess Royal an Jean o' Aberdeen for the mair gentie. There was a peck o' shortbread, butter-saps, wi weel-toasted oat-cakes, steamin' toddy, an' foamin yill. The daffin gaed on till neist day. Some, gey fou, gaed oot by the back an' through the burn, ithers wi' mair smeddum ran doon the front steps and lichtit on their hurdies, whilk fushionless pairts get mony a dunt whin fouk are daes't wi drink.

## 62

There wis supposed to be a passage fae the Ythan up ti the castle an supposed to be made by the Deevil. The Deevil was supposed . . . . Well, at that time there was supersteetious people, an they really thocht it wis true. And this lads 'at cam doon fae the north were MacAllisters, I think. Ay they were MacAllisters, so the leegend says. And they were both pipers. An the one brither gaed doon 'is passage, an he cam back an told them, says 'I'm afraid, I'm afraid ti gae doon there'. 'Afraid,' he says, 'a MacAllister afraid,' he says, 'if ye come back up here again,' he says. 'I'll kill ye.' 'Well,' he says, 'I'll tell ye, I'll gae doon an I'll play the bagpipes,' he says, 'an for as lang as the bagpipes is goin ye'll ken that I'm all right,' he says, 'but if the bagpipes stop ye'll ken fine that there's something wrong.' So he gaed doon an he played for a lang lang time. He heard him playin goin ben aa the road an supposed ti come oot at Meg's Spot – they ca't Meg's Spot, 'at's the name o this spot 'at this passage was supposed ti come oot at, syne. But they've niver seen ony mark o where there wis a hole comin out o the ground or nithin. But, however, that's jist how it is, it goes, an the pipes stoppit, an of course he never cam oot. An the ither brither gaed doon to look for him but he coudna get far enough ben, so that he missed, so he commits suicide i the hinner en. He says, 'I pit my brother till his

death.' He commits suicide. Well the leegend is, 't ye can hear the
bagpipes – now an again. 'At could be possible, but I never heard it,
I've been doon there at aa hoors, aa times . . . an I never heard it.

## MODERN LEGEND

## 63   The Pearls

From time to time a story goes the rounds that sounds too good to be
true.

It always happens to a friend of a friend or a relative of a relative.

Y'know the sort of thing. There's the one about the elephant that
sat on a red mini car because it thought it was a circus tub.

Or the one about the bloke who got a newish car for £1 because a
wife wanted to get her own back on a runaway husband.

Well, here's another that's on the go in Lanarkshire.

This woman, it seems, walked into Woolworths and bought a ten
bob 'pearl' necklace.

She wore it at a dinner dance.

During the meal a stranger admired it. He said he was a jeweller
and asked if he could examine it. Whereupon he pronounced it a
perfectly matched set of pearls 'worth a small fortune'.

The woman laughed and said they only cost a few bob in Woolies.

But the man was adamant. In the end he got the woman to agree to
have the pearls valued.

To her amazement, experts said they're worth £20,000.

The explanation is that the pearls had been stolen.

They'd got too hot for the thief to handle. So, with a detective on
his heels, he'd dropped the necklace on Woolies' counter to get rid of
it.

It's a smashing story.

The trouble is, when we tried to track it down last week we got
nowhere.

We'd dearly like to hear from the woman if the story is true.

But we suspect it's another of those tall tales that spring from
nowhere.

## 64   The Severed Head

There was a loony got out of the asylum and he was hiding up the old Denny back-road. The police were out looking for him because he was dangerous. They say he even killed his own mother with an axe. Anyway, he was hiding at an old house on the way out to Denny and just when it was getting dark, a car drew up with a man and a girl in it. They'd come to look at the house because it was for sale. When the man got out and started walking round about the patient got frightened so he picked up a spade that was lying around and he crept up to the man and hit him with it – took his head off. Then he thought he'd better finish off the girl too, so he went out to the car with the man's head. It was dark by now so he knocked on the window and showed her the man's head, and he laughed (because he was mad) but before he could open the door of the car a big police van arrived and they took him away. He's in Carstairs now and the folk looking after him are still scared of him. That happened only three or four years ago.

## 65   The Babysitter

There was a babysitter who was looking after three children one night. During the course of the evening she heard strange noises outside so she locked the doors of the house. Shortly after that she had a phone call from a man telling her she should go upstairs to see how the children were. She ignored the phone call and continued watching the television. A short while later the phone rang again and the same voice repeated the message to go upstairs and check the children. She decided to phone the police and they said they would intercept any calls should he phone again. Sure enough the phone rang a third time and the voice insisted that she went upstairs. A minute or two later the police rang telling her to get out of the house as quickly as possible. The girl ran out of the house screaming.

When the police arrived they discovered the three children with their throats cut. The police had traced the phone call to the extension in the upstairs bedroom where the man had lurked, killing one of the children before each phone call. The girl, unknowingly, by locking the doors had locked herself in the house with the killer.

# 2

# FOLKSONG

## INTRODUCTION

Folksong has been for centuries an important medium for Scottish cultural expression. Its richness has been widely recognised, not least by its being the only genre of folk literature represented in the literature anthologies. The practice of singing at one time permeated traditional life: at work, during the labour itself or the meal-breaks in the fields, at leisure, in the forenichts in kitchens and chaumers, and on festive occasions. Folksong is still a lively force today though in more limited contexts, for the last thirty years have seen the 'Folksong Revival', inspired by such stalwart collectors as Hamish Henderson. Many fine traditional singers, like the incomparable Jeannie Robertson, have been 'discovered' and given a wide audience, and the tradition has been both husbanded and extended in the folksong clubs.

Folksong has exercised a pronounced influence upon Scottish poets from medieval times to the present, and most markedly on Burns, Scott, and Hogg, all of whom not only collected songs but also wrote in modes derived, to varying degrees, from traditional song. This fruitful interrelation of high and folk literatures has, however, had one peculiar side-effect in that, as Rev. J.B. Duncan pointed out in 1908, the artsongs of the poets are often taken to represent the actual folk tradition:

> They [the folksongs] have moreover suffered from the contact
> of the literary song proceeding from Allan Ramsay, Burns,
> Baroness Nairne, Hogg, Tannahill, and the great horde of other
> imitators. In fact, it is this literary song that is now chiefly
> thought of when Scottish song is spoken of. Let no-one despise
> [it], rather let us all be deeply [grateful] for it; but there is this to
> be said, that it has never taken hold of the same class of people
> that sang so heartily the old folk-songs.[1]

89

Duncan there distinguishes with sharpness and confidence between folksong and literary song, but the precise definition of folksong has occupied many minds and drained much ink. It may be that no absolutely watertight definition can be arrived at, but the standard criterion for determining traditional material, the criterion of transmission, still seems to provide the surest guide; by this approach, then, folksongs would be those songs transmitted by word or mouth rather than by writing or print. This means, of course, that folksongs do not need to originate in a traditional context; they can come from a variety of sources so long as they are accepted within and transmitted by the traditional processes. Nowadays, because of the multiplicity of aural media (records, tapes, radio, television) and the number of possible channels of transmission, any hard-and-fast application of that definition as it stands is fraught with difficulty, and so it would be preferable to amend it slightly to read, those songs transmitted by word of mouth rather than by writing or print within small groups. Fortunately, in the historical perspective there is relatively less trouble in distinguishing the folksongs.

The songs that follow are an attempt to provide something akin to a definition-by-example; they are intended to demonstrate, besides their multifaceted appeal, the different *kinds* of song sung in the Scottish tradition. The selection is also intended to furnish a chronological spread of texts, from the sixteenth century to recent years, and to give a fairly wide regional representation, though that can not be done in any balanced fashion since certain regions have been much more heavily recorded than others. The division of the songs into classes is inevitably arbitrary to some extent and involves a certain overlapping, but the major kinds do stand out. The first class has the songs of custom, those songs which belong to a special, normally festive, occasion. Nos 1, 2, and 3 come from the Christmas-New Year period, a very active time in the traditional calendar, and are connected with seasonal practices in which groups circulated through the community. 'The Thigging Song' (no.2) was sung by young men who travelled round a district on New Year's Day collecting meal and money for invalids or old people in need, an illuminating example of how, through the mechanism of its customs, the traditional community looked after its weaker members and maintained its equilibrium, and had some fun into the bargain. Where nos 1-5 are associated in some way with the customs of the yearly calendar (no.4 hypothetically so), no.6, the marriage song from Cromarty, belongs to a rite of passage, a custom at a high point in the life of an individual.

The work songs come from seaward, landward, and domestic occupations. The sea shanty (no.7) was sung by sixteenth-century mariners and the dreg-song (no.8) by oyster-dredging fishermen of the eighteenth century. In the agricultural community, ploughmen, in the days of the oxen plough before the agrarian revolution, lightened their work and heartened their team with the two short songs for the owsen pleuch (no.9), while those driving the peats would amuse themselves with compositions like no.10. On the domestic front, the women performed the business of rearing a family and keeping a house with the aid of such songs as the lullaby, the cradle croon, and the spinning song (nos 11, 12, 13).

'Folksong' in general is often loosely equated with the songs that make up the next class, the lyric songs, which indeed constitute a most important part of the Scottish heritage. The examples in this section all relate to the theme of love in its many stages and guises. There are songs of affection and desire, regret and sharp disappointment, of courtship's pleasures and railleries and pain, of the penalties of being unmarried and the penalties of being married. Many, not just the two with clearly sexual metaphors, are imbued with a strong and natural sexuality, and throughout they manifest a sturdy stoical acceptance of life's buffets and rewards, an expressive testament to the emotional resilience of the ordinary folk who sang these far-from-ordinary songs. The lyric songs shade imperceptibly into the humorous lyrics, just as they in their turn shade into the comic songs. The humorous lyrics deal with the vagaries of male-female relationships from a wryly amused perspective, and often provide, in greater or lesser depth, a character sketch, whether of the obtusely practical suitor (no.23) or the obsessional bridegroom (no.24) or the wanton wife (nos 25, 26).

The comic songs display a fine relish for life's quiddities and include a nonsense (or thrawn) song (no.27), a convivial drinking song (no.28), two absurd songs, one about a character (no.29) and the other about an event (no.30), a burlesque version of the internationally found night-visit song (no.31), and a story of foolish behaviour reminiscent of the numskull tales (no.32). The narrative songs have a variety of stories. 'The Wedding of the Frog and the Mouse' (no.33), a fantastical tale, is mentioned in the 1549 *Complaynte*, while the allegorical theme of 'John Barleycorn' (no.34) also occurs in the sixteenth century, in a poem or song in the Bannatyne MS, 'Why should nocht Allane honorit be?' 'Buchan Forest' (no.35), on the other hand, recounts a particular event commemorated within a district, namely, a fox-hunt among the Kirkcudbrightshire-Ayrshire hills in the old Scottish style, with men and dogs; from present-day perspective, the song in its portrayal of past custom has not a little ethnographic interest. Told with a gentle humour, 'Flesher Robbie' (no.36) is a tale of rural courtship with an answering of the Session and a happy resolution; its refrain appears in a number of songs. Contrastingly defiant in tone is 'MacPherson's Lament' (no.37), the story of the execution at Banff in 1700 of James Mac-Pherson, leader of a roving gang, who was said to have composed his 'Rant' at the foot of the gallows and then offered his fiddle to anyone who would take it as a memorial of him; when no one accepted the offer, he broke it in pieces and threw it in the grave. This version contains an interesting traditional fusion of elements from the 'Lament' and from Burns's 'MacPherson's Farewell'.

From the eighteenth century on in Scotland, the broadside industry catered for the new markets created by the advent of mass literacy, and its products, composed for the most part in a subliterary style, introduced many English and Irish songs into Scottish tradition. The broadsides are represented by 'Billy Taylor' (no.38), which has the familiar theme of the girl disguising herself as a boy to follow her lover to sea or into the army, here given an unfamiliar twist in the ending, and 'The Poachers' (no.39), a transportation ballad about three Scottish poachers shipped to 'Van Diemen's Land' that sounds the new note of social protest found after the Industrial Revolution. While the work songs were sung during the labour itself, the occupational songs were sung about the labour or the occupation in general, though of course they may also have been sung in working time. They seem in origin to be a largely nineteenth-century phenomenon, but no.41, which stands apart from the others, is marked on the manuscript 'very old'. One clearly of the nineteenth century is 'The Wark o' the Weavers' (no.40), composed by David Shaw, a Forfar weaver (d. 1856, aged 70), which attained great popularity among the handloom weavers. The two songs from the mining industry show a stark contrast: 'Six Jolly Miners' (no.42) like 'The Wark o' the Weavers' extols cheerily the merits of the lads engaged in the industry, but 'The Coal-bearer's Lamentation' (no.41) is a rending cry of despair that may well derive from the days

when the Scottish colliers were bound in servitude.[2] 'The Greenland
Whale Fishery' (no.43) describes a typifying incident from that
hazardous marine occupation which drew its men from the east coast
ports and the northern isles. From the other end of the country,
Kintyre in Argyll, comes a bothy ballad, 'Killeonan' (no.44) which
quite caustically sketches in, stanza by stanza, the individual workers
at a particular farm and their lot in life.

The various song-kinds include a deedling song (no.45), one sung
for dancing in the absence of an instrument, a 'medlay' (no.46) which
was 'sung by several old people, the latter part in a deep, rough voice,
and with pantomimic action', an endless song (no.48), and songs for
non-singers (no.49). A little-known type is the play-song, here
represented by 'Lady Dundonald' (no.47) which illustrates again the
possible links of folksong and custom.

The classical ballads have attracted more attention than any other
genre of folksong, not surprisingly, given their artistic power, their
variousness of appeal, and the age and international dissemination of
many ballad-types. Though sometimes treated, with unfortunate
results, as a peculiar kind of written literature, the ballads need
to be seen for a clear understanding in the context of tradition, and
international tradition at that; in order to facilitate this aim the
Kommission für Volksdichtung has been engaged for some years in
establishing a ballad type-index for European and European-derived
balladries. Each country with a store of ballads tends, very naturally,
to view them as part of the national literary heritage, but they also
belong to the wider perspective of international ballad tradition. It
was from observation of the constant features of the genre across
Europe that Gerould evolved his descriptive definition of the ballad:
'A ballad is a folk-song that tells a story with stress on the crucial
situation, tells it by letting the action unfold itself in event and
speech, and tells it objectively with little comment or intrusion of
personal bias.'[3] Beyond its obvious exemplifying functions the brief
selection is intended to represent the stories of the sub-genres, to
furnish a chronological coverage of the texts (from 1630 to 1977), to
provide a good number of texts (ten) not found in Child, and to
recognise some outstanding singers. The magical and marvellous
sub-genre (nos 50-53) contains stories, both Scottish and international ('Thomas Rymer' and 'King Orfeo'), that involve witch-
craft, ghost lore, and otherworld lore. The ballads of the romantic
and tragic sub-genre (nos 54-57) have the customary powerful

mixture of murder, love, suicide, incest, and heroism. Representing the historical and semi-historical sub-genre are two stories dealing with events of (probably) the late thirteenth, and early fifteenth centuries, and two feud ballads (nos 58-61). The minor sub-genres section includes a religious ballad, a witcombat ballad, and a comic ballad (nos 62-64).

Where a tune accompanies a text at its source, it is given here. For more Scottish folksong tunes see Buchan and Hall,[4] Bronson,[5] and the discographies mentioned in the bibliography.

## Notes

1 P.N. Shuldham-Shaw and E.B. Lyle, 'Folk-song in the North-East: J.B. Duncan's Lecture to the Aberdeen Wagner Society, 1908', *SS*, 18 (1974), 8.
2 T.C. Smout, *A History of the Scottish People 1560-1830* (London, 1969), pp. 180-3, 430-40.
3 Gordon H. Gerould, *The Ballad of Tradition* (Oxford, 1932), p.11.
4 Norman Buchan and Peter Hall, *The Scottish Folksinger* (Glasgow, 1973).
5 Bertrand H. Bronson, *The Traditional Tunes of the Child Ballads*, 4 vols (Princeton, N.J., 1959-72).

## SONGS OF CUSTOM

## 1   New'r Even's Sang or Hoggeranonie Sang

1   Dis is guid New'r Even's night,
    Sant Mary's men are we,

Da morn is guid New'r (Even's) day*
  Before our Ladie.

2    Here are we a-beggin come,
      Sant Mary's men are we,
    Although we're gentlemen at home,
      Before our Ladie.

3    We're no come here for ony guid cheer,
      Sant Mary's men are we,
    But just ta honour da guid New Year,
      Before our Ladie.

4    Here hae we a kerryin horse,
      Sant Mary's men are we,
    Aa 'at's ill lie on his cross,
      Before our Ladie.

5    He had da cause we cam frae hame,
      Sant Mary's men are we,
    What may brak his neck bane,
      Before our Ladie.

6    Whar's da lass wi da yellow hair?
      Sant Mary's men are we,
    If we get her we'll seek nae mair,
      Before our Ladie.

*Miss Smith sang 'Even's' to fit the tune: read 'Da morn it is guid Newar day'?

## 2  Thigging Song

The following verses . . . were sung fifty years ago by the young men of our Strath when going the round of our district collecting meal and money for the poor and distressed about the New Year, and often I have seen five or six bolls of meal and two or three pounds of money collected in an afternoon, to be distributed to the most necessitous:

1    The auld year's out, and the new's in,
        Be soothan! Be soothan!
    An' a' the beggars are begun,
        An' we'll a' be soothan toun.

2    Rise up, gudewife, an' dinna be sweere,
        Be soothan! Be soothan!
    Bestow your charity on the peer,
        An' we'll a' be soothan toun.

3    If meal or money wi' ye be scant,
        Be soothan! Be soothan!
    We'll kiss your lasses ere we want,
        An' we'll a' be soothan toun.

4    If your ale be at the barm,
        Be soothan! Be soothan!
    We'll tak' a drink to had us warm,
        An' we'll a' be soothan toun.

5    The back o' my house's thacket wi' rye,
        Be soothan! Be soothan!
    I canna sing mair, my throat's so dry,
        An' we'll a' be soothan toun.

6    My sheen they're made o' an auld horse hide,
        Be soothan! Be soothan!
    My feet's sae cauld, I canna langer bide,
        An' we'll a' be soothan toun.

Another stanza was generally added about the party or parties the collection was made for, but it was various, and, in most instances, of indifferent composition.

## 3  The Hunting of the Wren

1   'Will ye go to the wood?' quo' Fozie Mozie,
    'Will ye go to the wood?' quo' Johnie Rednozie,

'Will ye go to the wood?' quo' Foslin' ene,
'Will ye go to the wood?' quo' brither and kin.

2 'What to do there?' quo' Fozie Mozie,
'What to do there?' quo' Johnie Rednozie,
'What to do there?' quo' Foslin' ene,
'What to do there?' quo' brither and kin.

3 'To slay the wren,' quo' Fozie Mozie,
'To slay the wren,' quo' Johnie Rednozie,
'To slay the wren,' quo' Foslin' ene,
'To slay the wren,' quo' brither and kin.

4 'What way will we get her hame?' quo'
    Fozie Mozie,
'What way will we get her hame?' quo'
    Johnie Rednozie,
'What way will we get her hame?' quo'
    Foslin' ene,
'What way will we get her hame?' quo' brither
    and kin.

5 'We'l hyre carts and horse,' quo' Fozie Mozie,
'We'l hyre carts and horse,' quo' Johnie
    Rednozie,
'We'l hyre carts and horse,' quo' Foslin'
    ene,
'We'l hyre carts and horse,' quo' brither and kin.

6 'What way will we get her in?' quo' Fozie
    Mozie,
'What way will we get her in?' quo' Johnie
    Rednozie,
'What way will we get her in?' quo' Foslin'
    ene,
'What way will we get her in?' quo' brither
    and kin.

7 'We'l drive down the door-cheeks,' quo' Fozie
    Mozie,

'We'l drive down the door-cheeks,' quo' Johnie
  Rednozie,
'We'l drive down the door-cheeks,' quo' Foslin'
  ene,
'We'l drive down the door-cheeks,' quo' brither
  and kin.

8   'I'll hae a wing,' quo' Fozie Mozie,
    'I'll hae anither,' quo' Johnie Rednozie,
    'I'll hae a leg,' quo' Foslin' ene,
    'And I'll hae anither,' quo' brither and kin.

## 4   Herrin's Heids

Oh, fit-'ll I dae wi' the her-rin's heids? I'll mak' them in-tae loaves o' breid,

I'll mak' them in-tae loaves o' breid, Sing fal the doo a day.

Her-rin's heids, loaves o' breid, An' a' sorts o' things.

*Chorus* The her-rin' it is the king o' the sea, The her-rin' it is the fish for me,

The her-rin' it is the king o' the sea, Sing fal the doo a day.

2   Oh, fit'll I dae wi' the herrin's eyes?
    I'll mak' them intae puddin's an' pies,
    I'll mak' them intae puddin's an' pies,
    Sing fal the doo a day.
    Herrin's eyes, puddin's an' pies,
    Herrin's heids, loaves o' breid,
    An' a' sorts o' things.

3   Oh, fit'll I dae wi' the herrin's fins?
    I'll mak' them intae needles an' pins.
    Herrin's fins, needles an' pins, etc.

4   Oh, fit'll I dae wi' the herrin's back?
    I'll mak' it a laddie an' christen him Jack.
    Herrin's backs, laddies an' Jacks, etc.

5   Oh, fit'll I dae wi' the herrin's belly?
    I'll mak' it a lassie and christen her Nellie.
    Herrin's bellies, lassies an' Nellies, etc.

6   Oh, fit'll I dae wi' the herrin's tail?
    I'll mak' it a ship wi' a beautiful sail.
    Herrin's tails, ships an' sails,
    Herrin's bellies, lassies an' Nellies,
    Herrin's backs, laddies an' Jacks,
    Herrin's fins, needles an' pins,
    Herrin's eyes, puddin's an' pies,
    Herrin's heids, loaves o' breid,
    An' a sorts o' things.

## 5   Corpus Christi Carol

The heron flew east, the heron flew west,
The heron flew to the fair forest;
She flew o'er streams and meadows green
And a' to see what could be seen:
And when she saw the faithful pair,
Her breast grew sick, her head grew sair;
For there she saw a lovely bower,
Was a' clad o'er wi' lilly-flower;
And in the bower there was a bed
With silken sheets, and weel down spread
And in the bed there lay a knight,
Whose wounds did bleed both day and
    night;
And by the bed there stood a stane,
And there was a set a leal maiden,

99

With silver needle and silken thread,
Stemming the wounds when they did bleed.

## 6 Marriage Song

The marriage feast lasted for a day or two. It was preceded by the betrothal feast and followed by visiting feasts.

A favourite marriage song was sung by the best man or the best maid. It opened:

1    'Hi'll gie to thee ha penny's worth ho' preens,
        To tack up thy flounces hor hony hother things,
    Hif thoo'll walk, if thoo'll walk, hif thoo'll
        walk with me honywhere'.

2    'But hi'll no' tak' yer penny's worth o' preens,
        To tack up my flounces hor hony hother things,
    Hi'll not walk wi' thee honywhere'.

3    'Hi'll gie to thee a braw new dress
        To sit hupon the cerpet, or to walk hupon
           the gress,
    Hif thoo'll walk', etc.

## WORK SONGS

## 7 Sea Shanty

than the marynalis began to veynd the cabil,
vitht mony loud cry. ande as ane cryit, al the
laif cryit in that samyn tune, as it hed bene
ecco in ane hou heuch. and as it aperit to me,
thai cryit thir vordis as eftir follouis.
veyra veyra, veyra veyra. gentil gallandis,
gentil gallandis. veynde i see hym, veynd i
see hym. pourbossa, pourbossa. hail al ande
ane, hail al and ane. hail hym vp til vs, hail

100

hym vp til vs. Than quhen the ankyr vas halit vp
abufe the vattir, ane marynel cryit, and al the
laif follouit in that sam tune, caupon caupona, caupon
caupona, caupun hola, caupun hola. caupun holt,
caupon holt. sarrabossa, sarrabossa. than
thai maid fast the schank of the ankyr.


## 8   The Dreg-Song

I rade to London yesterday
On a cruket hay-cock.
Hay-cock, quo' the seale to the eel,
Cock nae I my tail weel?
Tail weel, or if hare
Hunt the dog frae the deer,
Hunt the dog frae the deil-drum –
Kend ye nae John Young?
. . .
Willie Tod, Willie Tay,
Clekit in the month of May
Month of May and Averile,
Good skill o' reasons,
Tentlins and fentlins.
Yeery, ory, alie!
Weel row'd five men,
As weel your ten.
The oysters are a gentle kin,
They winna tak unless you sing.
Come buy my oisters aff the bing,
To serve the shirreif and the king,
And the commons o' the land,
And the commons o' the sea,
Hey *benedicete*! and that's good Latin.


## 9   Songs for the Owsen Pleuch

(a)     I hae gouden gear, I hae lan eneuch,
        Seven ousen gangin i' the pleuch,

Linkin, ower the lea,
An merry sall we be,
An if ye winna tak me,
Ye can lat me be.

(b)     The 'gadster' (goadman) and the ploughman whistled to
encourage the team, and the following are the words of a favourite
tune:

Baulky lands maks girsy corn,
An girsy corn maks a hole i' the kist,
An a hole i' the kist maks hungry wives,
An hungry wives maks hungry lads,
An hungry lads maks flobbery wark,
An flobbery wark it winna do –
Noo, wyn, Hawkie, dinna boo!

'Baulky land' is land which the plough has failed to turn over. 'Wyn',
the call to the oxen when the driver wished them to come towards
him, the opposite being 'Hop-off' or 'Haup'. 'Dinna boo' means
don't bend, i.e. keep straight.


## 10    A Peat Sang

A Gentleman informed me that the following stanzas were part of a
sang still sung in Buchan when the inhabitants are driving their
peats, and is called a Peat Sang. It was very long and mentioned
numerous localities generally distinguishing the possessors by some
epithet as in the two stanzas preserved, Canker'd & Bo (proud). . . .
The inhabitants call it a 'stroud'.

1    Canker'd Raxton as we gang by
Spiers at hus gin the peats be dry
We answer him atween the twa
But we maun gang by and far awa.

2    As we gang by yon bo Shethin
He says my lads ye'll be ahin
It's aye the faster we maun ca
That we maun gang by and far awa.

102

## 11 Lullaby: Ba-loo, Ba-lil-li

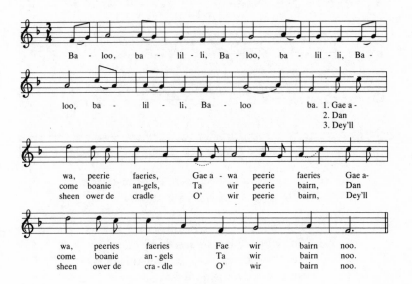

Ba - loo, ba - lil - li, Ba - loo, ba - lil - li, Ba -
loo, ba - lil - li, Ba - loo ba.

1. Gae a -
2. Dan
3. Dey'll

wa, peerie faeries, Gae a - wa peerie faeries Gae a-
come boanie an-gels, Ta wir peerie bairn, Dan
sheen ower de cradle O' wir peerie bairn, Dey'll

wa, peeries faeries Fae wir bairn noo.
come boanie an - gels Ta wir bairn noo.
sheen ower de cra - dle O' wir bairn noo.

## 12 Cradle Croon

Ride the country through and through,
And bring hame mony a Carlisle coo;
Through the Lowdens o'er the border,
Weel, my baby, may ye further,
Harry the loons of the low countree,
Syne to the border hame to me.

## 13 Spinning Song: De Norrawa Wheel

1   Tim-tim-ta ra-a, Tim-tim-ta-ree:
    De treed is snüddin' troo de e'e.
    An' tim-tim-ta ree-e, an' tim-tim-ta raa;
    De wap-tow hes a boanie caa.

2   Tim-tim-ta ra-a, Tim-tim-ta-ree;
    De pirm is bookin' i' de flee,

An' tim-tim-ta ree-e, an' tim-tim-ta raa;
Du's gaen fae me, du's gaen awa.

3    Tim-tim-ta ra-a, Tim-tim-ta-ree;
An twine de boanie treed wi' me.
An' tim-tim-ta ree-e, an' tim-tim-ta raa;
De sweerie fu' is gotten a'.

## LYRIC SONGS

## 14  O if my love

Cho.    O my love's bonny, bonny, bonny,
My love's bonny and fair to see.

1    O if my love was a pickle of wheat
And growing upon yon lilly-white lee,
And I myself a bonny sweet bird:
Away with that pickle I wad flie.

2    O if my love was a bonny red rose
And growing upon some barren wa',
And I myself a drap of dew:
Down in that red rose I would fa'.

3    O if my love was a coffer of gold,
      And I the keeper of the key: ·
      Then I would open it when I lest,
      And into that coffer I would be.

## 15   The Ley-Rigg

1    Will ye gang o'er the ley-rigg
      Wi' me, my kind deary O,
      And cuddle there fu' kindly,
      Myne ain kind dearie O?

Cho.   I'll row you east, I'll row you west,
       I'll row you the way you like best,
       And I'l row you o'er the ley-rig,
       Mine ain kind deary O.

2    At thornie dyke and birken tree
      We'll daff and ne'er be weary O,
      They'll skug ill een frae you and me,
      My ain kind dearie O.

Cho. I'll row you east, I'll row you west &c.

3    Nae herd wi' kent or collie there
      Shall e'er come near to fear ye O,
      But lav'rocks, singing in the air,
      Shall woo like me their dearie O.

Cho. I'll row you east, I'll row you west &c.

4    While others herd their eyes and lambs
      And toil for wardly gear, my jo,
      Upon the ley my pleasure grows,
      Wi' you, my kind dearie O.

Cho. I'll row you east, I'll row you west &c.

## 16   I lovèd a lass

1   I lovèd a lass, and I loved her sae weel
   I hated all others that spoke o' her ill;
   But noo she's rewarded me weel for my love,
     For she's gaun to be wed till anither.

2   When I saw my love to the church go,
   Wi'bride an' bride-maidens, they made a fine show;
   An' I followed them on wi' a heart fu' o' woe,
     For she's gaun to be wed till anither.

3   When I saw my love sit down to dine,
   I sat down beside her and poured out the wine,
   An' I drank to the lass that suld ha' been mine,
     An' now she is wed till anither.

4   The men o' yon forest they askit o' me,
   Hou many strawberries grew in the saut sea?
   But I askit them back wi' a tear in my ee',
     How many ships sail in the forest?

5   O dig me a grave and dig it sae deep,
   An' cover it over with flowers sae sweet,
   An' I'll turn in for to tak' a lang sleep,
     An' may be in time I'll forget her.

6   They dug him a grave an' they dug it sae deep,
   An' covered it over with flow'rets sae sweet,
   An' he's turned in for to tak' a lang sleep,
     An' may-be by this time he's forgot her.

## 17  Waly, Waly

1    Waly, waly up the bank,
      And waly, waly down the brae,
    And waly, waly yon burn-side,
      Where I and my love wont to gae.
    I lean'd my back unto an aik,
      I thought it was a trusty tree,
    But first it bow'd, and syne it brak,
      Sae my truelove did lightly me.

2    O waly, waly, but love be bonny,
      A little time while it is new,
    But when 'tis auld it waxeth cauld,
      And fades away like the morning dew.
    O wherefore shou'd I busk my head?
      Or wherefore should I kame my hair?
    For my true love has me forsook,
      And says he'll never love me mair.

3    Now Arthur-Seat shall be my bed,
      The sheets shall ne'er be fyl'd by me,
    Saint Anton's well shall be my drink,
      Since my true love has forsaken me.
    Martinmas wind, when wilt thou blaw,
      And shake the green leaves off the tree?
    O gentle death, when wilt thou come?
      For of my life I'm weary.

4    'Tis not the frost that freezes fell,
      Nor blawing snaw's inclemency;
    'Tis not sic cauld that makes me cry,
      But my love's heart grown cauld to me.
    When we came in by Glasgow town,
      We were a comely sight to see;
    My love was clad in the black velvet,
      And I my sell in cramasie.

5    But had I wist before I kiss'd,
      That love had been sae ill to win,

I'd lock'd my heart in a case of gold,
And pin'd it with a silver pin.
Oh, oh! if my young babe were born,
And set upon the nurse's knee,
And I my sell were dead and gane,
For a maid again I'll never be.

## 18   Rolling in the Dew

1    'What wid you dae
        If I were to lay you doon,
    Wi' your reid an rosy cheeks
        An your curly black hair?'
    'I'd be fit enough to rise again,
        Kind sir', she answered me,
    'Rolling in the dew
        Maks a milkmaid fair.'


2    'But what wid you dae
        If I were to bairn ye,
    Wi' your reid an rosy cheeks
        And your curly black hair?'
    'For you would be the daddie o't
        And I would be the mither o't,
    Kind sir', she answered me,
        'Rolling in the dew
    Maks a milkmaid fair.'

## 19   The Cuckoo's Nest

1. There is a thorn bush in oor kail-yard,

There is a thorn bush in oor kail-yard.

At the back o' thon bush there stands a lad and lass,

And they're bu-sy, bu-sy herry-in' at the cuc-koo's nest.

*Chorus* And its hey the cuck and ho the cuck and hey the cuc-koo's nest,

And its hey the cuck and ho the cuck and hey the cuc-koo's nest.

I'll gie o-ny bo-dy a shil-lin' and a bot-tle o' the best,

If they'll rum-ple up the fea-thers o' the cuc-koo's nest.

2   It is thorned, it is sprinkled, it is compassed all around,
   It is thorned, it is sprinkled, and it isn't easy found.
   She said: 'Young man, you're plundering;' I said it
      wasnae true,
   But I left her wi' the makin's o' a young cuckoo.


## 20   This field

'This field you're going to break upon has been eighteen
   years in lea,
This field you're going to break upon belongs no more to me.

And if you want a crop of it this very present year,
Just draw out your horses and then commence to feere'.
Then drawin out his horses, the number being three,

. . .

Twa big geldins gaun abreist and Whitey gaun afore,
For want o yird the missel pin was in its highest bore.


## 21    As I cam in by Fisherrow

1    As I came in by Fisherrow
     Mussleburgh was near me:
     I threw off my mussle-pock
     And courted wi' my deary.

2    O had her apron bidden doun,
     The kirk wad ne'er a kend it,
     But since the word's gane thro' the toun,
     My dear, I canna mend it

3    But ye maun mount the cutty-stool,
     And I moun mount the pillar,
     And that's the way that poor folks do,
     Because they hae nae sillar.

Cho. Up stairs, doun stairs,
     Timber-stairs fears me,
     I thought it lang to ly my lane,
     When I'm sae near my dearie!


## 22    O that I had ne'er been married

1    O that I had ne'er been married,
     I wad nevir had nae care,
     Now I've gotten wife and bairns
     They cry crowdie evermair.

Cho. Ance crowdie, twice crowdie,
     Three times crowdie in a day:

Gin ye crowdie ony may,
Ye'll crowdie a' my meal away!

## HUMOROUS LYRICS

### 23    Lass gin ye loo me, tell me noo

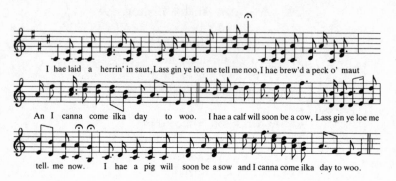

I hae laid a herrin' in saut, Lass gin ye loe me tell me noo, I hae brew'd a peck o' maut An I canna come ilka day to woo. I hae a calf will soon be a cow, Lass gin ye loe me tell me now. I hae a pig will soon be a sow and I canna come ilka day to woo.

1    I hae laid a herrin in saut,
    Lass gin ye loe me tell me noo,
    I hae brew'd a peck o' maut
    An I canna come ilka day to woo.
    I hae a calf will soon be a cow,
    Lass gin ye loe me tell me now.
    I hae a pig will soon be a sow
    and I canna come ilka day to woo.

2    I hae a house on yonder muir
    Lass gin ye loe me –
    I hae sparrows may dance on the floor
    And I canna come ilka day to woo
    I hae a butt and I hae a ben
    Lass gin ye loe me
    I hae three chickens and a fat hen
    And I canna &c

3    I hae a hen wi' a happity leg
    Lass gin ye loe me

Which ilka day lays me an egg
And I canna come &c
I hae a lairdship down in the Merse
Lass gin ye loe me
The eighteenth part o' a guse's grass
An' I winna come ony mair to woo.

## 24   He wadna want his Gruel

1   There lived a man into the west,
       And O! but he was cruel;
   Upon his waddin' nicht at e'en,
       He sat up, and grat for gruel.

2   They brought to him a good sheep's head,
       A napkin, and a towel, –
   'Gae tak' your whim-whams a' frae me,
       And bring me fast my gruel'.

   The Bride speaks.

3   'There is nae meal into the hous,
       What shall I do, my jewel?'
   'Gae to the pock, and shake a lock,
       For I canna want my gruel'.

4   'There is nae milk into the hous,
       What shall I do, my jewel?'
   'Gae to the midden, and milk the soo,
       For I wunna want my gruel'.

## 25   My Wife's a Wanton Wee Thing

My wife's a wanton wee thing,
My wife's a wanton wee thing,
My wife's a wanton wee thing,
    She'll never be guided by me!
She play'd the loon e'er she was married,

She play'd the loon e'er she was married,
She play'd the loon e'er she was married,
    She'll do it again e'er she die!

## 26   Fairly shot of her

I married a wife with a good commendation,
But now she's as peeck to a' the whole nation;
Hearken and hear, and I will tell ye a note of
    her,
Now she is dead, and I'm fairly shot of her.


    Cho. Fairly, fairly, fairly shut of her,
Now she is dead I will dance on the top of
    her,
Well's me now I am fairly shut of her,
Fairly &c.


## COMIC SONGS


## 27   A Thrawn Sang

There was a wee bird,
It took a fit in every han',
And whuppit awa to Ayr's lan'
Frae Ayr's lan' to Aberdeen,
And saw ferlies fifteen.

It saw an auld man in the byre bin'en the kye, and an auld wife in the
    close chackin' the mice to the hens throwing banes in her face.
The auld mare makin' the porridge, and the wee foal lickin' the stick.
There's an auld cat makin' cheese, and a wee kitten janglin' keys.
The dog in the ash-hole makin' brose, Doon comes a cinder and
    burns his nose.
The cock in the chimney-top kaimin' down his yellow hair.
Come down, sir, What are ye doin' up there?

## 28  We'll put the Sheep's Head in the Pat

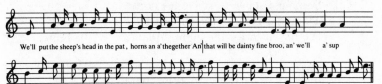

We'll put the sheep's head in the pat, horns an a' thegether An' that will be dainty fine broo, an' we'll    a' sup

thegether    We'll get a' fu' thegether, we'll be a' fu' thegether We'll no' stir frae the ingle neuk  until it be warmer weather.

We'll put the sheep's head in the pat, horns an a' thegether,
An' that will be dainty fine broo, an' we'll a' sup thegether.
We'll get a' fu' thegether, we'll be a' fu' thegether,
We'll no stir frae the ingle neuk, until it be warmer weather.

We'll round about Hawick thegether
We'll round about Hawick for ever
We'll up wi' the tane and the t'other
An we'll round about Hawick for ever.
    We'll a' get fu' &c.

## 29  Tam o' the Linn

1    Tam o' the Linn was a Scotsman born,
        Fa la linkum, feedledum.
    He had cap of a hunter's horn,
        Fa la linkum, feedledum.
    The wrong side out, and the right side in,
    'A very gude cap,' quo Tam o' the Linn.
        With my feedledum, &c.

2    Tam o' Linn's daughter scho sat on the stair,
    And, 'wow,' quo scho, 'Father am na I fair?
    There's mony ane wed wi an unwhiter skin.'
    'The deil whorl't aff,' quo Tam o' the Linn.

3    Tam o' Linn's daughter scho sat on the brig,
    And, 'wow,' quo scho, 'Father, am na I trig?'
    The brig it brak, and she tummel'd in –
    'Your tocher's paid,' quo Tam o' the Linn.

115

4    Tam o' the Linn's gaen doon to the moss,
      Seeking a stable to stable his horse,
      The night being mirk, the mare fell in,
      'Ye're stalled for the night,' quo Tam o' the Linn.

## 30   In Brechin did a Webster dwell

1    In Brechin did a Webster dwell, John Steinson was
       his name
      A mare he had, a lusty jade, baith sturdy stark
       an strang
      Baith lusty an trusty an he had spar'd her lang.

2    The webster bade his mare go work, quoth she I
       am not able
      For neither get I corn nor hay, nor stand I
       in the stable
      But hunts me an dunts me an dings me frae the town
      An fells me an tells me I am not worth my room.

3    The webster swore a bloody oath an' out he drew his
       knife
      If one word come out o' thy head I vow I'll take
       thy life
      The mare ay for fear fell fainting on the ground
      An' groanin an moaning fell in a deadly swoun.

4    They rumbled her an tumbled her an' shot her
       o'er the brae
      Wi rumbling an tumbling she to the ground did gae
      They nipped her an clipped her an took frae her
       the skin,
      The haunches an paunches they quickly brought them
       in –

5    But the night being cauld an the mare without
       her skin
      Darkness came o'er the land an fain wad she be in
      She rapped an she chapped wi her twa farther hooves

He heard her an feared her an' thought it had been
    thieves.

6    The webster's son was stout in heart, he up an to the
        door
    An' thrust his spear into her heart a lang claith yard an more

     —   —   —   —   —
    —   —   —   —   —

O mercy, mercy father for I ha' kill'd a man

     —   —   —   —   —
    —   —   —   —   —

What shall we do what can we do wi' this same
    wicked mare

     —   —   —   —   —

We'll wash her an dash her an saut her in a tub
We'll call in the neighbours all an we will call
    them in
John Dickson, John Davison, an kin' Patie Grun.
Christmass-day this greasy pack did a convene in
    haste
The hail tribe o' yarnstealers cam a' unto this
    feast.

## 31   As I Cam Ower the Muir o Ord

1    As I cam ower the Muir o Ord
    As I cam ower the Muir o Ord
    For I've come here withoot ony cause –
    Will ye rise an lat me in, o.
      Lat me in this ae nicht
      This ae only ae nicht:
      O lat me in this ae nicht
      An I'll never come back again, o.

2    Tae tak ye in that cannae be –
     My bedroom doors they chirp an cheep.
     My bedroom doors they chirp an cheep
     So I cannae let ye in, o.
         Gang ye hame this ae night
         This ae only ae nicht:
         So gang ye hame this ae nicht
         An never come back again, o.

3    Come oil yer locks till they are wet,
     For they 'ill neither chirp not cheep.
     Come slippin ben in yer stockin feet
     An let yer laddie in, o.
         O gang ye hame this ae nicht
         This ae only ae nicht:
         O gang ye hame this ae nicht
         An never come back again, o.

4    When I got in I was a king
     I drew ma bonnet weel ower ma een
     An the lassie lost a pair o sheen
     An the auld fowk heard nae din, o.
         O she likit that ae nicht
         That ae only ae nicht:
         For o she likit that ae nicht
         That she let her laddie in, o.

118

5    When I got in I was sae gled
I knockit the bottom clean oot o the bed
An the lassie lost her maidenhead
An the auld fowk heard nae din, o.
    For o she rued that ae nicht
    That ae only ae nicht:
    For o she rued that ae nicht
    That she let her laddie in, o.

## 32   The Widow's Dochter

1    There livit a widow woman in the West Mure land
She had never a daughter but ane
And she was telland her day and nicht
Neer to gie her maidenhead to nane

2    It happened on a day on a bonnie simmer's day
As she sat by her mother's knie
Thare is a jolly jinker in the King's life Guards
That has tane the maidenhead frae me

3    She took up the airn tangs
And gied her lunders thrie
Get out my house ye base like jade
Get out my house said she

4    O she's awa to the jolly jinker gane
As fast as she may hie
Sayand you maun gie me back what ye got last night
For my mammy has banished me

5    Or will ye have it in your hand
Or will ye have it on your knee
Or will ye have it in the dark corner
Where there is no one will not see

6    I'll have it not in my hand she says
Nor have it on my knei

119

But I will have it in the dark corner
Where no one will us see

7    He tuke her by the milk white hand
Led her away to the jolly jinker's bed
And laid her head where her heels was before
And gied her back her maidenhead

8    She's awa to her mother gane
As fast as she micht hie
I'm as leil a maid now deir mother she said
As the first nicht ye bore me

9    It happened on a day on a bonnie summer's day
This jolly jinker's ganeng to be wed

.   .   .   .   .   .   .   .   .
.   .   .   .   .   .   .   .

10    And she drest herself as braw as braw could be
With a fan in every hand
And she's awa to the green wud gane
And so merrilie as she sang

11    Wha is yonder the bride she says
That sings sae fine and braw
That is a widow woman's daughter in the
   West Mure land
But she tells her mammie aw

12    How could she do it for I could na do it
Or how could she do it for shame
I have lyne nine summer nichts wi my ain true love
And I neer telled that to nane

13    If you've lyin nine summer nichts with your an
   true love
Ye sall neer ly an wi me
And he's tane the widow woman's daughter in the
   West Mure land
And let his ain bride be

## NARRATIVE SONGS

### 33  The Wedding of the Frog and the Mouse

1    Frogie wad a wooing ride,
    Cuddy alone, Cuddy alone,
Frogie wad a wooing ride,
With Dirk and Pistol by his side.
    Syne, kick my Leerie, cow him down,
    Cuddy alone and I.

2    'Mistress Mouse, I am come to woo;
So Marriage ye man grant me now.'

3    'Uncle Rat is not at Home,
So marriage I can grant you none.'

4    'Go, cover the Table, go cover't wi' Cloath,
And here is a Penny to buy a white Loave.

5    Go, cover the Table, go cover it fine,
And bring us a Bottle of Claret Wine.'

6    Now guess you who sat at the Heid of them a'
But Mistress Mouse, so jimp and sma'.

7    Then guess you, who sat at the foot of the Table,
But Uncle Rat, so stout and able.

8    Then came the Duck ben and the Drake,
And our Bridegroom gave mony a Quake.

9    Then came in the old black Cat,
And the Kitlen on her Back.

10   The old Cat pulled the Rotten down,
And the Kitlen clave the Mouse's Crown.

11   Would it not make a Hale Heart wae
To see sick a Family so soon decay?

## 34  John Barleycorn

1   There came three merry men from the east,
    And three merry men they be;
And they have sworn a solemn oath
    John Barleycorn shall die.

2   They've ta'en a plough and plough'd him down,
    Put clods upon his head;
And they have sworn a solemn oath
    John Barleycorn was dead.

3   But the spring-time it came on at last,
    And showers began to fall;
John Barleycorn's sprung up again,
    Which did surprise them all.

4   Then the summer heat on him did beat,
    And he grew pale and wan;
John Barleycorn has got a beard
    Like any other man.

5   They've ta'en a hook, that was full sharp,
    And cut him above the knee;
And they've bound him intill a corn cart,
    Like a thief for the gallow-tree.

6   They've ta'en twa sticks, that were full stout,
    And sore they beat his bones;
The miller used him worse than that,
    And ground him between two stones.

7   The browster-wife we'll not forget;
    She well her tale can tell;
She's ta'en the sap out of his bodie,
    And made of it good ale.

8   And they have fill'd it in a cap,
    And drank it round and round;

And ay the mair they drank o'it,
    The mair did joy abound.

9    John Barleycorn is the wightest man
        That ever throve in land;
    For he could put a Wallace down
        Wi' the turning of his hand.

10    He'll gar the huntsman shoot his dog;
        The post-boy blow his horn,
    He'll gar a maiden dance stark-naked
        Wi' the tooming of a horn.

11    He'll change a man into a boy,
        A boy into an ass;
    He'll change your gold into silver,
        And your silver into brass

## 35   Buchan Forest

1    Buchan Forest, as we heard,
        A day of hunting set;
    It happened on a Monday,
        I wat it was na het.

2    Some came from Mennack,
        And some from Trool,
        And some from the Loch Doon,
    And when they met at Palskaig-head
        Some of them wanted shoon.

3    It happened on a wony Monday,
        It blew both snaw and hail;
    We raised him at the Saigy Goats,
        Put raches to his tail.

4    And doun Craignaw I wat he ran,
        Down by Loch Narroch strand –
    The staibler that we had set there
        Was mikle John McCom.

5    Now, John McCom, now let me by,
       For at thee I have no faid,
    For I am sure ye never was the worse of me
       Since ye cam to Glenhead.

6    I think this man he had no faid
       When he did let him by,
    For we were sair near Craiglee
       Before he raised the cry.

7    James Murray and George Gordon,
       They were two subjects true;
    They did well, and sped their heels,
       And ran to keep the view.

8    The foremost man cam up to them
       Was Maxcel of Straquhan;
    They stabled their men on every side,
       They put their terriers in.

9    They chattelt at his chamber day,
       They knew he was within;
    He did not love their chattling noise
       In chamber where he lay,
    He thought an' he were out again
       He would show them some more play!

10    Out he gat, and doun Craignaw,
       As swift as any naig,
    The mountain dog was good and true
       And catched him by the craig.

11    Straquhan took him by the hin' heels,
       To a stane he laid his head:
    This red-dog that we got here
       I think he be no bairn,
    For he has bear'd the faid for us
       Through Straiton and Carsfairn.

## 36   Flesher Robbie

1   It's fae Flesher Robbie that lived in Crieff
    A bonny, bonny lassie gaed to buy some beef.
    He took her in his airms, an' doon she did fa,
    An' the win' blew the bonnie lassie's plaidie awa,
    Plaidie awa, plaidie awa,
    An' the win' blew the bonnie lassie's plaidie awa.


2   The plaidie was lost, an' couldna be foun';
    The deuce is i' the plaid it's awa wi the win';
    'O what can I say to the auld folks ava,
    I canna say the win' blew the plaidie awa'.
    Plaidie awa, plaidie awa, &c.


3   When twenty lang weeks were a' gane an' past,
    That bonnie, bonnie lassie grew thick aboot the waist;
    An' Robbie got the wyte o' the hale o' it a',
    For the win' blew the bonnie lassie's plaidie awa.
    Plaidie awa, plaidie awa, &c.


4   Soon Robbie was summoned to answer the session,
    They a' cried oot, 'Noo mak a fair confession,
    For Robbie for to mak ane oot o' twa'.
    But Robbie said the win' blew the plaidie awa.
    Plaidie awa, plaidie awa, &c.


5   The lassie was sent for to speak for hersel;
    She lookit in's face, says 'Ye ken foo I fell;
    An' ye had the wyte o't, ye daurna say na,
    An' 'twas then 'at the win' blew my plaidie awa'.
    Plaidie awa, plaidie awa, &c.


6   He lookit in her face, an' he gae a bit smile,
    Says 'Dinna think bonnie lass that I'll you beguile;
    For the minister is here, he can mak ane oot o' twa,
    An that'll pay the plaid 'at the win' blew awa'.
    Plaidie awa, plaidie awa, &c.

125

7   So the whiskey was sent for to mak' a'thing richt,
    The minister an' elders they sat a' nicht;
    An' lang ere the cocks they begood for to craw,
    They were singin foo the win' blew the plaidie awa.
    Plaidie awa, plaidie awa, &c.

8   Noo Robbie an' his lassie they're joined hand in hand,
    They live as contentit as ony o' the lan';
    But when Robbie gets foo, an' he min's on the fa,
    An' he sings hoo the win' blew the plaidie awa,
    Plaidie awa, plaidie awa,
    An' he sings hoo the win' blew the plaidie awa.

## 37   MacPherson's Lament

With deliberation
For verse 1 only

Fare-weel, ye dun - geon's dark and strang, Mac - Pher - son's day - will no' be lang,

Up - on the gal - lows tree I'll hang. Sae ran - ting-ly, sae wan - ton-ly,

And sae daunt-ing-ly - gaed he,   He - played a tune and he danced it roond,

D. C. Fine For verses 2-8

Be - low   the gal - lows   tree. 2. It was by a wo - man's treach-erous hand

That I   was con-demned to - dee,   Be - low a ledge at a   win - dow she stood,

Chorus

And a blank - et she threw over me.   Sae ran - ting-ly, - sae wan-ton - ly.

2    It was by a woman's treacherous hand
      That I was condemned to dee,
      Below a ledge at a window she stood,
      And a blanket she threw ower me.

3    The Laird o' Grant, that Hieland sant,
      That first laid hands on me;
      He played the cause on Peter Broom,
      To let MacPherson dee.

4    Untie these bands fra' off my hands,
      An gie to me my sword,
      And there's no' a man in a' Scotland,
      But I'll brave him at a word.

5    There's some cam' here to see me hanged,
      And some to buy my fiddle,
      But before that I do part wi' her,
      I'll brak' it through the middle.

6    He took the fiddle into baith of his hands,
      And he broke it ower a stane,
      Says: 'There's nae ither hand shall play on thee,
      When I am dead and gane.'

7    O, little did my mither think,
      When first she cradled me,
      That I would turn a rovin' boy
      And die on the gallows tree.

8    The reprieve was coming over the brig o' Banff,
      To let MacPherson free;
      But they pit the clock at a quarter afore
      And hanged him to the tree.

## BROADSIDES

## 38   Billy Taylor

1    Billy Taylor was a sailor,
        Billy Taylor stout an gay:
     When our Billy was to marry
        He was pressed an sent away.⸪
        Refrain:     Sing wake falairal airal ido
        Wake falairal idle ay.

2    She's dressed herself in sailor's clothing,
        Dipped her hands in pitch an tar,
     Went on board like a tarry seaman,
        Straight on board a man-of-war,     Refrain.

3    In the vessel came a wrestle:
        She jumped out among the rest:
     Her silver buttons they flew open:
        The captain spied her lily-white breast.     Refrain.

4    Then the captain's called her to him:
        'Pray come tell what brings you here?'
     'Oh I am seeking Billy Taylor
        Now is pressed this seven long year.'     Refrain.

5    'You rise early the next morning,
        Early nigh the break of day:
     There you'll see young Billy Taylor
        Walkin with his true-love gay.'     Refrain.

6    She rose early the next morning,

128

Early by the break of day:
There she saw young Billy Taylor
    Walkin with his true-love gay.    Refrain.

7    Gun an pistol she demanded
    Gun an pistol by her side:
There she shot young Billy Taylor
    Walkin at his true-love's side,    Refrain.

8    Saying, 'Take you that, my false young fellow,
    Take you that, my false young man:
Seven long years I've served for you
    All aboard the *Mary Ann*.'    Refrain.

9    Now the captain's called her to him:
    'Pray come tell what you have done!'
'Oh I have shot young Billy Taylor
    With my double-barrelled gun.'    Refrain.

10    Now she is the captain's lady,
    Now she is the captain's bride,
Now she is the captain's lady
    Down aboard the *Mary Ann*,
        Sing wake falairal airal ido
        Wake falairal idle ay!

## 39   The Poachers

1    Come all ye gallant poachers that ramble void of care,
That walk out on a moonlight night, with your dog, your gun
    and snare;
The harmless hare and pheasant you have at your command.
Not thinking on your last career upon Van Dieman's Land

2    Twas poor Tom Brown from Glasgow, Jack Williams,
    and poor Joe,
We were three daring poachers, the country well
    did know:

At night we were trepanned by the keepers in
the sand,
And for fourteen years transported unto Van
Dieman's Land.

3    The first day that we landed upon this fatal shore
The planters they came round us, full twenty score
or more.
They rank'd us up like horses, and sold us
out of hand,
And yok'd us up to ploughs, my boys, to plough
Van Dieman's Land.

4    The houses that we dwell in here are built of
clod and clay:
With rotten straw for bedding, we dare not
say them nay:
Our cots are fenced with fire, and we slumber when
can,
And we fight the wolves and tigers which infest
Van Dieman's Land.

5    At night, when soundly sleeping, I had a pleasant
dream,
With my sweetheart I was courting down by a
purling stream;

Through Scotland I was roving, with her at my
  command –
But I awoke downhearted upon Van Dieman's Land.

6  There cam' a lass from sweet Dundee, Jean Stewart
    it was her name,
  For fourteen years transported, as you may know
    the same.
  Our captain bought her freedom, and married her
    offhand,
  And she gives us a' good usage here, upon Van
    Dieman's Land.

7  Although the poor of Scotland do labour and do toil,
  They're robbed of every blessing and produce of
    the soil;
  Your proud, imperious landlords, if we break
    their command,
  They'll send you to the British hulks, or to
    Van Daeman's Land.

8  So all you gallant poachers give ear unto my song,
  It is a bit of good advice, although it is not
    long,
  Throw by your dogs and snares, for to you I speak
    plain,
  For if you knew our hardships you would never poach
    again.


OCCUPATIONAL SONGS


## 40  The Wark o' the Weavers

1  Weel we're a' met thegither here to sit an' to crack,
  Wi' glasses in our hands and our wark upon our back;
  But there's no' a trade among us a' can either mend or mak'
  But what wears the wark o' the Weavers.

131

Cho.  If it warna the weaver what wad we do?
      We wadna get claith made o' our woo',
      We wadna get a coat neither black nor blue,
      Gin't warna for the wark o' the Weavers.

2    There's the Hiremen, they mock us, and crack aye aboot's,
     They say we're thin-faced, bleached-lookin' cloots;
     But yet for a' their mockery they canna do withoot's
     Na! they canna want the wark o' the Weavers.

   Chorus.

3    There's our Wrights, an' our Slaters, an' Glaziers an' a',
     Our Doctors, an' Ministers, an' them that live by Law,
     And our friends in South America – though them we never
     saw,
     Yet we ken they wear the wark o' the Weavers.

   Chorus.

4    There's our Sailors an' Sodgers, we ken they're very bauld,
     But if they hadna claes, faith, they couldna fecht for cauld;
     The high an' low, the rich and puir, a'-body young and auld,
     Mair or less need the wark o' the Weavers.

   Chorus.

5    Some folks are independent o' ither tradesmen's wark,
     For women need nae Barber, an' dykers need nae Clerk;
     But yet they canna do without a coat or a sark,
     Na! they canna want the wark o' the Weavers.

Chorus.

6    So the Weaving a trade is that never can fail,
     As lang's we need ae cloot to keep anither hale;
     So let us aye be merry owre a bicker o' guid ale,
     An' here's health an' lang life to the Weavers.

Chorus.

## 41    The Coal-bearer's Lamentation

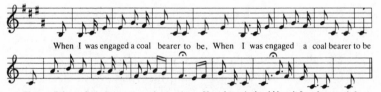

When I was engaged a coal bearer to be, When I was engaged a coal bearer to be

Thro all the coal-pits I maun wear the dron brat, If my heart it should break I wad never git free.

        When I was engaged a coal bearer to be,
        When I was engaged a coal bearer to be
        Thro all the coal-pits I maun wear the dron brat,
        If my heart it should break, I wad never git free.

## 42    Six Jolly Miners

1    We're six jolly miner lads an' miners you all know,
     We've travelled all the country round for many, many miles,
     We've travelled east, we've travelled west, this country all
          around
     To turn out the treasures that lies beneath the ground.

2    Oh, there's two of them from Airderie an' two frae Holytown,

We're six jol-ly mi-ner lads an' mi-ners you all know, We've tra-velled all the coun-try round for ma-ny ma-ny miles, We've tra-velled east, we've tra-velled west, this coun-try all a - round, To turn out the trea-sures that lies be-neath the ground.

> There's two o' them from Valleyfield, their equal can't be
>     found,
> For turnin' out the treasures that lies beneath the ground.

3   Now sometimes we've got money, sometimes we've none at
        all,
    But when we've got money we call our pals around,
    We call for liquor plenty and drink before we gang,
    So here's a health to all young men that works beneath the
        ground.

4   Now it's the huntsman's delight an' the soundin' of his horn,
    It's the fairmer's delight an' the sowin' of his corn,
    But it's the collier's delight for tae split the rock in two
    To turn out the treasures that lies beneath the ground.

5   Now I'll build my love a castle, a castle of renown,
    There's neither dukes nor earls will pull that castle down,
    For the king loves the queen an' the emp'ror does the same,
    But they a' loo a miner lad, an' wha could ye blame?


## 43   The Greenland Whale Fishery

1       In eighteen hundred and forty-four
            On March the twentieth day,

We hoisted our flag to our foretopmast
  And for Greenland sailed away, brave boys:
  And for Greenland sailed away.

2    Our captain walking the quarterdeck
       With a spyglass in his hand:
     'A whale, a whale, a whalefish,' he cries,
       'An he blows at every span, brave boys;
       He blows at every span.

3    'Overhaul, overhaul, let your davit tackles fall,
       Come launch your boats for sea,
     With line-coilers and the jolly Jack-o-Tars,
       And away to the fish we'll go, brave boys:
       Oh away to the fish we'll go.'

4    The whale bein struck and the line paid out
       She made a great flurry with her tail:
     The boat capsized, five men was lost,
       And the nice little apprentice boy, brave boys:
       And the nice little apprentice boy.

5    Sad news, sad news to our captain came
       Which grieved his heart full sore

135

At the losing of the poor apprentice boy –
But the whale grieved him ten times more, brave boys:
But the whale grieved him ten times more.

6    It is time to leave this cold country now
And for Greenland sail away,
Where the hail and the snow and the whalefishes blow
And the daylight is never done, brave boys:
And the daylight is never done.

## 44  Killeonan

1    There is a fairm near Stewarton,
Killownan is its name.
There's no such a hashin slashin place
Free Oatfield tae Killean.

Refrain:
With me tarrity, arrity, ing ding darrity,
Tarrity, arrity ay.

2    The first man aboot this place
He comes frae Strathbaan,
An he is ruein every day
That e'er the world began.

3    The second man aboot this place
He comes frae the North,

136

An he is ruein every day
That e'er he crossed the Forth.

4    The first pair aboot this place
They are a pair o' greys,
An when ye see them gan oot in chains
Ye wad sweir they were High Drumayes.

5    The second pair aboot this place
There's naethin but skin an bane
An when ye see them gan oot in chains
Ye wad sweir they wad never come hame.

6    There is a boy aboot this place
They ca him Baldy Bain,
An the wey he's hashed an slashed aboot
It's a God almighty shame.

7    The first lass aboot this place
She does naethin but feed the hens,
An tae gain an inch o' favour
She tells them a' she kens.

8    The second lass aboot this place
She does naethin but cook the grub,
An when it's cooked an ready
It wad scunner a collie dug.

9    There is an auld wife at this place
Her tongue gans like a bell,
An if she got a' that she deserves
She should be tied to the yetts o' hell.

10    Noo for the rest o' this sang, me boys,
Apply tae Patrick Graham.
A cheerier lad ye'll no get
Frae Oatfield tae Killean.

## VARIOUS SONG-KINDS

### 45   A Deedling Song

(a)   Your wee man's a bonnie wee man,
        My wee man's a deevil;
      That's the way the money goes –
        Pop goes the weasel.

(b)   Up and doon Jamaica Street,
        Riding on an eagle;
      That's the, etc.

### 46   A Medlay

There's auld Sir Simon the priest,
    And young Sir Simon the square;
The cat's a comical beast
    It's a' clad owre wi' hair.
Wha'll buy my fine broom besoms?
    Better never grew:
He fell in the fire and burned his big bow-ow-ow-ow;
He fell in the fire, etc.

### 47   A Play-Song: Lady Dundonald

This strange folly was generally sung by a man, with a woman's cap on his head, a distaff, and a spindle. The dialogue of which the subjoined is only a Fragment, was chanted in recitative. . . .

1   Weel it becomes the Lady Dundonald,
      To sit liltin' at her rock,
      And weel it becomes the Laird o' Dundonald,
      To wear his hodden gray frock!

Cho.    Lilty Eery, Lardy Lardy,
      Lilty Eery, Lardy Lam.

138

Enter *Marg'et*.

2    'My Lady, there is a lass at the door wants
To be feed.' –
'What fee does she want?' –
'Five punds.' –
'Five punds is o'er mony punds, to be
Drawing out the tail o' a rock.'

Lilty Eery, &c.

3    'Tell her I will gee her
Four punds, and spin a' the
Backs mysel.'

Lilty Eery, &c.

Enter *Marg'et*.

4    'My lady, what will I tell you noo,
Isna our kitchen lass wi' bairn!' –
'Wha may that be till?
The Laird, I needna speir.'

Lilty Eery, &c.

5    'He has fifteen at the fire-side else,
And that will mak sixteen,
And sae it will een;
It was me that made him a Laird;
But deel speed sic Lairds!'

Lilty Eery, &c.

6    'Hear, Marg'et!' –
'What does my Lady want noo?' –
'Bring ben the brandy bottle your waas,
And tak a dram yoursel',
And gar me tak twa.'

139

Lilty Eery, &c.

7    'I think we may as weel
     Tak our ain geer oursels,
     For it is gaein' whether or no.'

Lilty Eery, &c.

Enter *John*.

8    'My Lady, there is company come.' –
     'Fashious fock, John; I want nae company,
     I am spinning at my rock.'

Lilty Eery, &c.

9    'My Lady, the servants is going to their beds,
     They want the doup of a candle.' –
     'Tell them to put doups and doups thegither,
     And that will gie them licht.'

Lilty Eery, &c.

## 48   An Endless Song

Tune – The Laird o' Cockpen.
This is a good example of those endless songs, often sung by a singer
who has been coerced into a performance for which he knows he is
unfitted. Once started, however, he goes on and on till everybody is
scunnered, or helpless with laughter, and stops only when he is
exhausted.

There was a black hen, and she had a black fit,
And she biggit her nest in a blackberry tree ruit;
Black hen, and black fit, and blackberry tree ruit.

Cho. There was a black hen, and she had a black fit.
*D.C. ad lib.*

## 49   Songs for Non-Singers

(Said or sung by persons unwilling or unable to comply with
repeated requests.)

(a)     Tobacco pipes, tobacco pipes, tobacco pipes and porter;
        Mony ane can sing a sang, but few could sing a shorter.

(b)     For your diversion I'll sing ye a sang,
        For my diversion 'twill no' be lang;
        For your diversion my sang's begun,
        And for my diversion it now is done.


## CLASSICAL BALLADS


## 50   The Laily Worm and the Machrel of the Sea

1       'I was bat seven year alld
            Fan my mider she did dee,
        My father marrëd the ae warst woman
            The wardle did ever see.

2       'For she has made me the lailly worm
            That lays att the fitt of the tree,
        An o my sister Meassry
            The machrel of the sea.

3       'An every Saterday att noon
            The machrl comes to me,
        An she takes my laylë head,
            An lays it on her knee,
        An keames it we a silver kemm,
            An washes it in the sea.

4       'Seven knights ha I slain
            Sane I lay att the fitt of the tree;
        An ye war na my ain father,
            The eight an ye sud be.'

141

5    'Sing on your song, ye l[a]ily worm,
        That ye sung to me;'
     'I never sung that song
        But fatt I wad sing to ye.

6    'I was but seven year aull
        Fan my mider she [did] dee,
     My father marrëd the a warst woman
        The wardle did ever see.

7    'She changed me to the layel[y] worm
        That layes att the fitt of the tree,
     An my sister Messry
        [To] the makrell of the sea.

8    'And every Saterday att noon
        The machrell comes to me,
     And she takes my layly head,
        An layes it on her knee,
     An kames it weth a siller kame,
        An washes it in the sea.

9    'Seven knights ha I slain
        San I lay att the fitt of the tree;
     An ye war na my ain father,
        The eight ye sud be.'

10   He sent for his lady
        As fast as sen cod he:
     'Far is my son,
        That ye sent fra me,
     And my daughter,
        Lady Messry?'

11   'Yer son is att our king's court,
        Sarving for meatt an fee,
     And yer daugh[t]er is att our quin's court,
        A mary suit an free.'

12   'Ye lee, ye ill woman,

142

Sa loud as I hear ye lea,
For my son is the layelly worm
    That lays at the fitt of the tree,
An my daughter Messry
    The machrell of the sea.'

13  She has tain a silver wan
        An gine him stroks three
    An he started up the bravest knight
        Your eyes did ever see.

14  She has tane a small horn
        An loud an shill blue she,
    An a' the fish came her tell but the proud machrell
        An she stood by the sea:
    'Ye shaped me ance an unshemly shape,
        An ye's never mare shape me.'

15  He has sent to the wood
        For hathorn an fun,
    An he has tane that gay lady,
        An ther he did her burne.


# 51   Thomas Rymer

1   Oh True Thomas he lay on the Huntly bank,
    Beneath an eilton tree,
    Oh when he saw a lady fair
    Comin ridin ower the lea.

2   Her mantle it was of the forest green
    And her tresses oh sae fair,
    And from every tass of her horse's mane
    Hung twenty siller bells an mair.

3   True Thomas he doffed off he's hat;
    He got down upon his knee;
    He said, 'Lady, you're the greatest queen
    That ever I did see.'

Oh true Thom-as he lay on the Hunt - ly bank,

Be - neath an eil - ton tree;

Oh when he saw a la - dy fair

Com - in rid - in ower the lea

4    'Oh no, oh no, Thomas,' she said,
    'That name does not belong to me,
    For I have come from Elfin land;
    I have come to visit thee.

5    And you maun come, oh Thomas,' she said,
    'You maun come along wi me,
    For I am bound for Elfin land;
    It is very far away.

6    Oh mount up, mount up, oh Thomas,' she said,
    'And come along wi me;
    And you will come to Elfin land;
    It is very far away.'

7    So they rode, and they rode, and they merrily merrily rode,
    And they merrily rode away,
    Until they came to a great river
    That lay across their way.

8    'Oh what river is that,' True Thomas he said,
    'That lies across our way?'
    'Oh that is the river of tears,' she said,
    'That is spilled on this earth in one day.'

9    So they rode and they rode, and they merrily merrily rode,

And they rode for a night and a day,
Until they came to a red river
That lay across their way.

10    'Oh what river is that,' oh Thomas he said,
'That lies across our way?'
'Oh that is the river of blood,' she said,
'That is spilled on this earth in one day.'

11    So they rode and they rode, and they merrily merrily rode,
And they merrily rode away,
Until they came to a thorny road
That lay across their way.

12    'Oh what road is that?' oh Thomas he said,
'Oh please to me do tell!'
'Oh that is the road we must never lead,
For that road it leads to hell.'

13    Then they rode, and they rode, and they merrily merrily rode,
And they merrily rode away,
Until they came to a great orchard
That lay across their way.

14    'Oh light down, light down,' oh Thomas he said,
'For it's hungry that I maun be;
Light down, light down,' oh Thomas he said,
'For some fine apples that I do see.'

15    'Oh touch them not,' the Elfin queen said,
'Please touch them not, I say,
For they are made from the curses
That fall on this earth in one day.'

16    Then reachin up into a tree,
Into a tree so high,
She plucked an apple from a branch
As she went riding by.

17    'Oh eat you this, oh Thomas,' she said,

'As we go riding by,
And it will give to you a tongue
That will never tell a lie.'

18 So they rode and they rode, and they merrily merrily rode,
And they rode for a year and a day,
Until they came to a great valley
That lay across their way.

19 'What place is this?' oh Thomas he said,
'The likes I have never seen,'
'Oh this is Elfin land,'
Oh said the Elfin queen.

20 So Thomas got some shoes of lovely brown
And a coat of elfin green,
And for seven long years and a day
On earth he was never seen.

## 52   The Wife of Usher's Well

1   There lived a wife at Usher's Well,
    And a wealthy wife was she;
  She had three stout and stalwart sons,
    And sent them oer the sea.

2   They hadna been a week from her,
    A week but barely ane,
  Whan word came to the carline wife
    That her three sons were gane.

3   They hadna been a week from her,
    A week but barely three,
  Whan word came to the carlin wife
    That her sons she'd never see.

4   'I wish the wind may never cease,
    Nor fashes in the flood,
  Till my three sons come hame to me,
    In earthly flesh and blood.'

5    It fell about the Martinmass,
      When nights are lang and mirk,
    The carlin wife's three sons came hame,
      And their hats were o the birk.

6    It neither grew in syke nor ditch,
      Nor yet in ony sheugh;
    But at the gates o Paradise,
      That birk grew fair eneugh.

        *    *    *

7    'Blow up the fire, my maidens,
      Bring water from the well;
    For a' my house shall feast this night,
      Since my three sons are well.'

8    And she has made to them a bed,
      She's made it large and wide,
    And she's taen her mantle her about,
      Sat down at the bed-side.

        *    *    *

9    Up then crew the red, red cock,
      And up and crew the gray;
    The eldest to the youngest said,
      'T is time we were away.

10    The cock he hadna crawd but once,
      And clapped his wings at a',
    When the youngest to the eldest said,
      Brother, we must awa.

11    'The cock doth craw, the day doth daw,
      The channerin worm doth chide;
    Gin we be mist out o our place
      A sair pain we maun bide.

12    'Fare ye weel, my mother dear!

Fareweel to barn and byre!
And fare ye weel, the bonny lass
  That kindles my mother's fire!'

## 53   King Orfeo

1    There lived a Lady in yon Haa,
     Scowan Orlaa Grona;
     Her name was Lady Lisa Bell,
     Where gurtin grew for Norla.


2    One day the King a hunting went,
     They wounded the Lady to the heart.


3    The King of the Fairies we his dart,
     Wounded his Lady to the heart.


4    So when the King came home at noon,
     He asked for Lady Lisa Bell.


5    His nobles unto him did say,
     My Lady was wounded, but now she is dead.


6    Now they have taen her life fra me,
     But her corps they's never ha.


7    Now he have called his nobles aa,
     To waltz her corps into the Haa.


8    But when the Lords was faen asleep,
     Her corps out of the house did sweep.


9    Now he's awa' to the wood, wood were,
     And there he's to sit till grown o'er we hair.


10   He had not sitten seven long years,
     Till a company to him drew near.


11   Some did ride and some did ging,
     He saw his Lady them among.

12    There stood a Haa upon yon hill,
        There went aa the Ladie's tilt.

13    He is laid him on his belly to swim,
        When he came it was a gray stane.

14    Now he's set him down ful wae,
        And he's taen out his pipes to play.

15    First he played the notes of noy,
        Then he played the notes of joy.

16    And then he played the gaber reel,
        That might a made a sick heart heal.

17    There came a boy out of the Haa,
        Ye'r bidden to come in among us aa.

18    The formost man to him did say,
        What thou' ha' for thy play.

19    For my play I will thee tell,
        I'll ha' my Lady Lisa Bell.

20    Thy sister's son, that unworthy thing,
        To-morrow as to be crowned King.

21    But thou's take her and thou's go hem,
        And thou shalt be King o'er thy own.

## 54  Babylon, or, the Bonnie Banks of Fordie

1    There lived three Ladys in a Bower
        Annet & Margret & Margerie
    And they went forth for to pou a flower
        And the dew lies on the wood gay ladie

2    They hadnae pou'd a flower but one
        Till up there started a banish'd man

3 He took fair Annet by the hand
  He turn'd her about and he bade her stand

4 Its will ye be call'd a Banishd mans wife
  Or will ye be sticked by my penknife

5 I winnae be call'd a Banishd mans wife
  Ill rather be sticked by your penknife

6 O He's ta'en out his little penknife
  And frae fair Annet he's ta'en the life

7 He's taen fair Margret by the hand
  He's turn'd her about and he bade her stand

8 Its will ye be call'd a banishd man's wife
  Or will ye be sticked by my penknife

9 I winnae be call'd a banishd mans wife
  I'd rather be sticked by your penknife

10 O he's ta'en out his little penknife
  And frae this fair Lady he's ta'en the life

11 He's ta'en the youngest by the hand
  He's turn'd her about & he bade her stand

12 Its will ye be call'd a Banish'd man's wife
  Or will ye be sticked by my penknife

13 I winnae be call'd a Banish'd mans wife
  Nor will I be sticked by your penknife

14 If my three Brothers were at hame
  I had nae seen my sisters lie slain

15 And what are your three Bretheren
  That they wadnae seen their sisters lie slain

16 The Eldest o' them was a preacher fine

And mony a braw word he spoke in his time

17    The second o' them was the King of Spain
    And the youngest o' them was a Banish'd man

18    Woe to the day that I came here
    For I have kill'd my sisters Dear

19    He's ta'en out his little penknife
    And he has ta'en his ain sweet life

20    She howcked a hole fornent the moon
    And there she laid fair Annet down

21    She howked a hole fornent the Sun
    And there she laid her Brother John

22    She howked a hole among the sand
    And that is a' fair Margrets Land

23    She's ta'en out her little penknife
    And she has ta'en her ain sweet life

## 55   Sheath and Knife or Leesome Brand

1    Ther was a sister and a brother
      the sun gois to under the wood
    who most intirelie lovid othir
      god give we had nevir beine sib.

2    sayes 'sister I wald lay the by
      the sun gois to under the wood
    and thou wald not my deuds cry.'
      god give we had newer bein sib.

3    'Alas brother wald ye doe so
      the sun gois to under the wood
    I rathir nou death undergoe
      alas give we had newir bein sib.

4    the morrne is my fathirs feast
        the sun etc
    Weil in my clothis I most be least
        god give we had newir bein sib.

5    When they conwining al at ons
        to royal feasting in the hal
    it me behovith them amongs
        ge dekit in a goun of pa;

6    and when I lout me to my to
        the sun etc
    my lesse wil brak and go in tuo
        god giu etc

7    and when] I lout me to my kni
        the sun etc
    my lesse] will brak [and go in thrie
        god give etc

        .    .    .

8    and it will go from on to uthir
        the sun etc
    until it come to Jhon my brother
        lord give etc

9    and Jhon my brothir is most il
        the sun . . .
    he wil hus both burne on a hil
        lord god . . .

10    I sal go to my fathirs stable
        the sun . . .
    and tak a stid both wight and able
        lord giv . . .

11    and we sal ryd til tym we spend
        the sun . . .
    until we see our trystis end.'
        lord give . . .

12    She had not riden a myle but ane
        the sun . . .
    when she gan quakin gran and gran
        lord give . . .

13    'Is ther water into your shoes
        or comes the wind into your glowes

14    Or think ye me to simple a knight
        to ryd or go with you alnyght?'

15    'and when ye heire me loud loud cry
        ye bend your bow and ran tharby

16    and when ye se me ly ful stil
        so souing your horne come me til.

17    I wald give al my fathirs land
        for on woman at my command.'

18    when that he cam soon hir besead
        [the bab was borne the lady dead.]
        . . .

19    Ther he has tain his yong yong sonne
        and borne to a milk womane.

20    he dreu his sword him wonding sore
        from this tyme to wrid newir more.

21    'mother' quoth he 'can so mak my bed
        can se mak it long and nothing bread.

22    mother alas I tint my knife
        I lovid better then my lyffe.

23    mothir I have als tint my shead
        I lovid better then them bead.

24    ther is no cutlar in this land
        can mak a kniffe so at my command.'

25    he turnid his face to the wa
        gave up the goast and gaid his way.

26    the on was layid in Marie Kirk
        othir in Marie Queire
    out throch the on ther greu a birke
        and out throch hir a breir.
    ye may knou surlie by thir signes
        They wer tuo lowirs neire.

## 56   Child Waters

1    'I forbid you, ye gay ladies,
        That wear scarlet an brown,
    To leave your father's families,
        And follow young men frae the town.'

2    'I am a gay ladie,
        That wear scarlet an brown,
    Yet I will leave my father's castle,
        An follow Lord John frae the town.'

3    Lord John stands in his stable-door,
        Says I am boon to ride;
    Bird Ellen stands in her bowr-door,
        Says I'll run by your side.

4    He has mounted on his berry brown steed,
        An fast awa rade he;
    She's clad her in a page's weed,
        And ay as fast ran she.

5    Till they came till a wan water,
        An folks do ca it Clyde;
    He's lookd oer his left shoulder,
        Says Ellen will you ride.

6 'O I learned it when I was a bairn,
  An I learnt it for my weal,
 Weneer I came to a wan water,
  To swim like ony eel.'

7 But the firstin stap that ladie stappit,
  It was aboon her knee;
 'Ohon, alas!' says Bird Ellen,
  'This water's oer deep for me.'

8 The nextin stap that ladie stappit,
  It was up till her middle;
 'Ohon alas,' says Bird Ellen,
  'I've wat my gouden girdle.'

9 The thirdin step that ladie stappit,
  The water touched her pap;
 The bairn between her sides twa
  For caul begood to quake.

10 'Lye still, lye still, my ain dear babe,
  You gie your mother pain;
 Your father rides on high horse-back,
  And cares little for us twain.'

11 About the midst o Clyde's water
  There stands a yeard-fast stane;
 He has turnd about his berry brown steed
  And taen her up him behind.

12 'O tell me this now, good Lord John,
  An a word ye dinna lee,
 How far it is to your lodgin,
  Where this night you mean to be.'

13 'Do not ye see yon castle, Ellen,
  That shines so far and hie?
 There is a ladie there, he says
  Will sunder you an me.'

14 'Altho there be a ladie there,
  Should sunder you and me,

Betide my life, betide my death,
    I will go thither and see.'

15    'O my dogs sal eat the good white bread,
      An ye sal eat the brown;
    Then you will sigh, an say, alas!
      That ever you lovd a man!'

16    'O 't is I shall eat the good white bread,
      An your dogs sal eat the brown;
    But I neer shall live to cry alas,
      That ever I loved a man.'

17    'My horse shall eat the baken meat,
      And you shall eat the corn;
    You then will curse the heavy hour
      That ever your love was born.'

18    'O I shall eat the baken meat,
      An your horse sal eat the corn;
    And I still shall bless the happy hour
      That ever my love was born.'

19    O four an twenty gay ladies
      Welcomd Lord John to the ha,
    But a fairer lady then them a'
      Led his horse to the stable sta.

20    An four an twenty gay ladies
      Welcomd Lord John to the green,
    But a fairer lady than them a'
      At the manger stood her lane.

21    Whan bells were rung, an mass was sung,
      An a' were boun to meat,
    Bird Ellen at a bye-table
      Amo the foot-men was set.

22    'O eat an drink, my bonny boy,
      The white bread an the wine:'

'O I can neither eat nor drink,
   My heart's sae full of pine.'

23    'O eat an drink, my bonny boy,
   The white bread an the beer:'
'O I can neither eat nor drink,
   My heart's sae full of fear.'

24    But out it spake Lord John's mother,
   An a wise woman was she:
'My son, where gat ye that foot-page
   You have brought hame to me?'

25    'Sometimes his cheeks look rosy red,
   An sometimes pale and wan;
He looks mair like a ladie wi bairn,
   Than a young lord's serving man.'

26    He has looked oer his left shoulder,
   And a loud laugh laughed he;
Says, 'He's a squire's ae dear son,
   I got in the north countrie.

27    'Win up, win up, my bonny boy,
   Gi my horse corn an hay:'
'And so I will, my master dear,
   As fast as ever I may.'

28    She's taen the hay under her arm,
   And the corn in her right hand,
And she's hied her to the stable-door,
   As fast as she could gang.

29    'O room ye roun, my bonny broun steeds,
   Stand nearer to the wa;
For the pain that strikes between my sides
   Full soon will gar me fa.'

30    She has leand to the manger side
   And gien a grievous groan.

An even amo the great horse feet
   Bird Ellen brought home a son.


31    Then out it spake Lord John's mother,
     As she stood on the stair,
   'I think I hear a woman groan,
     And a bairn greeting sair.'


32    O quickly, quickly raise he up,
     Stayd neither for hose nor shoone,
   But hied him to the stable-door,
     Wi the clear light o the moon


33    'Now open the door, Bird Ellen,' he says,
     'O open and let me in,
   Or baith the door and the door cheeks
     Into the floor I'll fling.'


34    He is struck the door wi his right foot
     And pushed it wi his knee,
   Till iron bolts and iron bars
     In flinders he has gard flee:
   'Be not afraid, Bird Ellen,' he says,
     'For there's nane win in but me.'


35    The never a word spake that ladie,
     As on the floor she lay,
   But hushd her young son in her arms
     And turned his face away.


36    'Now up ye take my bonny young son
     And wash him wi the milk,
   And up ye take my fair ladie,
     And row her i the silk.'


37    'And smile on me now, Bird Ellen,
     And cast awa your care,
   For I'll make you ladie of a' my lands,
     And your son shall be my heir.'

38   'Blessed be the day,' sayd Bird Ellen,
      'That I followed you frae the town,
  For I'd rather far be your foot-page
      Than the queen that wears the crown.'

## 57  Fair Janet

1   Young Janet sits in her garden,
      Makin a heavie maen,
  Whan by cam her father dear,
      Walkin himself alane.

2   'It's telld me in my bower, Janet,
      It's telld me in my bed,
  That ye're in love wi Sweet Willie;
      But a French lord ye maun wed.'

3   'In it be telld ye in yer bower, father,
      In it be telld ye in your bed,
  That me an Willie bears a love,
      Yet a French lord I maun wed,
  But here I mak a leel, leel vow
      He's neer come in my bed.

4   'An for to please my father dear
      A French lord I will wed;
  But I hae sworn a solemn oth
      He's neer come in my bed.'

5   Young Janet's away to her bower-door,
      As fast as she can hie,
  An Willie he has followd her,
      He's followd speedilie.

6   An when he cam to her bowr-door
      He tirlt at the pin:
  'O open, open, Janet love,
      Open an let me in.'

7    'It was never my mother's custm, Willie,
        It never sal be mine,
    For a man to come the bower within
        When a woman's travelin.

8    'Gae yer ways to my sisters' bower,
        Crie, Meg, Marion an Jean,
    Ye maun come to yer sister Janet,
        For fear that she be gane.'

9    Sae he gaed to her sisters' bower,
        Cry'd, Meg, Marion an Jean,
    Ye maun come to yer sister Janet,
        For fear that she be gane.

10    Some drew to their silk stokins,
        An some drew to their shoon,
    An some drew to their silk cleadin,
        For fear she had been gane.

11    When they cam to her bower-door
        They tirlt at the pin;
    For as sick a woman as she was,
        She raise an loot them in.

12    They had na the babie weel buskit,
        Nor her laid in her bed,
    Untill her cruel father cam,
        Cried, Fye, gar busk the bride!

13    'There a sair pain in my back, father,
        There a sair pain in my head,
    An sair, sair is my sidies to;
        This day I downa ride.'

14    'But I hae sorn a solemn oath,
        Afore a companie,
    That ye sal ride this day, Janet,
        This day an ye soud die.

15    'Whae'll horse ye to the kirk, Janet?
        An whae will horse ye best?'
    'Whae but Willie, my true-love?
        He kens my mister best.'

16    'Whae'll horse ye to the kirk, Janet?
        An whae will horse ye there?'
    'Whae but Willie, my true-love?
        He neer will doo'd nae maer.

17    'Ye may saddle a steed, Willie,
        An see that ye saddle 't soft;
    Ye may saddle a steed, Willie,
        For ye winna saddle 't oft.

18    'Ye may saddle a steed, Willie,
        An see that ye saddle 't side;
    Ye may saddle a steed, Willie;
        But I thought to have been yer bride.'

19    When they war a' on horse-back set,
        On horse-back set sae hie,
    Then up spak the bold bridegroom,
        An he spak boustresslie.

20    Up then spak the bold bridegroom,
        An he spak loud an thrawn;
    'I think the bride she be wi bairn,
        She looks sae pale an wan.'

21    Then she took out her bible-book,
        Swoor by her fingers five
    That she was neither wi lad nor lass
        To no man was alive.

22    Then she took out her bible-book,
        Swoor by her fingers ten
    An ever she had born a bairn in her days
        She had born'd sin yestreen:
    Then a' the ladies round about
        Said, That's a loud leesin.

23    Atween the kitchin an the kirk
       It was a weel–met mile;
    It was a stra'd i the red roses,
       But than the camomile.

24    When the war a' at dener set,
       Drinkin at the wine,
    Janet could neither eat nor drink
       But the water that ran so fine.

25    Up spak the bride's father,
       Said, Bride, will ye dance wi me?
    'Away, away, my cruel father!
       There nae dancin wi me.'

26    Up then spak the bride's mother,
       Said, Bride, will ye dance wi me?
    'Away, away, my mother dear!
       There nae dancin wi me.'

27    Up then spak the bride's sisters, etc.

28    Up then spak the bride's brother, etc.

29    Then up spak the bold bridegroom, [etc]

30    Up then spak the Sweet Willie,
       An he spak wi a vance;
    'An ye'll draw of my boots, Janet,
       I'll gie a' yer lassies a dance.'

31    'I seen't other ways, Willie,
       An sae has mae than me,
    When ye wad hae danced wi my fair body,
       An leten a' my maidens be.'

32    He took her by the milk–white hand,
       An led her wi mickle care,
    But she drapit down just at his feet,
       And word spak little mair.

33    'Ye may gae hire a nurse, Willie,
       An take yer young son hame;
     Ye may gae hire a nurse, Willie,
       For bairn's nurse I'll be nane.'

34    She's pu'd out the keys o her coffer,
       Hung leugh down by her gair;
     She said, 'Gie thae to my young son,
       Thrae me he'll neer get mair.'

35    Up then spak the bold bridegroom,
       An he spak bousterouslie;
     'I've gien you the skaeth, Willie,
       But ye've gien me the scorn;
     Sae there's no a bell i St Mary's kirk
       Sall ring for her the morn.'

36    'Ye've gien me the skaeth, bridegroom,
       But I'll gee you the scorn;
     For there's no a bell i St Marie's kirk
       But sal ring for her the morn.

37    'Gar deal, gar deal at my love's burial
       The wheat-bread an the wine,
     For or the morn at ten o clock
       Ye'll deal'd as fast at mine.'

38    Then he's drawn out a nut-brown sword,
       Hang leugh down by his gair,
     He's thrust it in just at his heart,
       An word spak never mair.

39    The taen was buried i St Mary's kirk,
       The tother i St Mary's queer,
     An throw the taen there sprang a birk,
       Throw the tother a bonnie brier.

40    Thae twae met, an thae twae plaet,
       An ay they knitit near,

An ilka ane that cam thereby
   Said, There lies twa lovers dear.

41    Till by there came an ill French lord,
    An ill death may he die!
For he pu'd up the bonnie brier,

      .     .     .


## 58   Sir Patrick Spens

1    The king he sits in Dumferling,
    Drinking the blude reid wine: O
'O where will I get a gude sailor,
    That 'l sail the ships o mine?' O

2    Up then started a yellow-haird man,
    Just be the kings right knee:
'Sir Patrick Spence is the best sailor
    That ever saild the see.'

3    Then the king he wrote a lang letter,
    And sealld it with his hand,
And sent it to Sir Patrick Spence,
    That was lyand at Leith Sands.

4    When Patrick lookd the letter on,
    He gae loud laughters three;
But afore he wan to the end of it
    The teir blindit his ee.

5    'O wha is this has tald the king,
    Has tald the king o me?
Gif I but wist the man it war,
    Hanged should he be.

6    'Come eat and drink, my merry men all,
    For our ships maun sail the morn;
Bla'd wind, bla'd weet, bla'd sna or sleet,
    Our ships maun sail the morn.'

7   'Alake and alas now, good master,
        For I fear a deidly storm;
    For I saw the new moon late yestreen,
        And the auld moon in her arms.'

8   They had not saild upon the sea
        A league but merely three,
    When ugly, ugly were the jaws
        That rowd unto their knee.

9   They had not saild upon the sea
        A league but merely nine,
    When wind and weit and snaw and sleit
        Came blawing them behind.

10  'Then where will I get a pretty boy
        Will take my steer in hand,
    Till I go up to my tap-mast,
        And see gif I see dry land?'

11  'Here am I, a pretty boy
        That'l take your steir in hand,
    Till you go up to your tap-mast
        And see an you see the land.'

12  Laith, laith were our Scottish lords
        To weit their coal-black shoon;
    But yet ere a' the play was playd,
        They wat their hats aboon.

13  Laith, laith war our Scottish lords
        To weit their coal-black hair;
    But yet ere a' the play was playd,
        They wat it every hair.

14  The water at St Johnston's wall
        Was fifty fathom deep,
    And there ly a' our Scottish lords,
        Sir Patrick at their feet.

15    Lang, lang may our ladies wait
        Wi the tear blinding their ee,
    Afore they see Sir Patrick's ships
        Come sailing oer the sea.

16    Lang, lang may our ladies wait,
        Wi their babies in their hands,
    Afore they see Sir Patrick Spence
        Come sailing to Leith Sands.

## 59   The Battle of Harlaw

1    As I cam by the Garioch land
        And doon by Netherha'
    There were fifty thoosan Hielanmen
        A-marchin' tae Harlaw.

Chorus
Singin' didee-i-o
Sing fal la do
Sing didee-i-o-i-ay

2    It's did ye come frae the Hielans, man,
        Or did ye come a' the wey,
    And did ye see MacDonald and his men
        As they marched frae Skye?

3    For I've come frae the Hielans, man,
        And I've come a' the wey –

An' I saw MacDonald an' his men
As they marched frae Skye.

4    It's wis ye near and near enough,
Did ye their number see?
Come tell to me, John Hielanman,
What might their number be?

5    For I was near and near enough
An' I their number saw:
There were fifty thoosan Hielanmen
A-marchin' tae Harlaw.

6    For they went on an' furder on
An' doon an' by Balquhain:
It's there they met Sir James the Rose,
Wi' him Sir John the Graham.

7    If that be's true, said Sir James the Rose
We'll no come muckle speed.
We'll call upon wer merry men
And we'll turn wer horses' heids.

8    Oh nay, oh nay, said Sir John the Graham,
Sic things we maunna dee:
For the gallant Grahams were never bate
An' we'll try fit they can dee.

9    For they went on an' furder on
An' doon an' by Harlaw:
They fell full close on ilkae side,
Sic strikes ye never saw.

10    But the Hielanmen wi' their lang swords
They laid on us fu' sair;
They drove back wer merry men
Three acres breadth an' mair.

11    Lord Forbes tae his brother did say
O brither, dinna ye see?

They beat us back on every side,
And we'll be forced to flee.

12    O nay, O nay, my brither dear,
      O nay, that maunna be.
    Ye'll tak your guid sword in your hand
      And ye'll gang in wi' me.

13    For the twa brothers brave
      Gaed in amangst the thrang;
    They swope doon the Hielanmen
      Wi' swords baith sharp an' lang.

14    The first strike Lord Forbes gied
      The brave MacDonald reeled;
    The second strike Lord Forbes gied
      The brave MacDonald fell.

15    What a cry amongst the Hielanmen
      When they seed their leader fa';
    They lifted him an' buried him
      A lang mile frae Harlaw.

## 60   The Lads of Wamphray

1    Twixt the Girth-head and the Langwood en',
      Obilee, obilee,
    Lived the Gay Galliard and the Galliard's men;
      Obilee ye and o.
    But and the lads of Leverhay,
      Obilee, obilee,
    That drove the Crichtons' gear away,
      Obilee ye and o.

2    There is the lads of Eckanknow,
    They stell the sheep and pickit her pow;
    There is the san pocks of the mill,
    The Gay Galliard and Will o' Kirkhill.

3   It is the lads of Lethenha',
    The greatest rogues amang them a';
    But and the lads of Stefenbiggin,
    They broke the house in at the riggin.

4   The lads of Fingland and Hellbeck Hill,
    They were never for gude but aye for ill;
    'Twixt the Staywood bush and Langside Hill,
    They steal't the brokit cow and the
        branded bull.

5   It is the lads of the Girth-head,
    The deil's in them for pride and greed;
    For the Galliard and the gay Galliard's men,
    They ne'er saw a horse but they made it
        their ain.

6   The Galliard he's to Nithsdale gane,
    And nane wi' him but Willie his lane;
    To Sanquhar toun they rode richt wicht,
    And landit there at dead o' nicht.

7   They went to Simmy's of the Side,
    For he had a mare that they wad ride;
    'We'll do no hurt nor we'll tak' no wrang,
    But this nicht the mare wi' us maun gang.'

8   The Galliard he's to the stable gane,
    To steal Sim Crichton's winsome dun;
    But the nicht was dark and he couldna
        see plain,
    And instead of the dun, the blind he has ta'en.

9   'Come out now Simmy o' the Side,
    Come out and see a Johnston ride;
    Here's the bonniest mare in a' Nithside,
    And a gentle Johnston abune her hide.'

10  Simmy Crichton's mounted then,
    And Crichtons has raised mony a man;

The Galliard thocht his horse it had
  been wicht,
But the dun outstripped him quite out-richt.

11    As soon as the Galliard the Crichtons saw,
    Behind the saugh-bush he did draw;
    And there the Crichtons the Galliard hae ta'en,
    And nane wi' him but Willie his lane.

12    'O Simmy, Simmy, now let me gang,
    And I'll never mair do a Crichton wrang!
    O Simmy, Simmy, now let me be,
    And a peck o' gowd I'll gie to thee!

13    O Simmy, Simmy, now let me gang,
    And my wife shall heap it wi' her hand.' –
    But the Crichtons wadna let the Galliard be,
    And they hanged him hie upon a tree.

14    O think then Willie he was richt wae,
    When he saw his uncle guided sae;
    'But if ever I live Wamphray to see,
    My uncle's death avenged shall be.'

15    Back to Wamphray Willie is gane,
    And riders has raised mony a ane;
    Says he – 'My lads, if ye'll be true,
    Ye's a' be clad in the noble blue.'

16    Back to Nithsdale they have gane,
    And away the Crichtons' nowt hae taen;
    But Simmy Crichton's mounted then,
    And Crichtons has raised mony a man.

17    But when they cam' to the Wellpath-head,
    The Crichtons bade them licht and lead;
    And as they cam' through at Biddes strand,
    The Crichtons they were hard at hand.

18    And when they cam' to Biddes burn,

The Crichtons bade them fight or turn;
But when they cam' to Biddes-Law,
The Johnstons bade them stand and draw.

19    And out spoke Willie o' the Kirkhill,
'Of fighting, lads, ye'se hae your fill' –
And from his horse Willie he lap,
And a burnished brand in his hand he gat.

20    Out through the Crichtons Willie he ran,
And dang them doun baith horse and man;
O but the Johnstons were wondrous rude,
When the Biddes burn ran three days blude.

21    'I think my lads we hae done a noble deed;
We have revenged the Galliard's bleed,
For every finger of the Galliard's han',
I vow this day I've killed a man.

22    'We'll dae nae richt nor we'll tak' nae wrang,
But back to Wamphray we will gang.'
Then back to Wamphray they are gane,
And away the Crichtons' nowt hae taen.

23    As they cam' in at Evenhead,
At Ricklawholm they spread abroad;
'Drive on my lads it will be late,
And we'll hae a pint at Wamphray Gate.

24    For where'er I gang, or e'er I ride,
        Obilee obilee,
The lads of Wamphray are on my side;
        Obilee ye and o.
And if a' the lads that I do ken,
        Obilee obilee.
A Wamphray lad's the king of men,
        Obilee ye and o.'

## 61  Edom o Gordon

1   It fell aboot the Martinmas time,
    When the weather was chill and cauld,
Said Adam o' Gordon to his merry men
    'Where shall we draw to some fauld?

2   I think we'll go over to Castle Campbell
    The good lord's far awa';
I think we'll go over to Castle Campbell
    And ye my merry men a'.'

3   Lady Campbell look'd over her window
    All in a dress of black,
And there she spied Adam o' Gordon
    And all his merry men at his back.

4   'Go lock the doors, go bar the gates,
    Go bring the keys to me.'
They've lock'd the doors, they've barr'd the gates
    And brought the keys to she.

5   The dinner was na' weel set doon,
    The grace was hardly weel said,
When Adam o' Gordon and a' his merry men
    Stood at Lady Campbell's gate.

6   'Come doon the stairs, Lady Campbell,' he cried,
    'Come even to my hand:
For to-night ye shall serve my body,
    Ye shall serve at my command.'

7   'I winna come doon, I'll no' come doon:
    For neither lord nor loon,
I winna come doon for ony sheep-stealer
    That ever rode thro' lan'ward toon.'

8   'We neither meddled your sheep, madam,
    Nor did we yet your horse,

But ere tomorrow at twelve o'clock,
  Ye'll be burnt as sma' as dross.

9   'O! Johnnie the mason ye'll gang up,
    That kens the key o' the stane,
  O! Johnnie the mason ye'll gang up,
    And ken'le the flames on them.'

10  'O! woe be to ye, Johnnie the mason,
    An ill death may ye dee,
  For I got ye a false young child,
    I nurs'd ye on my knee.'

11  'O! weel do I mind o' your kindness, madam,
    When your good lord paid my fee,
  But noo I'm ane o' Gordon's men,
    I maun either do or dee.'

12  The flames were kindl'd on every side,
    The sparks flew wondrous high.
  Up spak the auld daughter to her mother,
    'It's here where we must die.

13  I once was contrac' to an English lord,
    But wedded I never shall be;
  I once was contrac' to an English lord,
    But a wedding I never shall see

14  Gae row me in a pair o' clean sheets,
    And tow me owre the wa',
  That a' my frien's may see and hear
    That I hae gotten a fa'.'

15  They've row'd her in a pair o' clean sheets,
    And tow'd her owre the wa'
  When ane o' Adam o' Gordon's men
    Kep't her on a spear sae sma'.

16  They've separated her heid frae her fair bodye
    And the tates o' her yellow hair,

And they threw it up to her mother again,
    And oh! but her heart it was sair.


17    Then up bespake the eldest son
      As he stood by his mother's side,
    'If I were in yonder field, mother,
      Wi' a bent bow in my hand,
    It's I would fight for you, mother,
      As long as I'd life to stand.'


18    Then up bespake the wily nurse,
      With the young babe on her knee,
    'It's throw them doon the keys, madam,
      Or the bonnie bairn will dee.'


## 62   The Maid and the Palmer

1    The may's to the well to wash an to wring
    The primrose o' the wood wants a name
    An' ay so sweetly did she sing
    I am the fair maid of Coldingham


2    O by there cam' an eldren man
    The primrose o' the wood wants a name
    O gie me a drink o' your cauld stream
    An' ye be the fair maiden of Coldingham


3    My golden cup is down the strand
    The primrose etc.
    Of my cold water ye sall drink nane
    Tho' I be etc.


4    O fair may bethink ye again
    The primrose etc.
    Gie a drink o' cauld water to an auld man
    If ye be etc.


5    O she sware by the sun an the moon
    The primrose etc.

That all his cups were flown to Rome
Yet she was etc.

6    O seven bairns hae ye born
    The primrose etc.
    An' as many lives hae ye forlorn
    An' ye're nae etc.

7    There's three o' them in your bower floor
    The primrose etc.
    It gars ye fear when ye woudna fear
    An' ye're nae etc.

8    There's ane o' them in yon well stripe
    The primrose etc.
    An' twa o' them in the garden dyke
    An' ye're nae etc.

9    There's ane o' them in your bed feet
    The primrose etc.
    It gars you wake when ye should sleep
    An' ye're nae etc.

10    Ye'll be seven year a cocky to craw
    The primrose etc.
    An' seven year a cattie to maiw
    An' ye're nae etc.

11    Ye'll be seven lang years a stane in a cairn
    The primrose etc.
    An' seven years ye'll go wi' bairn
    An' ye're nae etc.

12    Ye'll be seven years a sacran bell
    The primrose etc.
    An' ither seven the cook in hell
    An' ye're nae etc.

## 63    The Fause Knight upon the Road

1    'Whaur are ye gaun?' said the fause knicht,
    Said the fause knicht on the road.
  'A'm gaun t' schule,' said the child,
    But still he stood.

2    'What ha' ye got in your hands?' said the fause knicht,
    Said the fause knicht on the road.
  'I ha' bukes in ma hands,' said the boy,
    But still he stood.

3    'Wha's sheep are those?' said the fause knicht,
    Said the fause knicht on the road.
  'Ma mither's and mine,' said the boy,
    But still he stood.

4    'Whaur is ma share?' said the fause knicht,
    Said the fause knicht on the road.
  'All those that ha' blue tails,' said the boy,
    But still he stood.

5    'I wish ye were in the deepest well,' said the
      fause knicht,
    Said the fause knicht on the road.
  'I wish ye were in the bottom o' Hell,' said
      the boy,
    But still he stood.


## 64    The Keach i the Creel

1    The farmer's daughter gade to the market
  Some white fish for to buy
  The young squire followed after her
  As hard as he could hie, ricadoo
    Tun-un-nay, ricadoo,
    Tun-un-nay, ricadoo a dee a day,
    Raddle, ricadoo
    Tun-un-nay.

2    A gude mornin to you sweet heart she said
     For to see you I am richt glad
     But my faither he locks the door every nicht
     Puts the key below his head, ricadoo

3    But ye maun get a lang leather
     That's thirty feet and three
     And ye maun gang to the chimney top
     And your brither will let you down to me, ricadoo

4    He has got a lang leather
     That's thirty feet and three
     He has gane to the chimney top
     And his brither lute him down in the creel, ricadoo

5    But the auld wyfe she could nae rest
     For thoughts ran in her head
     I'll lay my life quo the silly auld wyfe
     There a man in our dochter's bed, ricadoo

6    The auld man he rose up himsel
     To see if it was true
     But she tuke the young squire in her arms
     An the curtains around him drew, ricadoo

7    Gude morrow to you auld faither she said
     Whar are ye gaun sae soon
     Ye disturbit me of my prayer
     And so did ye last noon, ricadoo

8    O woe to you he said,

And an ill death may you die
It was the braid book she had in her arms
She was prayand for you and me, ricadoo

9    But the auld wyfe she could nae rest
Till she got up hersel
But sumthing or anither tuke the auld wyfe's fit,
And into the creel she fell, ricadoo

10    The man upon the chimney top
He gade the creel a pou
I'll lay my lyfe quo the auld wyfe
The deil will hae us aw jest now, ricadoo

11    The man upon the chimney top
He lute the creel down fa
He brak three of the auld wyfe's ribs
Knock't her agane the wa, ricadoo

12    O the brume and the bonnie broom
And the broom that I like weel
An every auld wyfe that's jealous o her daughter
May be dangled in the same Peet creel, ricadoo

# 3

# FOLKSAY

## INTRODUCTION

Folksay deals with language in a traditional context. In a sense, of course, almost all language is traditional in that it is, by its very nature, in habitual spoken currency, but there exists an area worth specific demarcation. In practice, folksay concerns itself primarily with certain crystallizations of language in traditional currency that fall into some easily recognizable genres – the proverb and the riddle, for example – and ranges also over aspects of personal and place names to the habitual usages and patterns of folk speech.

Today we are likely to think of a riddle as an infrequent and fragmentary part of a conversation but at one time the 'speering of guesses' was a recognized household activity in the winter evenings, and the practice of having riddling sessions has continued until quite recently among the travellers.[1] In similar fashion we tend to be rather self-conscious in any use we may make of proverbs, unlike our forefathers who used them naturally and freely, and – at least in the early nineteenth century – enjoyed small proverb-telling sessions or 'rounds'.[2] The importance of proverbs in social groups not given to writing should be self-evident: for instance, they encapsulate the wisdom of the tribe, they convey moral precepts, and they provide guidelines for practical conduct. Like the riddle, which serves to stimulate and stretch the intellect, the proverb is, among other things, educational.

In folksay, as in other areas of folk literature studies, an earlier emphasis on compilation of material has evolved into interest in the functioning of the material in its social and cultural contexts, with particular stress on its place in the communicative process. Again, as with other areas of folk literature studies, one needs to know both the generic nature and variety of the material and the cultural context for a full understanding. Any attempt to convey both adequately within the limited compass of an anthology is bound to fall short of satisfaction, but the attempt is made. Section 1 introduces certain genres through a substantial collection from one quite small but well defined district, while section 2 contains samplings with explanatory commentary of the folksay of two distinct social groups, Fife mining communities and Border gypsies, which indicate how the language forms operate within the culture besides revealing the attitudes of the people in the groups to life around. In section 3 some basic contextual information accompanies the rhymes.

Section 1 contains examples of the proverb, proverbial phrase, proverbial comparison, wellerism, and conventional phrase. A proverb is 'a terse didactic statement that is current in tradition'. A proverbial phrase 'permits variation in person, number, and tense' ('Buyin/ he bocht a pig in a pyoke'). A proverbial comparison 'has a fixed traditional form, but contains no moral advice' ('Bare as the birks at yeel even'). A wellerism is a 'quotation proverb' designed 'to produce a humorous effect' ('Aberdeen, an' time till't, as said the wife when she saw the loch o' Skene'). 'Many locutions are conventionally used in particular situations or are accepted as traditional ways of expressing an idea': these are conventional phrases ('Twa kitchies ta ae bread!' would be said if a child put cheese as well as butter on an oatcake).[3]

Section 3 illustrates the minor genres of folksay, given here in rhyming form, though many genres also occur in prose. Because of the social changes of the nineteenth century rhymes nowadays tend, like other areas of folk literature, to be associated mainly with children, but they did once occupy a significant place in the life of the adult community, and one which deserves more attention than so far received. Rhymes fulfilled two, sometimes overlapping, sets of functions which we can distinguish, in broad terms, as the social and the cultural. Group B shows a major cultural function of rhyme in a traditional society – the transmission of knowledge – while group A demonstrates its range of functions in a social context through the eight categories: I rhymes relating to forms of folk belief involving a practice or luck-connected activity; II rhymes involving belief whose overt functions are to attempt expression of the unknowable or to avoid expression of the sacred; III rhymes of beneficent purpose; IV rhymes of maleficent or unfriendly purpose; V rhymes of social interaction; VI rhymes of work and commerce; VII rhymes of amusement; VIII rhymes relating to folk custom.[4]

Section 4 is devoted to riddles, all from the Southwest. The precise definition of the riddle has exercised many good minds from Aristotle onwards without any totally acceptable formulation emerging (appropriately enough perhaps), but a reasonably convenient way of looking at it is to see it as a statement, often with metaphorical and contradictory elements, describing a referent which has to be puzzled out by processes of correlation. Robert Georges and Alan Dundes have tried to probe more deeply into the nature of the riddle, and the ordering of the items here follows for the first part the general distinctions they make.[5] As the basic unit of analysis they propose the 'descriptive element', consisting of topic and comment: the topic being the apparent referent and the comment an assertion about it. (In no. 2, for example, the topic is 'hoddy-poddy', and the three comments are 'it has a wee black body', 'it has three legs', 'it has a timmer hat'.) Nos 1-4 show some basic examples of topic and comment relationship. Nos 5-8 are 'literal' while nos 9-18 are 'metaphorical' in that the riddle referent and the topic are the same in the first case but different in the second. These riddles do not involve contradiction, but nos 19-39 involve, as very many riddles do, various kinds of contradiction. Nos 40-47 include a catch riddle, and examples of various puzzles generally ranked among the 'guesses': verbal plays, naming puzzles, and an arithmetical puzzle.

# Notes

1 Kenneth Goldstein, 'Riddling Traditions in Northeastern Scotland', *Journal of American Folklore*, 76(1963), 330-6.
2 William Chambers, *Memoir of Robert Chambers* (Edinburgh, 1872), p.22; D.M. Moir, *The Life of Mansie Wauch* (1828; Edinburgh, 1911 ed.), p. 67.
3 Archer Taylor, 'Proverb', *Standard Dictionary of Folklore Mythology and Legend*, ed. Maria Leach (New York, 1972), pp.902, 905.
4 For an extended discussion see David Buchan, 'Social Function and Traditional Scottish Rhymes', in *Folklore Studies in the Twentieth Century*, ed. Venetia J. Newall (Woodbridge, Suffolk, 1980), pp.153-7.
5 'Toward a Structural Definition of the Riddle', *Journal of American Folklore*, 76(1963), pp. 111-18.

## I PROVERBS AND SAYINGS: CROMAR

Aberdeen, an' time till't, as said the wife when she saw the loch o'
    Skene (miles short of her objective).
A bonnie bride's seen (soon) busket.
Absence o' body is better than presence o' min' in an accident.
A len' (loan) sud gae lauchin' hame.
A clean dud's aye coothy, as said the wife when she turned over her
    sark.
A cloot abeen a cloot ta haud the win' aboot.
Ae bird i' the han's worth twa i' the bus.
Ae man can lead a horse ta the water but twenty couldna gar him
    drink.
Ae man's meat's anither man's pooshion.
Ae hoor i' the mornin's worth twa at nicht.
A fair exchange is nae robbery.
A feel an's siller's seen pairtet.
A freen in need's a freen indeed.
A gaen fit's aye gettin'.
A gi'en coo sudna be lookit i' the moo.
A green yeel maks a fat kirkyard.
A gweed follow's a beggar's brither.
A gweed sword, but it's i' the castle.
A hungry loose bites sair.
Aince wid, never wise.
A layin' hen's better than a stannin' mill.
A little pot's seen het.
A' complain for want o' siller but nane o' want o' sense.
A's fair in love an' war.
A's nae ill that's ill like.
A sicht o' ye's gweed for sair een.
A' Stewarts arena sib ta the king.
A's weel that en's weel, an' has a gweed beginnin'.
A' tarred wi' the same stick.
A'thegether, like Broon's kye when he had but ane.
A'thing thrives at thrice.
A' wark' an' nae play maks Jack a dull boy.
A man's a man for a' that.
A miss is as gweed as a mile.
A man pits his han' hamely tae his ain.

Ane at a time's gweed fishin'.
An eident drap will pierce a stane.
An aul' pyoke's aye skailin'.
A new besom sweeps clean.
An ill bell soons far.
A nod fae a lord is brakfast for a feel.
Are ye for? is nae a gweed follow.
A rowin' stane gathers nae fog.
A scatterin cock needs a gatherin hen.
As lang's ye stan' ya dinna bide.
As muckle's Paddy shot at, an' that was naething ava.
As peer's a kirk moose.
As the auld cock craws, the young cock learns.
As the feel thinks, the bell clinks.
A stitch in time saves nine.
As ye mak yer bed ye maun lie on't.
A wilfu' man maun hae his way.
A winkin' cat's nae aye blin'.
A wink's as gweed's a nod tae a blin' horse.
Bachelors' wives an' aul' maid's bairns are aye weel bred.
Bare as the birks at yeel even.
Beggers sudna be choosers.
Better teem hoose than ill tenant.
Better gang ta the kirk barefoot than ta hell shod.
Better half loaf than nae bread.
Better len' ta a foe than beg fae a freen.
Better oot o' the queets than oot o' the fashion.
Better rue sit than rue flit.
Better the en' o' a feast than the beginnin' o' a fray.
Better the ill kent than the gweed unkent.
Better wear sheen than sheets.
Big head, little wit, little head, less yet.
Birds o' a feather flock thegether.
Bread an' cheese is gweed ta eat when folk can get nae ither meat.
Broken bread maks hale bairns.
Brunt bairns dread the fire.
Butter ta butter's nae kitchie.
Buyin' a pig in a pyoke.
Cadgers are aye crackin' o' cruick-saikles.
'Can dee' is easy carriet.

Caul' kale het again.

Changes are lichtsome an' feels are fond o' them.

Clean cap oot, like the communicants o' Birse.

Coonsel's nae comman'.

Coont money after a' yer freens.

Corbies dinna pick oot ither corbies' een.

Crookin' o' moos is nae whistlin'.

Curses, like chickens come hame ta roost.

Cut yer coat accordin' ta yer claith.

Dinna coont yer chickens till they're hatched.

Dinna lie o' yer hip an' lippen till't.

East or wast, hame's best.

Eneuch's as gweed's a feast.

Experience teaches feels.

Fa gaes a-borrowin', gaes a-sorrowin'.

Fa gi'es wi' the sword, gets wi' the scabbar.

Fa has to eat a', needna care far he begins.

Facks are chiels that winna ding.

Faint hart never won fair lady.

Familiarity breeds contempt.

Fa pays the piper ca's the tune.

Far fools hae fair feathers.

Far wile is, wit wavers.

Fa would sup wi' the deil would need a lang speen.

Fat's deen's nae adee.

Fat's i'yer wame's nae i'yer tesment.

Fat's weel deen's seen deen.

Fed wi' a teem speen.

Fen drink's in, wit's oot.

Fen pride comes in at the door, love gaes oot at the lum.

Fen the tod preaches, tak tint o' the lambs.

Fen yer head's white ye'd like it curlin'.

Fen ignorance is bliss, tis folly ta be wise.

First throu' the wood an' last throu' the water.

Folk wi' lang noses are aye takin' ta them.

Forced prayers are nae devotion.

Gaur ye[r] head save yer heels.

Gaur yer wark set ye though it be but to muck the cat.

Gi'e him an inch an' he'll tak an ell.

Gi'e the deil his due.

Gin he dee o' a bursten skin, his will be the wyte that ca's him.

Gin ye binna thief, binna thief like.

Gin ye dinna steal yer neebor's kail dinna loup's dyke.

Gin ye ha'e pain tae yer paich, I pity ye.

Glib i' the tongue's aye glaiket i' the hert (mind).

Gnap at the win' (catch a shadow).

God fits the back tae the burden.

God tempers the win' tae the shorn lamb.

Gree greets. Ye'll be sun'ered yet.

Hae God, Hae a'.

Hair an' hair, maks the carl bare.

Hair an' horn grows on shargers.

Han'som is that han'som dis.

Haud aye the auld sack i' the water.

He disna aye ride fen he saidles.

He has a crap for a' corn an' a baggie for the rye.

He has mair jaw than judgment.

He hasna the gumption o' a suckin turkey.

He laughs best fa laughs last.

He'll mak a speen or spile a horn.

He's a chip o' the auld block.

He's a sicker horse that never snappers.

He's far ahin' that daurna follow.

He's far ahead that canna look back.

He's got ta the end o's tether.

He's nae sa daft as he's daft like.

He's nae willin ta ca' that lats the gad fa'.

He's scarce o' news that tells that his father wis hanged.

He that canna de as he would, maun even de as he may.

His auld bress will buy a new pan.

Hoppin like a hen on a het girdle.

Hunger's the best kitchie.

If a's true that's nae a lee.

If he's nae fit for meat, he's nae fit for wark, an if he's nae fit for wark,
    he's nae fit for me.

If 'ifs' an' an's were pots an' pans, ther'd be nae eese for tinkers.

If wis'es were horses, beggars would ride.

Ilka blade o'girs has its ain drap o' dew.

Ilka cock craws crusest on's ain midden-head.

It a' gangs by taste, as said the wife when she kissed the coo.

It gaed like a heely gaun pleuchie.

It gangs in at the ae lug an' oot at the ither.

It'll come again like Cuttie's note.

It's a gweed coat that hauds oot caul' an' cravin'.

It's a handy thing ta ha'e i' the hoose, as said the man aboot the coffin.

It's an ill bird that files its ain nest.

It's an ill win' that blaws naebody gweed.

It's a peer flock when the ewe carries the bell.

It's a sober horse that canna carry the fosser.

It's hard ta tak oot o' the flesh fat's been bred i'the bane.

It's ill feshin' ben fat's nae i' the but.

It's nae a' gowd that glitters.

It's nae a' lost that a freen gets.

It's nae better than it's ca'd (called).

It's nae eese ta keep a dog an' bark yersel'.

It's nae fool (foul) that water will wash off.

It's the early bird that gets the worm.

It's the life o' an auld hat ta be weel cocket.

Jouk an' lat the jaw gae by.

Kale at hame's nae kitchie.

Kissin' gangs by favour.

Lang fair, lang fool (foul).

Lang may yer lum reek.

Lat by-ganes be by-ganes.

Lat him queel i' the skin that he got het in.

Lat sleepin' dogs lie, lest they rise an' bite.

Lat the horns gang wi' the hide.

Learn young, learn fair, learn aul', learn sair.

Licht loads harry the wid (wood).

Lichtly come, lichtly gang.

Like a bad shillin', aye comin' back.

Like a whale in a ban' box.

Like drunken Geordie Pirie, 'slow but sure'.

Like the gowk, he has but ae leed an's aye at it.

Like the hielenman's gun, lacks naething but lock, stock and barrel.

Like the scrapin' o' a soo, muckle schreechin' for little oo (wool).

Like the sheep, aye busiest at the cote door.

Little best ale in Bervie when ae wife brews't a'.

Little dis the peer gweed an' as little de they get.

Little meat an' ill made ready ser's a lot o' folk.

Mair by luck than gweed management.

Mak a' face that will be face, for back will be face for nane.

Mak freens o' fremit folk.

Mak hay while the sun shines.

Makin' mountains o' mole heaps.

Mak yer feet yer freens.

Man proposes, but God disposes.

Man's extremity is God's opportunity.

Maybe's nae a honey bee.

Men' the aul' and hain the new.

Money maks the mare ta go whether she hae a tail or no.

Mony a ane speers the road he kens weel.

Mony a fair face that's scant o' grace.

Mony han's mak licht wark.

Mony littles mak a muckle.

Muckle whislin' for little red lan'.

Nae cadger cries 'Stinkin fish'.

Nae eese ta cry ower spilt milk.

Nae feel (fool) like an aul' feel.

Nae success without yer wife's consent.

Nane sa blin' as he fa winna see.

Ne'er cast a cloot till May be oot.

Never lat on but aye lat ower.

Never ower aul' ta learn.

Never venture, never win.

New lairds hae new laws.

Oot o' the pan into the fire.

Ower aul' a dog ta learn new tricks.

Ower gweed ta be true.

Ower het at hame.

Ower sweet ta be halesome.

Pairt sma an' ser' a'.

Penny wise an' poun' foolish.

Prayer an' provinder hinder nane.

Procrastination is the thief o' time.

Puttin' the cairt afore the horse.

Rome wasna a' bigget in ae day.

Scandal's like dirt; the mair it's stepped on, the wider it spreads.

Set a stoot hert till a stey brae.

Self praise's nae commen'.

Sellin' her hen on a rainy day.

She waited for hats till the bonnets gaed by and noo she can peck her
  tetherin'.

Short accounts mak lang freens.

Sic things micht be as swine ta flee, but they're nae a common bird.

Silence means consent.

Sing! I'll gaur ye sing wi' a tear i' yer ee.

Spang weel at the speen meat, bread'll keep.

Speak o' the deil an' he'll appear.

Speer nae questions an' ye'll be tell'd nae lees.

Steal a needle, steal a preen steal a coo ere a' be deen.

Still waters rin deep.

Sweer folks are aye bodin' ill weather.

Sweer ta bed an' twice as sweer ta rise.

Sweerty's waur than the gut.

Tak a tune o' yer ain fiddle: ye'll dance till't ere a' be deen.

Tak awa Aberdeen an' twal miles roon aboot, an' whaur are ye?

Tak care o' the aul', the new's dear.

Tak care o' the pence, the pouns will tak care o' themselves.

Tak fat ye hae an' ye'll never want.

Takin' in at the spiggot an' lattin' oot at the bung.

Tak nae mair i' yer cheek than yer teeth will chow.

Tak time by the fore-lock.

That story winna tell (Jamie Fleeman).

The best laid schemes o' mice an' men gang aft agley.

The best's aye the cheapest.

The bird that can sing and winna sing sud be gaurt sing.

The blacksmith's mare an' the shoe-maker's wife are aye worst shod.

The bucket gangs aye ta the wall till ae day.

The cat can look at the Queen.

The devil's corn gaes aye ta bran.

The dishes are dancin', the cook's gaen to be merrit.

The greatest thief cries aye first 'Fie'.

The hetter war, the seener peace.

The King may come ta the cadger's gate.

The langer here, the later there.

The less said, the seener men't.

The lift micht fa' an' smore the lavericks (larks).

The mair cooks, the waur kale.

The mair haste, the waur speed, quoth the tailor ta the lang threed.

Them that canna ride maun shank it.

Them that come wi' a gift needna stan' lang at the door.

Them that's bun maun obey.

The nearer the kirk, the farer fae gweed.

The preef o' the puddin's in the preein' o't.

The rank is but the guinea stamp, the man's the gowd for a' that.

There'll be nae word o' this i' the mornin'.

There's as gweed fish i' the sea as ever cam out o't.

There's aye some water far the stirkie droons.

There's room aye at the tap (top).

There's few bees i' the bike when the drones appear.

There's luck in odd numbers quo' Rorie O'Mor.

There's mair wayes o' killin' a dog than chokin' him wi' butter.

There's nae an ill but micht be waur.

There's nae ill in a merry min' as said the wife when she gaed ben the
  kirk whistlin'.

There's nane sick but them that ha'e a sair tae.

There's tricks in a' trades but the honest horse-couper's.

The truth will tell twice (Jamie Fleeman).

The win's aye in a peer body's face.

The wish is father ta the thocht.

They can de ill that canna de gweed.

They hinna muckle gear that get the gweed o't a'.

Time an' tide wait for nane.

Ta prime the pump is vain fin the cistern's dry.

This winna pay the laird an' keep the fairm.

Trust in God and de the richt.

Turn aboot's fair play.

Twa kitchies ta ae bread!

We a'maun gang the same gaet.

Weel begun's half deen.

Weel is that weel dis (does).

Wilfu' waste maks woefu' want.

Ye aye mak yer ain pairt gweed.

Ye can mak a kirk or a mill o't.

Ye canna mak a silk purse oot o' a soo's lug.

Ye canna pit an aul' head on young shouthers.

Ye canna tak the breeks aff a hielanman.

Ye'd speer the tail fae a docket dog.

Ye hae sitten yer time as mony a gweed hen has deen.

Ye hae the vrang soo by the lug.
Ye maun creep afore ye gang.
Ye may wash aff dirt, but never dun hide.
Ye micht eat yer auld sheen if ye'd butter them weel.
Ye needna eat the coo an' worry o' the tail.
Yer ain han's sickerest.
Ye're ca'in yer hogs ta an ill market.
Ye're i' yer ain licht like the guid-wife wi' the lichtet candle.


## II FOLK SPEECH

### (a) Fife Mining

'Marry for love and wark for siller' runs the Fife proverb, setting forth the principles on which matrimony should be undertaken.

On hearing of an intended marriage, the customary enquiry is, as to the man, 'Wha's he takkin'?' but in the case of a woman, 'Wha's she gettin'?' Other common sayings are: 'She's ower mony wer-rocks (bunions) to get a man': and, 'Mim-mou'ed maidens never get a man; muckle-mou'ed maids get twa.' 'When ye tak' a man, ye tak' a maister,' is a woman's proverb. But when once the wedding ring was on, it was unlucky to take it off again. 'Loss the ring, loss the man.'

> 'Change the name an no' the letter,
> Change for the waur and no' the better.'

It was quite common in the parish for a married woman to be referred to by her maiden name in preference to the surname she was entitled to use by marriage.

When labour was in progress, various proverbs, consolatory and otherwise, were always used; such as, 'Ye'll be waur afore ye're better'; 'The hetter war, the suner peace'; 'Ye dinna ken ye're livin' yet', etc.

'Nurse weel the first year, ye'll no nurse twa', was the advice given by experienced elders to young mothers.

When the child was born, it was frequently greeted with the words, 'Ye've come into a cauld warl' noo.'

If the child is pronounced to be like father or mother, some one present will say, 'Weel, it couldna be like a nearer freen'!' (Friend, *Scot.*, a relative.)

If the little stranger is a well-developed child, we are told: 'That ane hasna been fed on deaf nuts.' (Deaf nuts are worthless withered nuts.)

Early teething portends sundry troubles. 'Teeth sune gotten, teeth sune lost'; 'Sune teeth, sune sorrow'. And as regards the mother: 'Sune teeth, sune anither'; or, 'Sune teeth, sune mair'.

To cut the upper teeth before the lower is very unlucky, for

> 'He that cuts his teeth abune
> Will never wear his marriage shoon.'

When a milk-tooth comes out, it should be put in the fire with a little salt, and either of the following verses repeated:

> 'Fire, fire, burn bane,
> God gi' me my teeth again.'

Or

> 'Burn, burn, blue tooth,
> Come again a new tooth.'

An addition to a miner's family, if a boy, is described as 'a tub o' great'; if a girl, as 'a tub o' sma' '.

A family of two is described as 'a doo's cleckin' ' (i.e. a pigeon's hatch).

A family of three is looked on as ideal: 'twa to fecht an' ane to sinder' (separate). Sometimes another child is allowed, and it becomes 'twa to fecht, ane to sinder, an' ane to rin an' tell'.

The last of the family is described as 'the shakkins o' the poke' (bag). 'Losh, wumman! this'll surely be the shakkins o' the poke noo!'

> Better haud weel than mak' weel.
> Better wear shoon than sheets.
> Feed a cold and starve a fever.

If ye want to be sune well, be lang sick: i.e. keep your bed till you are better. 'He's meat-heal ony way', is said of an invalid whose illness is not believed in. Nervous people are said to be 'feared o' the death they'll never dee'.

'He'll no kill', and 'He has a gey teuch sinon (sinew) in his neck', are said of hardy persons.

'Let the sau (salve) sink to the sair', was said jestingly as a reason for drinking whisky instead of rubbing it in as an outward application.

## (b)  Border Gypsy

Gipsy sayings used by an old wife when on the 'clap o' ninety' – and this was fifty years ago.

Thack (thatch) is better nor sclate, and the tent is better than thack.

He crossed knives at denner, but it was the other man got the hurt.

He'll no' gang tae St James's Fair: he sald a meer there ance. (He is afraid of meeting the man he cheated.)

Horners are aye horners. (The maker of horn spoons is always looked on as outside the law.)

Better the suppin' end nor the whistle end. (The old horn spoons had a whistle at the end of the handle of the spoon.)

The lang road disna need the box-bed at the end o't. (You'll sleep anywhere.)

Better a brown hare than a white ane. (Better the summer than the winter – the mountain hare takes on a white coat in the winter-time.)

The priest's curse disna haud out of the parish.

And, somewhat similar – The writ rins nae further than the baillie.

They can tak' the feathers, they canna get the bird. (The bird is eaten.)

## III   MINOR GENRES: RHYMES

## A      I                    1   Charm

This old 'freit' was used in connection with witches when calves were born. I heard it once said, and saw the ceremony performed, by an old man, who went round the byre and threw a pickle salt over each of the calves.

> Buckle up, buckle doon,
> Flee awa', and ne'er look roon';

192

Gin the jauds should come ava,
Hang them a' against the wa'.

## 2   Cure

A hantle o' the cures needit rhymes – or words o' some kin' – yt had
tae be said ower whun the chairm wus bein put on; but they wur ey
verra carefu no tae say them yt a buddy could mak oot the words
richt; A suppose for fear they wud learn them an work the spell
theirsels.

There's only twa or three yt A ever heard the words o'.

Here's yin yt yino' my sons got fae an aul buddy at Kirkmichael, in
the Water o' Ae.

It was for stoppin bluid whun onybuddy wus woundit. They put
a Taedstane on the wound an said:

> The water's mud, an rins afluid,
> An sae dis thy bluid.
> God bad it stan, an so it did.
> In the name o' the Father, Son, and Holy Ghost
> Stan Bluid.

## 3   Safeguard

The cross of the Saviour, tradition says, was made of the bourtree
(elder). It is not misliked, often being planted about dwellings, but it
is deemed unlucky to cut it. Before trimming it to shoot out anew in
Spring, it was customary to mention the fact to the free-growing
elder in the following words:

> Bourtree, bourtree crooked,
> Never straight and never strong,
> Ever bush and never tree
> Since our Lord was nailed on thee.

That rhyme exonerated the gardener from ill intent.

193

## 4   Prohibition

The laverock and the lintie,
The robin and the wren;
If ye harry their nests,
Ye'll never thrive again.


## 5   Divination

Hemp seed, I sow thee,
Hemp seed, I sow thee,
And he who is my true love
Come after me and pu' me.

On Hallowe'een a person who wished to ascertain his or her matri-
monial prospects, went out to the peat stack, and sowing a handful of
hemp seed called out the above incantation. Then from behind the
left shoulder stood forth the apparition of the future spouse in the
attitude of pulling the hemp.


## 6   Omen

Gang and hear the gouk yell,
Sit and see the swallows flee,
See the foal before its mother's e'e,
'Twill be a prosperous year for thee.


## II   7   Prophecy

(Attributed to Thomas the Rhymer)

When the Gows o' Gowrie come to land,
The Day o' Judgment's near at hand.

The Gows – sometimes 'Gees' and sometimes 'Yowes' – are two
large blocks of stone, lying in the channel of the river Tay, and
opposite the village of Invergowrie. Changes on the shoreline have
already stranded one of the boulders . . . .

194

## 8 Psalmody Rhyme

All people that on earth do dwell,
Rax oot yer han's an help yersel;
Or else, you may depend upon't,
You'll get a scon, an naething on't.

It use't tae be thocht an awfu sin tae use the verses o' the Psalms at the
Singin-skule, tae learn the tunes wi; an sae the Precentors an Singin-
maisters use't tae mak up rhymes tae learn us wi instead.

## III    9   Blessing

[Spoken before the breaking of a bottle of whisky on the prow at the
launching of a fisher boat.]

> Fae rocks an saands
> An barren lands
> An ill men's hands
> Keep's free.
> Weel oot, weel in,
> Wi a gueede shot.

## 10   Prayer

The Skyeman's Prayer

> Oh that the peats would cut themselves,
> The fush shump on the shore,
> And that we in our peds might lie
> For aye and evermore,
>    Och, ochay, Amen.

## 11   Grace

Lang life, and happy days, Plenty meat and plenty claes;
A haggis and a horn spune, And aye a tattie when the ither's dune.

## 12   Toast

The life o' man, the deid o' fish, The shuttle, soil, and plew;
Corn, horn, linen, yarn, Lint and tarry 'oo.

## IV      13   Curse

> If evyr maydenis malysone
> Did licht upon drye lande,
> Let nocht bee funde in Furvye's glebys,
> Bot thystl, bente, and sande.

Tradition says that the proprietor to whom the parish belonged
left three daughters as heirs of his fair lands; they were however
bereft of their property, and thrown houseless on the world. On
leaving their home they uttered the curse contained in the foregoing
words. In course of no long time a storm, which lasted nine days,
burst over the district, and turned the parish of Forvie into a desert of
sand; this calamity is said to have fallen on the place about 1688.

## 14   Taunt

> Wassla waiter wuns the day;
> Eassla waiter canna play,
> For eatin' sodden dumplin's.

[This taunt was issued by one side in the annual Hawick ball game
(those living on the west of the Water of Slitrig) against the other
(those from the east of the river).]

## 15   Blason Populaire

There use't tae be a rhyme tae cry at the Castle Douglas folk:

> Whun Wyllie Douglas, pawkie loon,
> Had got tae hae a shirt,
> He made aul' Causeway-en a toon,
> An ca't it Castle-Dirt.

An Castle-Dirt's the name it gets tae the present day.

## V    16    Rhyme of Situation

The following was a formula of acknowledgment made at the doors
of churches, in former times, as a reparation for scandal:

> First I ca'd her honest woman –
> 'Twas true, indeed;
> Niest I ca'd her (jade) and thief –
> Fause tongue, ye lee'd!

The words were . . . varied [in the case of a man] and according to
the nature of the slander.

## 17    Rhyme of Conversation

> Seek your sa' where you got your ail,
> And beg your barm where you buy your ale.

The reply of a person who is asked for assistance by one who
formerly shunned him.

## 18    Rhyme Used to Children

Said by a mother when combing her child's hair.

> Haily, paily, sits on the sands,
> Combs her hair with her lily-white hands.

## VI    19    Work Rhyme

The winder of a cribbie, a quantity of yarn made up on a crib, a reel
for winding yarn, kept count by repeating:

> Up the Cribbie, doon the Cribbie
> Cribbie ye are yin
> Up the Cribbie, doon the Cribbie
> Cribbie ye are twa. [and so on]

## 20   Vendor's Cry

[A nineteenth century itinerant cobbler, wife, and son chanted line
by line:]

(Boy)      My father mends bellises;
(Woman)  It's true 'at the lad does say;
(Man)     And I'm the boy 'at can dae it,
           Wi' my tiddy-fal-lal-de-lal-lay.

## 21   Oath

I trapse (or rapse) my word abune my breath,
I've touched cauld airn (iron) afore ye!
(Here the boot tackets are touched.)

## VII   22   Nonsense Rhyme

Have ye ever seen the Devil
Wi his widen spade an shovel
Shovellin tatties in a bushel
An his sleeves rowed up;
Have ye ever seen his wife
Wi a double-bladed knife
Goin to tak his life
An her sleeves rowed up.

## 23   Tongue-Twister

Kittok sat in pepper pock
pikel pepper Kittock.

## 24   Game Rhyme

A piece of stick was made hot in the fire and handed from one to
another of the circle, idle by want of light, sitting around the hearth.

> About wi' that, about wi' that,
> Keep alive the Priest's cat.

one of the party by the fireside said, and passed the brand from hand to hand. When the flame died the person who held the stick was liable to a fine. In days of old, when the priest's cat in the flesh died, there was great lamentation throughout the country-side, as it was supposed to turn into some supernatural being who would work mischief among the human flock.

## 25 Narrative Rhyme

An Auld Maid's Seven Ages

> Fa'll I hae?
> Fa'll I tak?
> Fa'll I get?
> Fa'll get me?
> Fa'll tak me?
> Fa'll hae me?
>    No naebody!

## VIII 26 Periodic Custom Rhyme

The guisers chanted in chorus:

> Rise up, guidwife, an' shak' yer feathers,
> Dinna think that we are beggars;
> We are guid folks come to play,
> Rise up an' gie's oor Hogmanay.
> Hogmanay, Trol-lol-lay.

Like all other customs of this kind, these visits have been increasingly abandoned to children, and indeed a late version of the rhyme substitutes the words 'We're girls and boys come out today' for the third line quoted above.

## 27  Rite of Passage Rhyme

An ancient burial formula . . . was used on the island of Yell as late as the eighteenth century . . .:

> Yurden du art fur af yurden du vis skav'd
> Oktoa yurden nu ven dœd [?vende at – Jakobsen]
> Op fra yurden skal du Opstaa,
> Naar Herren laar syne bastnan blaa.

its meaning appears to be:

> Earth thou art, for of earth thou wast made –
> To earth thou now returnest.
> From the earth thou shalt arise
> When the Lord shall blow the last trumpet.

## 28  Occasional Custom Rhyme

[Chanted during the custom of Riding the Stang, which was an old punishment inflicted by the community on wife-beaters, the stang being a fir pole, snedded, but with the branch stumps left to the length of an inch or so.]

> Ocht yt's richt'll no be wrang,
> Lick the wife an ride the Stang.

At the words 'wife' an 'stang' they liftit it as heich as they could, an than loot it suddently fa' again; an he cam doon wi a thud every time on some o' the ens o' the brenches yt had been left sticking oot for his benefit, an the scraichs o' him wus fearfu.

The stang wus through atween his legs, ye ken.

## B    1    History: a Disruption rhyme

> The Wee Kirk,
> The Free Kirk,
> The Kirk withoot the steeple;
> The Auld Kirk,
> The cauld Kirk,
> The Kirk withoot the people.

200

## 2 Geography: farms in Fife

Ladernie, Lother, Lathones,
Minziemill, Seggiehill,
Pittormie stands alone;
When you see the lichts o Dersiemair
Ye're at the gates o Dron,
Ye'll hear the cock at Middlefiddy
Cryin Kilmaron.

## 3 Law: a tenure for the lands of Keilor granted by a King James

Ye Haddens o' the Moor ye pay nocht
But a hairen tither – if it's socht
A red rose at Yule, and a sna'ba' at Lammas.

## 4 Medicine

The buttered peas o' Lauderdale,
Are better than the best o' kail,
When Tammie's pith begins to fail.

## 5 Belief

Rowan tree and red thread
Mak' the witches tyne their speed.

## 6 Weather

When the mist tak's the hills,
Guid weather spills;
When the mist tak's the howes,
Guid weather grows.

7   Occupational knowledge: a rhyme for dry-dykers

> Pin weel, pack sma',
> Lay ae stane abune twa.

8   General knowledge: rhyme describing how to sain a corpse

> Thrice the torchie, t[h]rice the saltie,
> Thrice the dishes toom for loffie –
> These three times ye must wave round
> The corpse, till it sleep sound.
> Sleep sound and frown nane
> Till to heaven the souls gane.
> If you want that soul to die,
> Procure the torchie frae the Elleree.
> But gin ye want that soul to live,
> Between the dishes place a sieve
> And it shall have a fair, fair shrive.

9   Practical Conduct: rhyme on the training of a child

> Thraw the widdie (withie) when it's green,
> Atween three and thirteen.

## IV   RIDDLES

1   What is't that stan's oot o' the wud and eats in it?
> A sow eating out of its trough.

2   Hoddy-poddy, wee black body,
Three legs and a timmer hat.
> A little pot with wooden lid.

3   What is't that's neither withoot nor within and it's aye on the dyke dryin'?
> The window.

4   What's red below, black in the middle, and white abune?
      A girdle of scones on the fire.

5   What's as white's milk,
  And as sleek's silk,
  And hops like a mill shillin'?
      A magpie.

6   As roon as a riddle,
  As black as a coal,
  A lang neck, and a pumping hole.
      A greybeard (jar for liquor).

7   As white as snaw, but snaw it's not;
  As red as bluid, but bluid it's not;
  As black as ink, but ink it's not.
      A bramble.

8   Mouthed like a mill door, lugged like a cat,
  Though you guess to ne'rday, ye'll no' guess that.
      A potato pot.

9   The sma' lean faither,
  The big baggit mither,
  And the three sma' bairns.
      Pot and crooks (chain from which hung kettle etc.).

10   Hip-chip-cherry, a' the men in 'Derry
  Couldna climb (like) hip-chip-cherry.
      The reek (smoke).

11   Ayont yon dyke, a dusty dyke,
  I heard a fellow rout,
  And aye he spewed, and aye he spat,
  And aye he turned about.
      A meal-mill.

12   Nine taps, nine tails,
  Nineteen score o' nails,
  Ae elbow, ae fit,

What a gruesome beast was it!
    The Scottish thistle.


13    As I gaed ower the heather hill
    I met the bull of Beverlin,
    I dashed his heid against a stane,
    White as milk cam' back again.
        Corn ground between two stones.


14    Four-and-twenty white kye
    Standin' at a stall,
    Oot cam' the reid bull
    And licked ower them all.
        The teeth licked by the tongue.


15    Doon in yon meadow, yellow an' green,
    The King couldna name it, nor yet could the Queen;
    They sent for a wise man oot o' the east:
    He said it had horns, but it wasna a beast?
        A whin bush.


16    Wee man o' leather gaed through the heather,
    Through a rock, through a reel,
    Through an auld spinnin' wheel,
    Through a sheep shank bane –
    Sic a man was never seen.
        A beetle.


17    As I went ower ayont yon dyke,
    I fun a wee pen-knife;
    It could kill a hare, it could kill a bear,
    It could kill a hunner men an' mair.
        Hunger.


18    In comes two legs, carrying one leg,
    Lays down one leg, on three legs,
    Out goes two legs, in comes four legs,
    Out goes five legs, in comes two legs,
    Snatches up three legs, flings it at four legs,
    And brings back one leg.

A woman (two legs) brings in a leg of mutton (one leg), places it on a stool (three legs), as she goes out (two legs) a dog (four legs) enters and runs off with mutton (five legs), woman returns (two legs), throws stool (three legs) at dog (four legs), and brings back piece of mutton (one leg).

19  The fairest flower in a' the garden,
That e'er the sun shone on,
Was made a wife the first day of her life,
And died before she was born.
    Eve.

20  There was a man o' Adam's race
Which had a strange dwelling place,
'Twas neither in Heaven, earth, nor hell,
Now tell me where that man did dwell.
    Jonah in the whale's belly.

21  A deep, deep dungeon, a dark, dark cave,
A leevin' man, and a leevin' grave,
    Jonah in the whale's belly.

22  We are two sisters' sons, we are two brothers dear,
Our father was our grandfather, it's queer our kin's so near.
    The sons of Lot's two daughters.

23  What's a' holes and carries water?
    The crooks.

24  The bull bulled me,
The cow calved me,
The smith made me,
And I grew in the wud.
    The bellows (made of hide, iron, and wood).

25  I gaed away abune grun and I cam hame below't.
        A man goes to cut a sod and returns carrying the sod
        on his head.

26  What gangs away wi' the carriage, comes back wi' the carriage,

is of no use to the carriage, and yet the carriage cannot do without it?

The sound.

27    As wee as a mouse, as high as a house,
And yet it canna get into the kirk door.

A star.

28    As I went ower yon muir I met a wee boy who was roaring and greeting. I asked him what was wrang wi' him, and he said his faither had died seven years before he was born, and he got bread and cheese at his burial.

The boy's father was a dyer.

29    What is't that never was and never will be,
I hae't in my han' tae let ye see?

The fingers all one length.

30    There is a wee hoose that's fu' o' meat,
And there's neither door nor window in't.

An egg.

31    Doon in yon meadow there lies twa swine,
Ane's my faither's, the aither's mine;
The mair ye gie them the mair they cry,
The less ye gie them the quater they lie.

Two guns.

32    Doon in yon meadow grows a bunch o' willow wands;
Naebody can count them but God's ain hands.

The hairs of the head.

33    Hickerty- pickerty pinned the yett,
Hickerty-pickerty pinned it weel;
Hickerty-pickerty pinned the yett,
Withoot aither ern or steel.

Frost.

34    Lang legs, an' short thees [thighs], A wee heid, an' nae ees?

A pair of tongs.

35    Faither and mither, sister and brither,
      A' lie in ae bed, and never touch ane anither.
           The bars of the grate.


36    There was a man who had no eyes,
      And he went out to view the skies;
      He saw a tree wi' apples on't,
      He took nae apples of't
      And he left nae apples on't.
                The man had one eye, and he took one apple off a
                tree which had two on it at first.


37    Jenny wi' the white petticoat and the red nose,
      The langer she stands the shorter she grows.
           A candle.


38    A lang man, legless, cam staffless owre the hill;
      Quo' he, 'Gudewife, keep in your hens, your dowgs do me nae
      ill'?
           A worm.


39    In times of old, the Scripture doth record,
      There lived one who never did offend the Lord,
      Who spoke the truth and never did sin commit,
      Yet in God's presence he shall never sit.
           Balaam's ass.


40    Like a cherry, like a chess,
      Like a bonny blue gless,
      Like a cow amang the corn,
      Blawing Billy Buck's horn:
      Spell that wi' four letters.
           T-h-a-t.


41    There was a joiner made a door and it was ower big; he took a
      bit off, and it was ower wee; he took another bit off and it
      answered.
                The piece taken off at first was too small a piece, and on
                taking another piece off the door fitted.

42 The bat, the bee, the butterflee,
  The cuckoo and the gowk,
  The myre-snipe, the heather bleat;
  How many birds is that?
    Two.


43 The Queen o' Sheba had a ship
  An' her daughter sailed in it,
  I'm aye telling ye, but ye're no kennin'
  The name o' the daughter in that ship sailin'.
    Ann.


44 As I gaed ower yon heathery hill
  I met John Reekum-teekum-tanguil
  Carrying away a poor demaujil;
  I took up my hunjil-cunjel-caujel,
  And made John Reekum-teekum-tanguil
  Lay down the poor demaujil.
    A fox carrying a lamb away, when a man with a stick
    attacks the fox and causes it to lay the lamb down.


45 As I stood on my timper tillies,
  And looked through my wimper willies,
  I saw a muckle big bag
  In the whirly-whig-whag,
  I sent my little tig-tag
  To bring the muckle big bag
  Oot o' the whirly-whig-whag.
    A woman on tiptoes looking through a window sees a
    cow among the turnips, and sends her little dog to bring
    the cow out.


46 I met a man wi' a drove o' sheep. I says, 'Gude mornin' to you
  wi' your score o' sheep.' He says, 'havena a score, but if I had as
  many more, and half as many, and two sheep and a half, I
  would have a score.' How many had he?
    7

47   A blind man saw a hare,
A dumb man cried 'Where?'
A legless man ran and catched it,
And a naked man put it in his pocket.

     A catch riddle, to which no answer can be give

# 4

# FOLK DRAMA

## INTRODUCTION

At Halloween and Guy Fawkes time guisers still present us with a wierdly picturesque sight and a cry which may be either 'a penny for the guy' or 'a penny for the guisers', but whereas nowadays these disguised ones are children, up to the nineteenth and even into the twentieth century guising was practised by the adults of a community. Guising activities took different forms but the most notable is the performing of the folk play, which occurred in Scotland usually at Christmas–New Year time but sometimes at Halloween, the end of the Celtic year.

The play is really a folk custom with a text. Men of a village or district took their performance round the dwellings of their locality in a 'luck-visitation', which served at least one basic function in redefining and bonding the community at a significant time, when one year ended and another began. This custom has a 'text' in that words accompany the action but the action of the performance is more important than the text, which usually consists of brisk doggerel. It is likely, in fact, that the words are later rationalized accretions to the action.

There are three kinds of folk play in the British Isles: the Hero-Combat Play, the Sword Dance Play, the Wooing Play. In the Hero-Combat Play, by far the most widespread, 'the action consists of one or more champions overcoming one or more opponents who are revived by a doctor'. In the Sword Dance Play 'the linked sword dance . . . is the basis. A man is executed by the lock of swords round his neck, and is revived by either a doctor, a Clown, or a "Female" ' (i.e. a man dressed as a woman). Cawte, Helm, and Peacock do not list any Sword Dance Play among the Scottish entries in *English Ritual Drama. A Geographical Index*, the type being largely localized in northeastern England, but there exists one curious relative of the play in the Papa Stour Sword Dance ceremony, which has aroused considerable controversy and is discussed in the Notes. The Wooing Play has this descriptive definition: 'the wooer of a young "Female" is rejected in favour of a Clown, and enlists in the army. The Clown is occasionally accused of being the father of the bastard child of an older "Female". This he rejects. The action then normally follows' the Hero-Combat Play. The Wooing Plays are localized in the English East Midlands though traces appear elsewhere. In all three kinds of play the core of the action is the death and resurrection of one of the characters.[1]

Cawte, Helm, and Peacock list for Scotland only 16 Hero-Combat texts, besides fragments and references to performance, a total of 25 entries covering 15 counties.[2] According to these accounts the known performance dates range from the 1780s to the First World War with only one isolated reference to a Halloween performance at Leven in Fife thereafter, in 1930. Contemporary field-work, however, has turned up recollections of dramatic guising from earlier this century. For instance, Emily Lyle's 1979 article in *Tocher* contains four sets of memories of performances in the Borders and West Lothian.[3] And in 1979 a trouvaille was discovered by students from Stirling University when they recorded from Mr Andrew Rennie (aged 90), retired blacksmith, of Kippen, Stirlingshire, a complete text of the play as it had been performed in Kippen before the First World War. The text has been printed, along with Maidment's, by Rob Watling as *Two Stirlingshire Hero-Combat Plays*.[4]

In the Hero-Combat Play a presentation and quête (a collection of gifts) flank the central action's two main elements of the combat and the cure, where a kind of crudely stylized tragedy balances a kind of crudely imaginative comedy. The Scottish texts generally have as characteristic features, such as here in the two early nineteenth-century versions from Roxburghshire and Stirling, appearances of Alexander the Great and Galatian among the champions, the attempt to throw the blame for the killing on an innocent bystander (Stirling text only), and some hard bargaining in the Doctor episode. Galatian in fact lends his name to the group of black-faced guisers, the Goloshans, and one can still hear grandmothers reprove a mud-clarted child with 'My, you're like a Goloshan'.

The possible meanings of the folk play have provoked consider-able speculation. The centrality of the death and resurrection to the action led to the belief that the play was a ritual designed, by mimetic action, to promote fertility in field and fold in the ensuing year, and that latterly the idea of fertility had shaded into the idea of luck. Over twenty years ago there arose, largely on the basis of European parallels, the Life-Cycle Theory, so called because 'the various parts of the different customs [i.e. the three kinds of play] fall into a pattern representing all the stages needed to portray the human life-cycle', involving as they do three generations and the three critical high-points of existence, birth, marriage and death. Since the publication of *Christmas Mumming in Newfoundland*,[5] however, with its inno-vatory contextualist approach, a reaction has set in against what is seen as outdated emphases on the hypothesized origins of the play, and on the play as 'survival' or 'fertility rite', emphases sometimes pointed to as evidence that much British thinking on tradition has not advanced very far since the turn of the century. In their stead is, primarily, an emphasis on the 'contemporary meaning' of those plays still performed, to be obtained through a study of the context and functions of the performances; in an examination of a current Cheshire play, for example, Susan Pattison has shown how the meaning of the play relates directly to the idea of community.[6] Both contemporary and historical perspectives can contribute to our understanding of the folk play in general, and to any study of the Scottish material; and such a study there should be since Scotland furnishes a compact body of texts within a distinctive context of guising and custom.

# Notes

1 E.C. Cawte, A. Helm, and N. Peacock, *English Ritual Drama. A Geo-graphical Index* (London, 1967), pp. 37, 37–8.

2 Cawte, Helm, and Peacock, pp.66–7. From their list of counties the geographically anomalous Orkney can be excised, for the Deerness refer-ence derived from Leishman's composite text proves on examination to be based on one line from a New Year song, not a hero-combat play. To the counties list, however, can be added Aberdeenshire: see David Buchan, 'The Folk Play, Guising, and Northern Scotland', *Lore and Lan-guage*, I:10(1974), 10–14.

3 'The Goloshans', *Tocher*, no.32(1979), 107–12.

4 Stirling: Stirling University Bibliography Centre, 1980.

5 Herbert Halpert and G.M. Story, eds, *Christmas Mumming in Newfoundland* (Toronto, 1969).

6 Susan Pattison, 'The Antrobus Soulcaking Play: An Alternative Approach to the Mummers' Play', *Folk Life*, 15(1977), 5-11.

# 1   HERO-COMBAT PLAY: ROXBURGHSHIRE

## The Game of Gysarts

In the southern counties of Scotland a number of young men dress themselves in a fantastic manner and paint or disguise their faces, and in this situation go through towns, villages, farmsteads and cottages, and enter into every house where they think that the inhabitants will allow them a small pittance, for which they perform a kind of dramatic game, and call themselves Gysarts. Tradition says that it is very unlucky to let the Gysarts go out of a house where they have performed and acted that tragedy (which they sometimes call Galatian, or Alexander of Macedon) without giving them some money to drink to the success of the family.

The Gysarts always dress themselves in white. They appear like so many dead persons, robed in their shrouds, who have risen from their narrow homes; and the simile is still improved from their faces being all painted black or dark blue. Their mutches are sometimes adorned with ribbands of diverse colours, but these seldom enter into their dress as the plain mutch is the most common.

A sword is a necessary article of their dress, which they wear below their shroud or gown. The evening is the usual time that the Gysarts make their appearance, though I have seen them perform in the sunshine in some villages.

*Dramatis Personae*

> Alexander of Macedon
> St George of England   } servants
> Gallashen
> A Doctor
> A Boy

*Scene First*
Enter a servant with a besom who sweeps the floor singing as follows:

1    Redd up rocks redd up reels (or) Redd up stocks, redd up stools
     Here comes in a pack o' fools.  Here comes in a pack of fools – &c
     A pack o' fools was never here before
     Meikle head an little wit stands behind the door.

2    Redd room, and redd room,
     And gie's room to sing;
     We'll shew ye the best sport,
     Acted at christmas time.

Sometimes one and sometimes all of them repeat at the same time,
when they first enter into a house, the preceding verse.

Enter the commander of the band

              Activous and Activage,
              I'll shew you the best sport,
              Ever acted on any stage.
              If you don't believe the word I say
              Call for Alexander of Macedon
              And he will shew ye the way.

Enter Alexander of Macedon

         Here comes I, Alexander of Macedon,
         Who conquered the world, all, but Scotland alone,
         And when I came to Scotland,
         My heart it grew cold, my heart it grew cold,
         To see that little nation, sae crouse an sae bold,
         Sae crouse and sae bold, sae frank an sae free,
         I call for Gallashen, and he will fight wi' me.

Sometimes I have heard Galashen pronounced Slashen.

Enter Gallashen who kills Alexander

              Here comes I Galashen,
              Galashen is my name,
              Wi sword an buckler by my side,
              I hope to win the game.
              My head is clothed in iron,
              My body's clothed wi steel,
              My buckler's made o' knuckle-bone
              My sword is made o' steel.

I call for great St George of England and he will
fight wi me.

Some Gysarts in the character of Galashen repeat the lines thus.

My head is made o' Iron, my bodies made o' steel, my a—e is made
o' knuckle bone &c.

Galashen is next killed by St George.

Enter St George of England

Here comes I, great St George of England,
See my bloody weapon, it shines clear,
It reaches up to my very ear,
Let any man come fence me here.

Enter a Boy

As I was at a fencing school,
I saw a boy turn out a fool,
A fool, a fool, as you may see,
I deliver him up to fight wi thee.

This dragon, of a boy, enters the lists with St George and stabs him,
to the astonishment of the party present. He falls down on his knees,
repeating as he looks at the dead body of St George –

Ohon, ohon, I've kill'd a man,
I've killed my brother's eldest son.

The servants are ordered to take up the body of St George, but to
their surprize, He says –

I am, I am, I am not slain,
For I'll rise and fight that boy again.

The boy says to him –

To fight wi me ye are not able,
For my sword will split yer haly table.

Then the boy transfixes him with his spear, as he is in the act of rising
to fight him.

215

A Doctor is next called for, by another of the company, and a second crys fifty pounds for a Doctor.

Enter a Doctor

Here comes I, a Doctor, as good a Doctor as Scotland ever bred.
What diseases, says one to him, can you cure?
He answers, I can cure the Itch, the stitch, the maligrumphs, the
    lep [probably leprosy], the pip, the roan, the blaen, the
    merls, the nerels, the blaes, the splaes, and the burning pintle.
Another asks him, What more diseases can you cure?
He answers, I can cure a man that has lain seven years in his grave
    and more.

They next ask him what sum he will take to cure this man, pointing to the body of St George as it lies upon the ground: – after looking at the body, he answers, I will take £10 to make a complete cure. They offer him six pounds, which he refuses, then eight, and lastly nine: He says, nine and a bottle o' wine will do, and immediately he touches him with a small rod or wand, and orders him to rise up and gives him the new appelation of Jack, as he rises.

The other killed chieftains are reanimated by a touch of the Doctor's wand, and instantly spring up, all except poor Jack, who rises slowly, and complaining of a severe pain, in the lumber region of his back.

The Doctor says to him what 'ailes yer back?':
He answers, there is a hole in it wad hold a head of a horse threefold: –
The Doctor replies this is nonsense, Jack, you must tell me a better tale than this; and accordingly Jack proceeds thus:

I have been east, I have been west,
I have been at the Sherckle-dock,
And many were there, the warse o the wear
And they tauld me, the Deel there, marries a' the poor folk.

They ask him what he saw at the Sherckle-dock: When he goes on thus: I saw roast upo' rungs, q — s upon tongues, ladies p — g Spanish needles, ten ells lang, auld wives flying in the air, like the peelings o' ingins (onions), swine playing upo' bagpipes, cats gaun upon pattens, and hens drinking ale.

*Scene the last*

At the termination of Jack's speech the Gysarts are desired to drink with the family, after which they are presented by each person in the house with a small sum of money for their trouble. They lastly form themselves into a ring and as they dance round all of them sing the following carol:

> As we came by yon well we drank,
> We laid our gloves upon yon bank;
> By came Willie's piper to play.
> Took up our gloves and ran away;
> We followed him from town to town,
> We bade him lay our bonny gloves down;
> He laid them down upon yon stone,
> Sing ye a carol, ours is done.

Sometimes each of the Gysarts sings a carol before leaving the house, of the preceding sort. Every evening from Christmas to Fasternseen is allowable for the Gysarts to make their perambulations.

## 2  HERO-COMBAT PLAY: STIRLING

*Dramatis Personae*:

Sir Alexander
Galations
Admiral
Farmer's Son
Doctor

*Sir Alexander*

> Keep silence, merry gentlemen, unto your courts, said I:
> My name's Sir Alexander, I'll show you sport, said I.
> Five of us all, fine merry boys are we,
> And we are come a-rambling your houses for to see:
> Your houses for to see, Sir, and pleasure for to have,
> And what you freely give to us we freely will receive.
> The first young man that I call in, he is the farmer's son;
> And he's afraid he lose his love, because he is too young.

217

*Farmer's Son*

>    Altho' I am too young, Sir, I've money for to rove,
>    And I will freely spend it before I lose my love.

*Sir Alexander*

>    The next young man that I call in, he is a hero fine;
>    He's Admiral of the Hairy Caps, and all his men are mine.

*The Admiral*

>    Here am I the Admiral – the Admiral stout and bold,
>    Who won the battle of Quinbeck, and wear a crown of gold.

*Sir Alexander*

>    The next young man that I call in, is Galations of renown,
>    And he will slay our Admiral, and take his golden crown.

*Galations*

>    Here comes in Galations, Galations is my name;
>    With sword and pistol by my side, I hope to win the game.

*The Admiral*

>    The game, Sir; the game, it is not in your power;
>    I'll draw my bloody dagger, and slay you on the floor.

*Galations*

>    My head is made of iron, my body's made of steel;
>    I'll draw my bloody weapon, and slay you on the field.

*Sir Alexander*

>    Fight on, fight on, brave warriors! fight on with noble speed!
>    I'll give any ten hundred pounds to slay Galations dead.

[*Here Galations and the Admiral fight, and Galations falls, being stabbed*]

*Sir Alexander*

>    Galations ye have killed, and on the floor have slain:
>    Ye will suffer sore for him, as sure's your on the plain.

*The Admiral*

>    Oh no: it was not I, Sir; I'm innocent of the crime;
>    'Twas that young man behind me that drew his sword so fine.

*Farmer's Son*

>    Oh, you awful villain! to lay the weight on me;
>    For my two eyes were shut, Sir, when this young man did die.

*Sir Alexander*
How could your eyes be shut, sir, when you stood looking on?
When their two swords were drawn, you might have sindered them.
Since Galations ye have killed, Galations ye must cure;
Galations ye must raise to life in less than half an hour.
*Spoken*   Round the kitchen, and round the hall,
          For an old greasy doctor I do call.

*Doctor*
   Here comes I, the best old greasy doctor in the kingdom.

*Sir Alexander*
   What can you cure?

*Doctor*
   I can cure the rout, the gout, the ringworm, cholic, and the scurvy;
and can gar an old woman of seventy look as gay as a young woman
of sixteen.

*Sir Alexander*
   What will you take to cure this dead man?

*Doctor*
   Ten pounds and a bottle of wine.

*Sir Alexander*
   Will five not do? nor six?

*Doctor*
   Six won't take down a Highlandman's breeks to let the devil fart
out fire.

*Sir Alexander*
   Seven? Eight? Nine?

*Doctor*
   No.

*Sir Alexander*
   Ten?

*Doctor*
   Yes, ten! and a bottle of wine.

*Sir Alexander*
   What will you give him?

219

*Doctor*

I'll give him –: and I have a small bottle in my breek pouch full of
Inky Pinky* (*sings*) a little to his nose, and a little to his toes
(*applying it accordingly*). Start up, Jack, and sing.

*Galations*

> Once I was dead, and now I'm come alive;
> Blessed be the doctor that made me to revive.

*Omnes*

We will all join hands, and never fight more,
But we will all 'gree as brethren, as we have done before;
We thank the master of this house, likewise the mistress, too,
And all the little babies that round the table grow.
Your pockets full of money, and your bottles full of beer,
We wish you a good Hogmanay, and a happy New Year.

[Exeunt

*Epilogue*

> Here comes in little diddlie dots,
> With his pockets full of groats,
> If you have anything to spare,
> Put it in there.

---

* Inky Pinky, about seventy or eighty years since, was used by the
brewers in Stirlingshire to designate the smallest kind of beer; the medium
was termed Middle-moy, and the best, or strongest, Ram-tambling.


## 3   SWORD DANCE CEREMONIAL: PAPA STOUR, SHETLAND

To the Primate's account of the sword-dance, I am able to add the
words sung or chanted on occasion of this dance, as it is still performed in Papa Stour, a remote island of Zetland, where alone the
custom keeps its ground. It is, it will be observed by antiquaries,
a species of play or mystery, in which the Seven Champions of
Christendom make their appearance, as in the interlude presented in
*All's Well that Ends Well*. This dramatic curiosity was most kindly
procured for my use by Dr Scott of Hazlar Hospital, son of my friend
Mr Scott of Mewbie, Zetland. Mr Hibbert has, in his *Description of*

*the Zetland Islands*, given an account of the sword-dance, but somewhat less full than the following:

*Words used as a prelude to the sword-dance, a Danish or Norwegian ballet,*
*composed some centuries ago, and preserved in Papa Stour, Zetland.*

*Personae Dramatis*

(Enter Master, in the character of St George)

> Brave gentles all within this boor,
> If ye delight in any sport,
> Come see me dance upon this floor,
> Which to you all shall yield comfort.
> Then shall I dance in such a sort,
> As possible I may or can;
> You, minstrel man, play me a porte,
> That I on this floor may prove a man.

(He bows, and dances in a line.)

> Now have I danced with heart and hand,
> Brave gentles all, as you may see,
> For I have been tried in many a land,
> As yet the truth can testify;
> In England, Scotland, Ireland, France, Italy, and Spain
> Have I been tried with that good sword of steel.

(Draws, and flourishes.)

> Yet, I deny that ever a man did make me yield;
> For in my body there is strength,
> As by my manhood may be seen;
> And I, with that good sword of length,
> Have oftentimes in perils been,
> And over champions I was king.
> And by the strength of this right hand,
> Once on a day I kill'd fifteen,
> And left them dead upon the land.
> Therefore, brave minstrel, do not care,
> But play to me a porte most light,
> That I no longer do forbear,
> But dance in all these gentles' sight;
> Although my strength makes you abased,

Brave gentles all, be not afraid,
For here are six champions, with me, staid,
All by my manhood I have raised.
(He dances.)
Since I have danced, I think it best
To call my brethren in your sight,
That I may have a little rest,
And they may dance with all their might;
With heart and hand as they are knights,
And shake their sword of steel so bright,
And show their main strength on this floor,
For we shall have another bout
Before we pass out of this boor.
Therefore, brave minstrel, do not care
To play to me a porte most light,
That I no longer do forbear,
But dance in all these gentles' sight.
(He dances, and then introduces his knights, as under)
Stout James of Spain, both tried and stour,
Thine acts are known full well indeed;
And champion Dennis, a French knight,
Who stout and bold is to be seen;
And David, a Welshman born,
Who is come of noble blood;
And Patrick also, who blew the horn,
An Irish knight, amongst the wood;
Of Italy, brave Anthony the good,
And Andrew of Scotland king;
St George of England, brave indeed,
Who to the Jews wrought muckle tinte.
Away with this! Let us come to sport,
Since that ye have a mind to war,
Since that ye have this bargain sought,
Come let us fight and do not fear.
Therefore, brave minstrel, do not care
To play to me a porte most light
That I no longer do forbear,
But dance in all these gentles' sight.
(He dances, and advances to James of Spain.)
Stout James of Spain, both tried and stour,

Thine acts are known full well indeed,
Present thyself within our sight,
Without either fear or dread.
Count not for favour or for feid,
Since of thy acts thou has been sure;
Brave James of Spain, I will thee lead,
To prove thy manhood on this floor.
(James dances.)
Brave champion Dennis, a French knight,
Who stout and bold is to be seen,
Present thyself within our sight
Thou brave French knight,
Who bold hast been;
Since thou such valiant acts hast done,
Come let us see some of them now
With courtesy, thou brave French knight,
Draw out thy sword of noble hue.
(Dennis dances, while the others retire to a side.)
Brave David a bow must string, and with awe
Set up a wand upon a stand
And that brave David will cleave in twa.
(David dances solus.)
Here is, I think, an Irish knight,
Who does not fear, or does not fright,
To prove thyself a valiant man,
As thou has done full often bright;
Brave Patrick, dance, if that thou can.
(He dances.)
Thou stout Italian, come thou here;
Thy name is Anthony, most stout;
Draw out thy sword that is most clear,
And do thou fight without any doubt;
Thy leg thou shake, thy neck thou lout,
And show some courtesy on this floor,
For we shall have another bout
Before we pass out of this boor.
Thou kindly Scotsman come thou here;
Thy name is Andrew of Fair Scotland;
Draw out thy sword that is most clear,
Fight for thy king with thy right hand;

223

> And aye as long as thou canst stand,
> Fight for thy king with all thy heart;
> And then, for to confirm his band,
> Make all his enemies for to smart.

(He dances.) (Music begins.)

*Figuir*

The six stand in rank with their swords reclining on their shoulders. The master (St George) dances, and then strikes the sword of James of Spain, who follows George, then dances, strikes the sword of Dennis, who follows behind James. In like manner the rest – the music playing – swords as before. After the six are brought out of rank, they and the master form a circle, and hold the swords point and hilt. This circle is danced round twice. The whole, headed by the master, pass under the swords held in a vaulted manner. They jump over the swords. This naturally places the swords across, which they disentangle by passing under their right sword. They take up the seven swords and form a circle, in which they dance round.

The master runs under the sword opposite, which he jumps over backwards. The others do the same. He then passes under the right-hand sword, which the others follow, in which position they dance, until commanded by the master, when they form into a circle, and dance round as before. They then jump over the right-handed sword, by which means their backs are to the circle, and their hands across their backs. They dance round in that form until the master calls 'Loose', when they pass under the right sword, and are in a perfect circle.

The master lays down his sword, and lays hold of the point of James's sword. He then turns himself, James, and the others, into a clue. When so formed, he passes under out of the midst of the circle; the others follow; they vault as before. After several other evolutions, they throw themselves into a circle, with their arms across the breast. They afterwards form such figures as to form a shield of their swords, and the shield upon their heads. It is then laid down upon the floor. Each knight lays hold of their former points and hilts with their hands across, which disentangle by figuirs directly contrary to those that formed the shield. This finishes the ballet.

*Epilogue*

> Mars does rule, he bends his brows,

224

He makes us all agast;
After the few hours that we stay here,
Venus will rule at last.

Farewell, farewell, brave gentles all.
That herein do remain
I wish you health and happiness
Till we return again.

# ABBREVIATIONS

| | |
|---|---|
| *FFC* | *Folklore Fellows Communications* |
| *FLJ* | *Folk-lore Journal* |
| *JAF* | *Journal of American Folklore* |
| *MRC, TRC* | *Miscellanea (Transactions) of the Rymour Club* |
| *PRS* | Robert Chambers, *Popular Rhymes of Scotland* |
| *SS* | *Scottish Studies* |
| *TDGS* | *Transactions and Journal of the Proceedings of the Dumfries and Galloway Natural History and Antiquarian Society* |

# BIBLIOGRAPHIES AND NOTES

## FOLK LITERATURE
### Bibliography

Useful introductions to the study of folk literature are provided by the relevant chapters in works, all American, devoted to traditional culture in general: Jan Harold Brunvand, *The Study of American Folklore: An Introduction* (2nd ed.: New York, 1978), American and contemporary in orientation but a readable elementary entrée; Richard M. Dorson, ed., *Folklore and Folklife: An Introduction* (Chicago, 1972), a collection of essays, some excellent, on the genres, the theories, and the methodology; Alan Dundes, ed., *The Study of Folklore* (Englewood Cliffs, N.J., 1965), a collection of essays illustrating the varieties of scholarly concern and including some basic writings in the discipline; and Barre Toelken, *The Dynamics of Folklore* (Boston, 1979), which incorporates the behavioural and interactional emphases of much contemporary American folkloristics.

The texts and studies of Scottish tradition appear in widely scattered books and periodicals but the more recent material has been listed in the annual bibliographies, now discontinued, in *Scottish Studies*, and since 1970 in the 'Folk Literature' section of *The Bibliotheck's Annual Bibliography of Scottish Literature*, and the annual review 'The Year's Work in Scottish Literary Studies: Folk Literature' in the periodical of the Association for Scottish Literary Studies, initially *Scottish Literary News*, now *Scottish Literary Journal*.

Two earlier works devoted largely to examples of the genres of tradition are Robert Chambers, *Popular Rhymes of Scotland* (Edinburgh: 1st ed. 1826, 4th ed. 1870; Detroit, 1969), and *Miscellanea of the Rymour Club* which became the *Transactions* in the third volume (Edinburgh: I, 1911; II, 1919; III, 1928). Three of the pre-First World War publications of the Folklore Society cover Scottish regions: Walter Gregor, *Notes on the Folk-Lore of the North-East of Scotland* (London, 1881); George F. Black, *County Folklore III . . . the Orkney and Shetland Islands* (London, 1901); John E. Simpkins, *County Folklore VII . . . Fife, Clackmannan and Kinross* (London, 1914). A fourth, William Henderson, *Notes on the Folklore of the Northern Counties and the Borders*

227

(London, 1879) incorporates Scottish material derived from the Thomas Wilkie MSS. One of these regions receives a more recent treatment in Ernest Marwick, *The Folklore of Orkney and Shetland* (London, 1975). An invaluable complementary book for the study of folk literature is Alexander Fenton's *Scottish Country Life* (Edinburgh, 1976) which deals with the material culture of Scottish tradition. Periodicals containing Scottish folklore are *Tocher* (1971– ), *Scottish Studies* (1957– ), *Chapbook* (1964–9), and *Folklore* (1890– ), which was formerly *Folk-lore Journal* (1883– ) and before that *Folk-lore Record* (1878– ); for the Scottish material in this consecutive trio see the relevant index headings in Wilfred Bonser, *A Bibliography of Folklore as contained in the first eighty years of the Publications of the Folklore Society* (London, 1961) and *A Bibliography of Folklore 1958-1967* (London, 1969). Many local books and periodicals (Transactions of Field Clubs, etc.) incorporate the stories, songs, and speech of their region's traditional culture; there are too many to list even a tithe of them here, but the ascriptions of individual items in the anthology will supply a number of pointers. A useful source for the regional material is Arthur Mitchell and C.G. Cash, *A Contribution to the Bibliography of Scottish Topography* (Publications of the Scottish History Society, 2 ser., XIV, 2 vols, Edinburgh, 1917). In the following notes a work's bibliographical data is normally given in full only in the first reference and thereafter in short form.

## FOLK NARRATIVE

## Bibliography

The standard indexes referred to in the introduction are: Antti Aarne and Stith Thompson, *The Types of the Folktale* (2nd rev. ed.: Helsinki, 1961); Ernest Baughman, *Type and Motif Index of the Folktales of England and North America* (The Hague, 1966); and Reidar Christiansen, *The Migratory Legends* (Helsinki, 1958).

The best short introduction to the subject is Linda Dégh, 'Folk Narrative', in *Folklore and Folklife: An Introduction*, ed. Richard M. Dorson (Chicago, 1972), pp. 53–83. Max Lüthi's *Once Upon a Time* (Bloomington, Ind., 1976) provides a series of very readable essays for the newcomer. For long the basic book in English, Stith Thompson's *The Folktale* (New York, 1946) is still, more than thirty years on, very useful, though its historic-geographic emphasis needs to be seen, for full perspective, in the light of later methodological approaches. An excellent example of the contextualist approach that originated in part at least from the writings of the Swedish folklorist Carl von Sydow is Linda Dégh's *Folktales and Society: Story-telling in a Hungarian Peasant Community* (Bloomington, Ind., 1969). The structuralist approach appears at its most stimulating in a work whose age belies its modernity, Vladimir Propp's *Morphology of the Folktale* (1928; Austin, 1968). On legend, the best available book is *American Folk Legend: A Symposium*, ed. Wayland Hand (Berkeley, 1971).

Richard M. Dorson has acted as General Editor for the University of Chicago Folktales of the World series, which presents the narrative material of various national traditions, and he has also, drawing in part from these volumes, edited *Folktales Told Around the World* (Chicago, 1975) which offers a panoramic view of international folk narrative. Katharine M. Briggs, *A Dictionary of British Folktales* (4 vols; London, 1970-1) is a large storehouse of British folk narrative, exclusive of material in the Celtic languages. Narratives in Scots and Gaelic and English from the archives of the School of Scottish Studies have been appearing since 1971 in *Tocher*. Hannah Aitken's *A Forgotten Heritage* (Edinburgh, 1973) contains a perceptive choice of Scots language texts and Sir George Douglas's *Scottish Fairy and Folk Tales* (1893; Wakefield, 1977) a selection of stories mainly from nineteenth-century printed sources. From the earlier nineteenth century are the texts, taken from tradition or manuscript, in Chambers *PRS*, and in Peter Buchan, *Ancient Scottish Tales* (1908; Norwood, Pa., 1973) where the narratives have been comprehensively englished. A considerable amount of narrative material, especially legend, exists in local books and regional antiquarian journals.

## Notes

1  AT 425, *The Search for the Lost Husband*. No provenance given. Chambers, *PRS*, pp.95-9. Chambers prints another version, pp.99-101, 'The Red Bull of Norroway'. The tale-type is studied by Jan-Öjvind Swahn, *The Tale of Cupid and Psyche* (Lund, 1955).

2  AT 480, *The Kind and the Unkind Girls*. Fife. Chambers, *PRS*, pp.105-7. The tale-type is the subject of a historic-geographic monograph by Warren Roberts, *The Tale of the Kind and the Unkind Girls* (Berlin, 1958).

3  AT 500, *The Name of the Helper*. Dumfriesshire. Chambers, *PRS*, pp.72-5, from Charles Kirkpatrick Sharpe who gives it as heard from his nurse Jenny at Hoddam Castle. Edward Clodd looks at the tale-type for, in the manner of his time, evidence of primitive survivals in *Tom Tit Tot, an Essay on Savage Philosophy in Folktale* (London, 1898).

4  AT 500, *The Name of the Helper*. Wigtownshire. Walter Gregor, 'Preliminary Report on Folklore in Galloway, Scotland', Appendix III to the Fourth Report on the Ethnographical Survey of the United Kingdom, *Proc. Brit. Assoc. for 1896* (London, 1897), p.613. Obtained in 1895 from John Thomson, aged 70, a workman for Sir Herbert Maxwell in the parish of Mochrum. The contrast between this and the previous version of the tale-type illustrates the difference between a text which conveys the style and flavour of the actual narration and one, like this, which merely records the essentials of the narrative.

5  AT 501, *The Three Old Women Helpers*. No provenance given. Chambers, *PRS*, pp.76-7.

6  AT 510B, *The Dress of Gold, of Silver, and of Stars (Cap o' Rushes)*. Fife. Chambers, *PRS*, pp.66-70. A version from the Cinderella story-complex studied by Anna Birgitta Rooth, *The Cinderella Cycle* (Lund, 1951) and Marian Roalfe Cox, *Cinderella* (London, 1893). Behind the initial scene here, with its shadowy suitor, is in the norm of the tale-type as summarised by Aarne-Thompson the episode of 'the father who wants to marry his own daughter'. The implications of the incest theme for *King Lear*, which is based on a version of the Cinderella story, are discussed by Alan Dundes, ' "To Love My Father All": A Psychoanalytic Study of the Folklore Source of *King Lear*', *Southern Folklore Quarterly*, 40(1976), 353-66.

7  AT 560, *The Magic Ring*. Perthshire/Angus. *Tocher*, no. 23(1976), 266-75 and no. 24(1976), 320-3. Copyright School of Scottish Studies, University of Edinburgh, SA 1975/13/5-14/1 and SA 1975/200 B. Recorded in Montrose from Bessie Whyte, of Perthshire travelling stock, by Peter Cooke and Linda Headlee on 28 February 1975; passages between asterisks are supplied from a fuller version recorded by Alan Bruford at a ceilidh in Edinburgh on 29 November 1975. See *Tocher*, no.23, 249-76, for a feature on Bessie Whyte; see also her book *The Yellow on the Broom* (Edinburgh, 1979).

8  AT 2, *The Tail-Fisher*. Sutherland. Miss Dempster, 'The Folklore of Sutherlandshire', *FLJ*, 6(1888),249-50. Recorded from J. Macleod, fisherman, Laxford. This and the other stories in which the clever fox confronts the stupid bear or wolf are examined by Kaarle Krohn in the first historic-geographic study, *Bär (Wolf) und Fuchs* (Helsingfors, 1886).

9  AT 6, *Animal Captor Persuaded to Talk*. Sutherland. Dempster, pp.250-1. From J. Macleod.

10  AT 56, *The Fox through Sleight Steals the Young Magpies*. Sutherland. Dempster, p.251.

11  AT 62, *Peace among the Animals — the Fox and the Cock*. Sutherland. Dempster, p.250. From J. Macleod and D.M.

12  AT 124, *Blowing the House in*. Perthshire. Briggs, *Dictionary*, A2,572-3. Copyright School of Scottish Studies, University of Edinburgh. Recorded for the School of Scottish Studies from Bella Higgins, Blairgowrie, of a travelling family, by Hamish Henderson. This version shows in interesting fashion how the telling of a tale can reflect the culture from which it comes, in this case, that of the travellers.

13  AT 236*, (Tales with imitation of bird sounds.) Selkirkshire. James Cockburn, 'Border Folk-Lore', *Scottish Notes and Queries*, 4(1890-1), 152. Heard from an old man who was born and lived to manhood at Deuchar Mill in Yarrow.

14  The first episode is a very bald statement of AT 750B, *Hospitality Reward-*

*ed*; the second belongs to tale-types 780-789 *Truth Comes to Light* and may be provisionally assigned AT 783\*. Clackmannanshire. Simpkins, pp.246-7, from W.M. Metcalfe, *Ancient Lives of Scottish Saints* (Paisley, 1895). These stories of course can also be classed as saints' legends.

15 AT 922, *The Shepherd Substituting for the Priest Answers the King's Questions*. Perthshire. *Tocher*, no.21 (1976), 169-71. Copyright School of Scottish Studies, University of Edinburgh, SA 1955/37/1. Recorded in 1955 at Blairgowrie from John Stewart, a traveller, by Maurice Fleming. For a study of all Scottish versions, both in Scots and in Gaelic, see Alan Bruford, ' "The King's Questions" (AT 922) in Scotland', *SS*, 17(1973), 147-54. There is a feature on John Stewart and family in *Tocher*, no.21, 165-88.

16 AT 924, *Discussion by Sign Language*. Aberdeenshire. Neil Maclean, *Life at a Northern University* (Glasgow, 1874), pp.265-7. An international tale here localised in student tradition. Hugh Miller was acquainted with the story for he refers to 'the well-known story of the Professor of Signs and the Aberdeen butcher' in *Scenes and Legends of the North of Scotland* (Edinburgh, 1891 ed.), p.42.

17 AT 1137, *The Ogre Blinded (Polyphemus)*. Kirkcudbrightshire. Walter Gregor, 'Further Report on Folklore in Galloway, Scotland', Appendix I to the Fifth Report on the Ethnographical Survey of the Unted Kingdom, *Proc. Brit. Assoc. for 1897* (London, 1898), p.489.

18 AT 1291, *One Cheese Sent to Bring Back Another*, and AT 1291D, *Other Objects Sent to Go by Themselves*. Sutherland. Dempster, pp.168-9. This compilation includes besides the tales a number of numskull motifs: J1943 var. *Examining the sundial by candle-light;* J2066.7 *Dupe waits for rear wheels of wagon to overtake front wheels;* J2213.5.1 *More than twenty commandments;* J2466.3 *The long day;* J1784(a) *Man sees rabbit for first time.*

19 AT 1452, *Bride Test: Thrifty Cutting of Cheese*. Orkney. *Tocher*, no.1(1971), 31. Copyright School of Scottish Studies, University of Edinburgh. SA 1969/53/B6. Recorded from Mrs Ethel Findlater, Dounby, in 1969 by Alan Bruford.

20 AT 1562A, *The Barn is Burning*. Angus. Jean C. Rodger, *Lang Strang* (Forfar, n.d.), pp.45-6.

21 AT 1653F, *Numskull Talks to Himself and Frightens Robbers Away*. Aberdeenshire. *Tocher*, no.6(1972), 176-8. Copyright School of Scottish Studies, University of Edinburgh. SA 1959/15/A4. Recorded from Jeannie Robertson, Aberdeen, in 1959 by Hamish Henderson. There is a feature on Jeannie Robertson as a storyteller in *Tocher*, no.6, 169-78.

22 AT 1696, *'What Should I have Said (Done)?'*. Kirkcudbrightshire. J. Mathewson, *MRC*, II, 66-8.

23 AT 1735A, *The Bribed Boy Sings the Wrong Song*. Orkney. Alan Bruford, ' "The Parson's Sheep" ', *SS*, 14(1970), 88-9. Copyright School of Scottish Studies, University of Edinburgh, SA 1969/154/A2. Recorded by

Alan Bruford in 1969 from Gilbert Voy, aged 75, a native of Inganess in the East Mainland of Orkney who had spent fifty years in the Glasgow area.

24  Perthshire. C[hristina] R[obertson], *Dunning Folk Lore* (n.p., 1897), p.9.

25  Renfrewshire. *The Laird of Logan*, compiled by John D. Carrick, William Motherwell, and Andrew Henderson (new ed.: Glasgow, 1878), p. 143.

26  Kinross. Simpkins, pp.380-1, from David Beath, *The Bishopshire and its People* (Kinross, 1902).

27  Dumfriesshire. Recorded 25 March 1976 from R.C., a Dumfriesshire man, who can trace the story's telling back to a farm worker in the shire who told it to the factor of a neighbouring estate circa 1900.

28  Aberdeenshire. Recorded 20 August 1972 from Mrs J.G., Alford.

29  AT 1889B, *Hunter Turns Animal Inside Out*. Perthshire. [? Duncan Macara] *Crieff: Its Traditions and Characters* (Edinburgh, 1881), p.68. William Smeaton was well known locally as a tale-teller.

30  AT 1889L, *Lie: the Split Dog*. Perthshire. John Monteath, *Dunblane Traditions* (Stirling, 1835), pp.105-6. Like William Smeaton in Crieff, Bilzy Young, who died about 1800, had a local reputation as a tale-teller.

31  AT 1890D, *Ramrod Shot* plus series of lucky accidents. Angus. Alexander Lowson, *Tales Legends and Traditions of Forfarshire* (Forfar, 1891), p.90.

32  AT 1890F, *Lucky Shot*. Wigtownshire. Gordon Fraser, *Lowland Lore* (Wigtown, 1880), p.139.

33  AT 2014A, *The House is Burned Down*. Midlothian. Robert Chambers, *Minor Antiquities of Edinburgh* (Edinburgh, 1833), p.274.

34  AT 2034A var., *Mouse Bursts Open when Crossing a Stream*. Aberdeenshire. David Rorie, 'Stray Notes on the Folk-Lore of Aberdeenshire and the North-East of Scotland', *Folklore*, 25(1914),354. This kind of tale was a great favourite in the entertainment of children.

35  Perthshire. *Dunning*, p.4. The Dunning tower dates from the twelfth century.

36  Perthshire. James Kennedy, *Folklore and Reminiscences of Strathtay and Grandtully* (Perth, 1928), p.4. See also the saints' legends of no.14.

37  Perthshire. *Dunning*, pp.4-5. Brownies figure quite prominently in Scottish supernatural legends. Hogg utilises Border traditions about brownies imaginatively in *The Brownie of Bodsbeck*.

38  Clackmannanshire. J.C., 'Rhymes and Superstitions of Clackmannanshire, &c', *Scottish Journal of Topography, Antiquities, Traditions* (Edinburgh, 1848), II,275.

39  Perthshire. *Dunning*, p.5.

40  ML 6035 var., *Fairies assist a Farmer in his Work*. Clackmannanshire. Simpkins, pp.313-15, from J.C., *The Edinburgh Topographical Traditional and Antiquarian Magazine* (Edinburgh, 1848), 40-1.

41  ML 5080, *Food from the Fairies*. Dumfriesshire. John Corrie, 'Folk Lore of Glencairn', *TDGS*, 7(1890-1),77.

42 Perthshire. *Dunning*, pp.5–6.
43 Perthshire. *Dunning*, p.6. The story of the hare and the siller saxpence is one of the most common of Scottish legends; it is one manifestation of ML 3055 *The Witch that was Hurt*. 'Scoring abune the breath' was a practice for deactivating a witch's power in which blood was drawn from the upper part of the suspected witch's face.
44 Dumfriesshire. Corrie, p.76. This is a memorat, an account of a personal experience.
45 ML 3045, *Following the Witch*. Ayrshire. J. De Lancey Fergusson, *The Letters of Robert Burns* (Oxford, 1931), II,24. This story comes from the same letter to Captain Grose (no.401) in which Burns gives the two legends behind 'Tam o' Shanter', and is a version of the legend (found in a number of relatings throughout Scotland including a 1695 account from Moray) which inspired Hogg's 'The Witch of Fife'.
46 Aberdeenshire. William Watson, *Glimpses o' Auld Lang Syne* (Aberdeen, 1905), p.58. Another memorat.
47 Dumfriesshire. Corrie, p.78. An account of seeing a wraith.
48 Kincardine. Walter Gregor, *FLJ*, 2(1884), 378. Communicated to Gregor by Alexander Walker, Aberdeen. An example of a legend which validates belief, in this case belief about a folk medicine.
49 Perthshire. *Dunning*, p.10.
50 AT 1416, *The Mouse in the Silver Jug*. Perthshire. *Crieff*, pp.62–4. Here an international tale has attached itself to James V who in his persona of The Guidman o' Ballengeich is the subject of many legends on the King in Disguise theme. In Fife a version of AT 922 (see no.15) was told about King James and the Priest of Markinch.
51 Lanarkshire. Janet Hamilton, *Poems, Sketches and Essays* (new ed.: Glasgow, 1885), p.364. This story of Covenanting times and the other Janet Hamilton stories are examples of legends passed down within a family tradition. She lived in the village of Langloan, near Coatbridge.
52 Perthshire. Monteath, pp.18–19. These legendary anecdotes of the Battle of Sheriffmuir (13 November 1715) were handed down in the tradition of the district where the battle was fought.
53 Lanarkshire. Hamilton, pp.416–17.
54 Perthshire. Monteath, pp.29–30. Passed down in the tradition of the burgh of Dunblane.
55 Lanarkshire. Hamilton, pp.371–2. The famines were those of the years 1739 and 1740.
56 Invernesshire. *Legends of Badenoch* (5th ed.: Kingussie, 1965), pp.23–4. An out-of-the-ordinary pressgang legend.
57 Caithness. *Tocher*, no.3(1971),74. Copyright School of Scottish Studies, University of Edinburgh. SA 1971/257/A1 and SA 1969/48/B17. Recorded from Mrs David Gunn, John O' Groats, 1971. There are many Scottish legends dealing with illicit distilling and smuggling.

58 Dumfriesshire. James R. Wilson, 'Further Original Letters, &c, of the Burns period', *TDGS*, 7 (1890-1), 66. Taken down by Dr Grierson, Thornhill, in 1863 from Mrs Wallace, then aged 75 and widow of a Thornhill weaver. Mr Bacon was the proprietor of Brownhill Inn.

59 Angus. Lowson, pp.87-8. Told here as a personal anecdote about Tam Swankie is the international motif J2213.5.1 *More than twenty commandments* also attached to the Assynt man (no.18).

60 Aberdeenshire. Alex. McConnachie, *Bennachie* (Aberdeen, 1890), pp.61-2. This account of the local giant, and his counterpart on Tap o' Noth, has aetiological and hero tale motifs.

61 Perthshire. *Dunning*, pp.9-10.

62 Aberdeenshire. School of Scottish Studies Archives: SA/1961/40/A12. Copyright School of Scottish Studies, University of Edinburgh. Recorded from Geordie Stewart, Huntly, by Hamish Henderson. This legend of the musician who disappears underground occurs throughout Scotland and appears in Ireland, Wales, England, and North America; it seems to have some connection with the Celtic festival of Lughnasa. See David Buchan, 'The Legend of the Lughnasa Musician in Lowland Britain', *SS*, 23(1979), 15-37.

63 Lanarkshire. *Sunday Post*, 4 August 1968, p.16. This fortunate accident story has interesting links with tales by De Maupassant and Henry James.

64 Stirlingshire. Recorded from E.R., a student aged 20, 29 November 1976; told to her in March or April 1975 by an elderly man, a native of the Stirling area who said he knew the wife of the victim. In the commonest Scottish versions of the tale the couple are parked in a lovers' lane and the car won't start or it runs out of petrol and the boyfriend leaves to find some, instructing the girl not to leave the car for any reason. After a while she hears a tapping or banging which continues through the night, until headlights flash on the car and through a loudhailer she is told to run towards the lights without looking back. She runs, but looks back, and sees either the maniac banging her boyfriend's head on the car-roof or his body swinging from a tree against the car. This story, a variant of 'The Boyfriend's Death', is also related to 'The Hook', where the couple escape narrowly from the maniac; both types are discussed by Linda Dégh in *Indiana Folklore*, I (1968), 92-106, and 'The Hook' by Alan Dundes and Linda Dégh in their articles in *American Folk Legend*, ed. Hand.

65 Dunbartonshire. Recorded from J.D., a student aged 20, November 10 1976; told to her by a friend as having happened in Cumbernauld. Also reported as having happened in Aberdeen and Barnton, a suburb of Edinburgh. This story, as well as 'The Boyfriend's Death' and 'The Hook', are discussed by Jan Harold Brunvand in *The Vanishing Hitchhiker: American Urban Legends and their Meanings* (New York, 1981).

## 2 FOLKSONGS

# Bibliography

An excellent general anthology of Scottish folksong is Norman Buchan and Peter Hall, *The Scottish Folksinger* (Glasgow, 1973). Publications of folksong in the eighteenth century include David Herd, *Ancient and Modern Scottish Songs* (2nd ed.: 2 vols; Edinburgh, 1776) and James Johnson, *The Scots Musical Museum* (6 vols; Edinburgh, 1787-1803); Hans Hecht later edited *Songs from David Herd's Manuscripts* (Edinburgh, 1904). The early nineteenth century saw a remarkable series of books: Walter Scott, *Minstrelsy of the Scottish Border* (3 vols; Kelso and Edinburgh, 1802-3); Robert Jamieson, *Popular Ballads and Songs* (2 vols; Edinburgh, 1806); Charles Kirkpatrick Sharpe, *A Ballad Book* (Edinburgh, 1823); James Maidment, *A North Countrie Garland* (Edinburgh, 1824); William Motherwell, *Minstrelsy, Ancient and Modern* (Glasgow, 1827); George Ritchie Kinloch, *Ancient Scottish Ballads* (Edinburgh, 1827) and *The Ballad Book* (Edinburgh, 1827); Peter Buchan, *Ancient Ballads and Songs of the North of Scotland* (2 vols; Edinburgh, 1828). A considerable amount of material from this period remains inedited, though volume I of *Andrew Crawfurd's Collection of Ballads and Songs*, ed. E.B. Lyle (Edinburgh, 1975) has appeared and an edition of the Glenbuchat MSS is being prepared. In the twentieth century the field collecting of the Aberdeen-shire dominie Gavin Greig produced *Folk-Song of the North-East* (2 vols; Peterhead, 1909, 1914), a gathering of articles printed in the *Buchan Observer*, and *Last Leaves of Traditional Ballads*, ed. Alexander Keith (Aberdeen, 1925); in progress is the huge and highly desirable project of publishing the entire folksong MSS of Gavin Greig and his collaborator, Rev. J.B. Duncan. Collected folksongs appear also in *MRC*, John Ord, *Bothy Songs and Ballads* (Paisley, 1930), Peter Kennedy, *Folk Songs of Britain* (London, 1975), Ewan MacColl and Peggy Seeger, *Travellers' Songs from England and Scotland* (London, 1977), and, from the archives of the School of Scottish Studies, in *Tocher*.

The standard compilations of the ballad texts and tunes are Francis J. Child, *The English and Scottish Popular Ballads* (5 vols; Boston, 1882-98) and Bertrand H. Bronson, *The Traditional Tunes of the Child Ballads* (4 vols; Princeton, N.J., 1959-72). Anthologies of ballads are: G.L. Kittredge and H.C. Sargent, *English and Scottish Popular Ballads* (Cambridge, Mass., 1904), a condensation of Child; MacEdward Leach, *The Ballad Book* (New York, 1955); Albert Friedman, *The Viking Book of Folk Ballads* (New York, 1956), reprinted as *The Penguin Book of Folk Ballads* (Harmondsworth, 1977); William Beattie, *Border Ballads* (Harmondsworth, 1952), selected from Border tradition; and David Buchan *A Scottish Ballad Book* (London, 1973), selected from Northeast tradition.

D.K. Wilgus gives an illuminating account of much twentieth-century writing on folksong in *Anglo-American Folksong Scholarship since 1898* (New Brunswick, N.J., 1959). Useful starting-points for British material are Cecil Sharp, *English Folk Song: Some Conclusions* (London, 1907), and A.L. Lloyd, *Folk Song in England* (London, 1967). There exists, unfortunately, no introductory book on Scottish folksong, but Francis Collinson has a general chapter in *The Traditional and National Music of Scotland* (London, 1966) and Thomas Crawford includes folksong in his admirable study of the song culture of eighteenth-century Scotland, *Society and the Lyric* (Edinburgh, 1980), which has a complementary anthology, *Love, Labour and Liberty* (Cheadle, 1976). Innovative articles on Burns and folksong by Mary Ellen B. Lewis are: ' "The Joy of my Heart": Robert Burns as Folklorist', *SS* 20(1976), 45–67; 'Some Uses of the Past: The Traditional Song Repertoire of Robert Burns', in *Folklore Today*, eds Linda Dégh et al. (Bloomington, Ind., 1976), pp.325–33; and 'What to do with "A Red Red Rose": A New Category of Burns's Songs', *Scottish Literary Journal*, 3(1976), 62–75.

Two books about traditional narrative song in America, G. Malcolm Laws, *Native American Balladry* (rev. ed. Philadelphia, 1964) and *American Balladry from British Broadsides* (Philadelphia, 1957) provide classification schemes which are extensively used by students of British folksong; a companion volume, Tristram P. Coffin, *The British Traditional Ballad in North America* (new ed., with supplement by R. Renwick: Austin, Tex., 1977) documents the recordings of the classical ballads. Broadsides are dealt with by Leslie Shepard, *The Broadside Ballad* (London, 1962) and Claude M. Simpson, *The British Broadside Ballad and its Music* (New Brunswick, N.J., 1966). The bothy songs have received recent attention from: David Kerr Cameron, *The Ballad and the Plough* (London, 1978); Hamish Henderson, 'The Bothy Ballads', *Journal of Peasant Studies*, II(1975), 497–501; and Bob Munro, 'The Bothy Ballads', *History Workshop*, no.3(1977), pp. 184–93.

The classical ballads have habitually attracted more notice than the other genres of folksong and have consequently an extensive bibliography. Basic works are Gordon H. Gerould, *The Ballad of Tradition* (Oxford, 1932) and M.J.C. Hodgart's lucid handbook *The Ballads* (2nd ed.: London, 1962). William Entwistle supplies a panoramic survey in *European Balladry* (2nd impr.: Oxford, 1951) and David Buchan discusses the regional tradition of Northeast Scotland and oral composition in *The Ballad and the Folk* (London, 1972). Bertrand Bronson investigates the music in *The Ballad as Song* (Berkeley, 1969) and Lowry C. Wimberly the folk belief in *Folklore in the English and Scottish Ballads* (Chicago, 1928). Three recent collections of papers are: *The European Medieval Ballad*, ed. Otto Holzapfel (Odense, 1978), *Ballad Studies*, ed. E.B. Lyle (Cambridge, 1976), and *Ballads and Ballad Research*, ed. Patricia Conroy (Seattle, 1978).

Studies of modern singers include: Herschel Gower, 'Jeannie Robertson: Portrait of a Traditional Singer', *SS*, 12 (1968), 113–26; H. Gower and James

Porter, 'Jeannie Robertson: The Child Ballads', *SS*, 14 (1970), 35–58, 'Jeannie Robertson: The "Other" Ballads', *SS*, 16 (1972), 139–59, 'Jeannie Robertson: The Lyric Songs', *SS*, 21 (1977), 55–103; Ailie Munro on Jeannie Robertson's daughter in 'Lizzie Higgins and the Oral Transmission of the Child Ballads', *SS*, 14 (1970), 155–88; Hamish Henderson, 'Willie Scott', *Tocher*, no.25 (1977), pp. 33–48; James Porter, 'The Turriff Family of Fetterangus', *Folk Life*, 16 (1978), 5–25.

Hamish Henderson provides valuable discographies in 'Scots Ballad and Folk-Song Recordings', *Scottish Literary News*, I (1971), 42–51, and 'Scots Folk Song – a Selected Discography', in *Tocher* from no.25 onwards.

# Notes

*Songs of Custom*

1 Shetland. *Tocher*, no.20 (1975), 142–3. Copyright School of Scottish Studies, University of Edinburgh, SA 1975/168/A5. The tune and stanza 1 were recorded from Miss Mary Smith, Elvister, Walls, in 1975 by Alan Bruford, and the remaining stanzas taken from a manuscript copy written in her youth. Alan Bruford notes 'the Smith family used to sing this in neighbouring houses when they were children, though the custom of men going round singing it was otherwise forgotten by then locally'.

2 Aberdeenshire. *Banffshire Journal*, 12 November 1889, p. 6; letter from J.F., Corgarff, headed 'Folk-lore in Strathdon'. For an account of New Year's Day thigging see also Gregor, *North-East*, pp. 160–2.

3 *Herd's MSS. Songs*, pp. 200–1. The song is related to the Christmas-New Year seasonal custom of imprisoning a wren and carrying it round the community. Scottish traces of the custom are recorded for nineteenth-century Galloway in the 'deckan o the wran' ceremony, but it is well documented elsewhere; see, for example, Trefor M. Owen, *Welsh Folk Customs*, 3rd ed. (Cardiff, 1974), pp. 63–8, which includes variants of the song in Welsh.

4 Aberdeenshire. Buchan and Hall, pp. 146–7. From Lottie Buchan, Peterhead. A.L. Lloyd, commenting that 'a remarkable number of folk ritual songs have survived in twentieth-century England', discusses this and 'The Hunting of the Wren' as 'formerly ceremonial' songs which 'become harmless social entertainments' in *Folk Song in England*, pp. 93–7.

5 Selkirkshire. James Hogg, *The Mountain Bard* (1807), pp. 13–14, from the recitation of his mother. See also Richard L. Greene, *The Early English Carols*, 2nd rev. ed. (Oxford, 1977), pp. 196–7, 423–7.

6 Ross and Cromarty. Donald A. Mackenzie, 'Cromarty Dialects and Folk-Lore', *TRC*, III, 81–2.

*Work Songs*

7 *The Complaynte of Scotland*, p.40. This sixteenth-century shanty for the weighing of the anchor is followed in the *Complaynte* by one for the unfurling of the sails.

8 *Herd's MSS. Songs*, pp. 190-2. This 63 line song (here excerpted) was sung by oyster-dredging fishermen, but similar gallimaufries were sung by other workers. See Francis Collinson, 'The Oyster Dredging Songs of the Firth of Forth', *SS*, 5 (1961), 1-17.

9 Aberdeenshire. (a) Donald R. Farquharson, *Tales and Memories of Cromar and Canada* (Chatham, Ontario, n.d.), p. 35, heard from 'nonagenarian Willie Ley, last survivor of' the pre-iron plough days; (b) R.M. Lawrance, *TRC*, III, 187.

10 Aberdeenshire. Joseph Robertson MSS (1829-32), p. 98.

11 Shetland. E.S.R. Tait, 'Songs and Lullabies', *Shetland Folk Book*, I (Lerwick, 1947), 51; noted down by Mrs E.J. Smith, Schoolhouse, Sandness, from her mother's singing.

12 Borders. Eve B. Simpson, *Folk Lore in Lowland Scotland* (London, 1908), p. 203; the moss-trooper's conditioning began early.

13 Shetland. Tait, p. 50; noted down in Bressay by Mrs E.J. Smith. $2^4$ 'refers to the movement of the wheel over the floor, owing to the action of the treadle. The wheel has sometimes to be pulled back to the spinner.'

*Lyric Songs*

14 *Herd's MSS. Songs*, pp. 98-9. A traditional relative of Burns's 'Red, Red Rose'.

15 *Herd's MSS. Songs*, pp. 100-1. A traditional relative of Burns's 'The Lea-Rig'.

16 Shetland. *MRC*, I, 179-80; learned by A. Briggs Constable, W.S., from John Henderson of Spiggie, Dunrossness, in 1885.

17 Allan Ramsay, *The Tea-table Miscellany* (Glasgow, 1768 ed.), I, 231-2. This song has connections with the classical ballad 'Jamie Douglas' (Child 204).

18 Aberdeenshire. Herschel Gower and James Porter, 'Jeannie Robertson: The Lyric Songs', *SS*, 21 (1977), 70-1. Copyright School of Scottish Studies, University of Edinburgh. SA 1955/154/B8. Recorded from Jeannie Robertson by Hamish Henderson in 1955.

19 Aberdeenshire. Buchan and Hall, p. 69. As sung by Jeannie Robertson.

20 Perthshire. A fragment recorded from Sandy Watt, a retired farmworker, Glenfarg, 18 April 1978, by Sheila Douglas. This, like the previous, demonstrates the fresh and healthy eroticism to be found in traditional song. Thomas Crawford (*Society and the Lyric*, p. 123) quotes from Duncan McNaught's 1911 Introduction to *The Merry Muses* a

six-line version then current in Ayrshire.

21 *Herd's MSS. Songs*, p. 114.
22 *Herd's MSS. Songs*, p. 112.


*Humorous Lyrics*

23 Borders. Lady John Scott MSS, NLS MS 835, p. 115.
24 Dumfriesshire. Sharpe (1823), pp. 16-17.
25 *Herd's MSS. Songs*, p. 111.
26 *Herd's MSS. Songs*, p. 110.


*Comic Songs*

27 Lanarkshire. *MRC*, II, 100. A fragment from Crawfordjohn (1820-30) supplied by Dr Knight, Uddingston.
28 Borders. Lady John Scott MSS, NLS MS. 835, p. 59.
29 Perthshire. Charles Kirkpatrick Sharpe, *A Ballad Book*, ed. David Laing (Edinburgh, 1880), pp. 44, 137. From 'the late Mr Drummond of Strageth'.
30 Aberdeenshire. Jamieson Brown MS, Appendix, pp. iv-v; sent by Professor Robert Scott, King's College, Aberdeen, to Robert Jamieson, 9 June 1805. The action of this absurd comic song would seem to bear some relation to customs discussed by E.C. Cawte in *Ritual Animal Disguise* (Cambridge, 1978). '&' is silently expanded throughout.
31 Moray. *Tocher*, no. 2 (1971), 58-9. Copyright School of Scottish Studies, University of Edinburgh, SA 1952/30/B4. Recorded from James Bowie (Blin Jimmy), Elgin, by Hamish Henderson in 1952.
32 Wigtownshire/Renfrewshire. *Crawfurd's Collection*, I, 182-3. Taken down by Crawfurd from John Smith, a tailor, in the 1820s.


*Narrative Songs*

33 Borders. Frank Miller, 'The Macmath Song and Ballad MS.', *TDGS* (1925), 100-1. Macmath found this version in the papers of the eighteenth-century collector, John, Duke of Roxburghe.
34 Moray. Jamieson, II, 240-2. Learned by Jamieson when a boy in Moray, 'before', as he stresses, 'the Poems of Burns were published'; he prints besides in a composite text from two sources a related song, 'Allan o' Maut'.
35 Kirkcudbrightshire. 'Macmath MS', pp. 96-8. Originally written down by John Murray, shepherd at Knocknarling, in the parish of Kells, on paper watermarked 1823.
36 Aberdeenshire. Murison MS, pp. 30-2.

37 Moray. Peggy Seeger and Ewan MacColl, *The Singing Island* (London, 1960), p. 89. From Jimmy McBeath, Elgin.

*Broadsides*

38 Laws N11. Orkney. *Tocher,* no. 26 (1977), 85-6. Copyright School of Scottish Studies, University of Edinburgh. SA 1970/229/A4. Recorded from James Henderson and Jock Dass, singing together, by Alan Bruford in 1970.
39 Laws L18. Aberdeenshire. Ord, pp. 384-5.

*Occupational Songs*

40 Angus. *MRC*, I, 39-40. Recorded by George B. Gardiner from Mr Spence, hairdresser, Brechin, the melody being noted by Mr Hollingworth, an organist there.
41 Lady John Scott MSS, NLS MS 835, p. 23.
42 Fife. Recorded from Jock Breen, retired miner, Valleyfield, 22 March 1972, by Jill Goldy; he learned it in France during the First World War from a Glaswegian, Barney Kearnin.
43 Laws K21. Orkney. *Tocher*, no.26 (1977), 90-1. Copyright School of Scottish Studies, University of Edinburgh. SA 1967/117/A3. Recorded from John Halcro in 1967 by Alan Bruford.
44 Argyll. *Tocher*, no.3 (1971), 80-1. Copyright School of Scottish Studies, University of Edinburgh. SA 1952/156/4. Recorded from Willie Mitchell, Campbelltown, by J.S. Woolley in 1952; 'High Drumayes' may refer to a stallion that then travelled Kintyre.

*Various Song-Kinds*

45 Lanarkshire. *MRC*, I, 123. Collected in the district of Crawford by Rev. Wm C. Fraser.
46 Lanarkshire. *MRC*, I, 123. Collected in the district of Crawford by Rev. Wm C. Fraser.
47 Sharpe (1823), pp. 24-7.
48 Midlothian. *MRC*, I, 206. From B.J. Home, Edinburgh.
49 Aberdeenshire. *MRC*, II, 108. From Annie Shirer, Mintlaw.

*Classical Ballads*

50 Child 36. Aberdeenshire. 1802-3. The Old Lady's MS. The only text ever recorded of this transformation ballad.
51 CH 37. Argyll. *Tocher*, no. 27 (1977), 175-8. Copyright School of Scottish Studies, University of Edinburgh. SA 1977/147/B3. Recorded from Duncan Williamson, a Kintyre traveller, by Mrs Linda Headlee William-

son, 28 July 1977. A splendid example of the way in which the travellers
have nurtured to the present day songs which were otherwise last recorded in Scotland in the early nineteenth century.

52  CH 79A. West Lothian. Scott, *Minstrelsy*, II (1802), 111; from an old
woman living near Kirkhill.

53  CH 19. Shetland. Patrick Shuldham-Shaw, 'The Ballad "King Orfeo" ',
*SS*, 20 (1976), 125-6. This text was taken down at Gloup fishing station in
1865 by Bruce Sutherland of Turfhouse, North Yell, and printed in the
*Shetland News* of 25 August 1894. The relationship of the ballad variant of
the Orpheus story to the medieval romance 'Sir Orfeo' has been made
clearer by the discovery of a sixteenth-century text of the Scottish
romance 'King Orphius'; see Marion Stewart, 'King Orphius', *SS*, 17
(1973), 1-16.

54  CH 14. Midlothian. Frank Miller, 'The Mansfield Manuscript', *TDGS*, 3
ser., 19 (1933-5), 71-2. The MS was compiled by Elizabeth St Clair in
Edinburgh between 1770 and 1780.

55  CH 15/16. Fife. Helena Mennie Shire, ed., *Poems from Panmure House*
(Cambridge, 1960), pp. 13-19. This, one of the two oldest Scottish ballad
texts, was written into his Music Commonplace Book by Robert
Edwards in Fife about 1630.

56  CH 63Bb. Aberdeenshire. Alexander Fraser Tytler Brown MS. This
version was recorded from Mrs Anna Brown in 1800, seventeen years
after her Ba version, with which it can be instructively compared.

57  CH 64H. Borders. Abbotsford MSS: Scotch Ballads, Materials for
Border Minstrelsy; in the handwriting of William Laidlaw, 'from Jean
Scott'.

58  CH 58B. Herd's MSS. It can be reasonably argued that this is the oldest
historical ballad-story in Scottish tradition, dealing with events of the late
thirteenth century. See Knut Liestøl, 'Den skotske ballad "Sir Patrick
Spens" ', *Arv*, 4 (1948), 28-49.

59  CH 163. Aberdeenshire. Bronson, *Tunes*, III, 123-4. Copyright School of
Scottish Studies, University of Edinburgh. Sung by Jeannie Robertson.
Collected by Hamish Henderson and transcribed by Francis Collinson.
The battle took place in 1411 and the ballad is discussed in David Buchan,
'History and Harlaw', *Ballad Studies*, pp. 29-40.

60  CH 184. Dumfriesshire. Tom Wilson, 'Memorials of Sanquhar Churchyard', *Dumfries and Galloway Courier and Herald* 6 August 1910; from a
MS provided by T.B. Stewart of Pennyland from the papers of his
great-grandfather, William Johnston, the Laird of Roundstonefoot. It
recounts some Border pastimes of 1593 involving the feuding Johnstons
of Wamphray and Crichtons of Sanquhar.

61  CH 178. Clackmannanshire. Simpkins, pp. 341-3; taken down from an
old woman in the mid-nineteenth century. Reported as sung by the

people of Dollar at the end of the eighteenth century about the local Castle Campbell. The story derives from events in the Aberdeenshire feud between the Gordons and the Forbeses that included the 1571 burning of Corgarff Castle. The murdered chatelaine, wife of John Forbes of Towie, was Margaret Campbell, whose surname probably led by association to the localization of the story at Castle Campbell in Clackmannan.

62 CH 21. Aberdeenshire. From the Glenbuchat MSS (King's College, Aberdeen) which were collected by the local minister at the beginning of the nineteenth century; discussed in David Buchan, 'The Maid, the Palmer, and the Cruel Mother', *Malahat Review*, no. 3 (1967), 98-9. Religious ballads are none too common in Scottish tradition but this story is based on the meeting (John IV) of Christ and the Woman of Samaria, who is here fused with Mary Magdalen.

63 CH 3. Invernesshire/Oklahoma. Ethel and Chauncey O. Moore, *Ballads and Folk Songs of the Southwest* (Norman, Okla., 1964), pp. 11-12; copyright 1964 by the University of Oklahoma Press; recorded from James McPherson, born in Inverness about 1861, who moved when a boy to Ohio and then to Oklahoma. Normally classed as a riddling ballad, the story involves a wit-combat (between boy and Devil) rather than the solution of riddles proper. This version exemplifies how the songs and the other genres of Scottish folk tradition were carried abroad by generations of Scottish emigrants. In the Moores' volume there are no fewer than twenty ballad texts of verified Scottish derivation.

64 CH 281. Renfrewshire. *Crawfurd's Collection*, pp. 64-6. Recorded 12 December 1826 from Mary Macqueen, Mrs Storie, who emigrated to Canada in 1828. The story of this comic ballad is found in a fourteenth-century fabliau.

## 3  FOLKSAY

## Bibliography

The standard work in the area has been for long Archer Taylor, *The Proverb and Index to the Proverb* (1931, 1934; Hatboro, Penn., 1962), which can be supplemented by his *Selected Writings on Proverbs*, ed. Wolfgang Mieder (*FFC* no.216; Helsinki, 1975); Taylor also provides a concisely packed introduction to the subject in the entry under 'Proverb' in Maria Leach, ed., *Standard Dictionary of Folklore* . . . (New York, 1949). A seminal article for the study of proverbs as communication is E. Ojo Arewa and Alan Dundes, 'Proverbs and the Ethnography of Speaking Folklore', *American Anthropologist*, 66(1964), Special Publication No.6 Part 2, eds John Gumperz and Dell

Hymes, 70–85. Other modern considerations are to be found in the journal *Proverbium* (edited from Helsinki) in such articles as Nigel Barley, 'A Structural Approach to the Proverb and Maxim', 20(1972), 737–50, and ' "The Proverb" and Related Problems of Genre Definition', 23(1974), 880–4 Ágnes Szemerkényi, 'A Semiotic Approach to the Study of Proverbs', 24(1974), 934–6, and Alan Dundes, 'On the Structure of the Proverb', 25(1975), 961–73.

Scotland possesses quite a wealth of folksay compilations, though relatively little in the way of analysis of the material. The major works are: M.L. Anderson, ed., *The James Carmichaell Collection of Proverbs in Scots* (Edinburgh, 1957) (material from the early seventeenth century); Erskine Beveridge, ed., *Fergusson's Scottish Proverbs* (STS 2 ser 15; Edinburgh, 1924) (texts of 1598 and 1641); Chambers *PRS*; Andrew Cheviot, *Proverbs, Proverbial Expressions, and Popular Rhymes of Scotland* (Paisley, 1896); Alexander Henderson, *Proverbs of Scotland* (Edinburgh, 1832); George Henderson, *The Popular Rhymes, Sayings, and Proverbs of the County of Berwick* (Newcastle, 1856); Alexander Hislop, *The Proverbs of Scotland* (3rd ed.; Edinburgh, 1870); James Kelly, *Collection of Scottish Proverbs* (London, 1721); *MRC*; Allan Ramsay, 'A Collection of Scots Proverbs', *Works*, V(1972), eds Alexander Kinghorn and Alexander Law. A modern local collection, Alexander Fenton, 'Proverbs and Sayings of the Auchterless and Turriff Area of Aberdeenshire', *SS*, 3(1959), 39–71, contains a valuable and extensive bibliography, which includes full references to the other early (sixteenth- and seventeenth- century) collections of Bannatyne, Blau, Fortescue, and Maxwell. Bartlett J. Whiting draws together scattered material in 'Proverbs and Proverbial Sayings from Scottish Writings before 1600' in *Mediaeval Studies* 11(1949), 123–205 and 13(1951), 87–164. W.F.H. Nicholaisen, who has produced the excellent *Scottish Place-Names* (London, 1976), has also investigated names and naming in a traditional context in 'Place-Name Legends: An Onomastic Mythology', *Folklore*, 87(1976), 146–59. A trove for folksay of course is the *Scottish National Dictionary* whose editor, David Murison, discusses 'The Scots Tongue – The Folk-Speech' in *Folklore*, 75(1964), 37–47.

The basic compendium of riddles is *English Riddles from Oral Tradition* (Berkeley, 1951) by Archer Taylor, who also compiled *A Bibliography of Riddles* (FFC no.126; Helsinki, 1939). For riddles in ballads and folktales see Child, passim, and Thompson, *The Folktale*, pp.156–63. Scottish riddles appear in folksay books already mentioned, such as Chambers *PRS* and *MRC*, and often in regional books and articles. Two relatively recent articles of considerable interest are: Calum I. Maclean and Stewart F. Sanderson, 'A Collection of Riddles from Shetland', *SS*, 4(1961), 150–86, and Kenneth S. Goldstein, 'Riddling Traditions in Northeastern Scotland', *JAF*, 76(1963), 330–6.

# Notes

I   Proverbs and Sayings: Cromar. From Donald R. Farquharson, *Tales and Memories of Cromar and Canada* (Chatham, Ontario, n.d.), pp. 208-14. He describes it as 'a list of Proverbs and sayings in common use in the District of Cromar in Aberdeen-shire, Scotland in the middle of the 19th century, as recalled by [his] late sister Betty (Mrs F.B. Stewart) and members of her family' (p.208).

IIa Folk Speech: Fife Mining. Condensed from David Rorie, 'The Mining Folk of Fife' in Simpkins, pp.397-407.

IIb Folk Speech: Border Gypsy. From C.K. Moore, 'Rhymes and Sayings', *MRC*, II, 198-9.

III Minor Genres: Rhymes.

A   1 *MRC*, II, 169. Stirlingshire. From the Rev. W.B. Dempster of Slamannan.

    2 R. DeB. Trotter, *Galloway Gossip: the Stewartry* (Dumfries, 1901), pp. 127-8. Kirkcudbrightshire. A taedstane is a kind of stone once believed to have come from the heads of very old toads which was held to have special – magical or curative, for instance – properties.

    3 Eve B. Simpson, *Folk Lore in Lowland Scotland* (London, 1908), p.151.

    4 Simpson, p.163.

    5 Cheviot, p.165.

    6 Jeannie M. Laing, *Notes on Superstition and Folk Lore* (Brechin, 1885), p.86.

    7 *MRC*, II, 142. Angus.

    8 Trotter, p.77. Kirkcudbrightshire.

    9 Gregor, *North-East*, p.197.

    10 *MRC*, II, 153. This is a parodic prayer which could also be classed as a blason populaire. For examples of prayers (one thirty lines long, the other eleven) used by a late sixteenth-century wise woman of Keith in Lothian see Chambers, *PRS*, pp.345-7.

    11 *MRC*,II,143. Fife and the Lothians.

    12 *MRC*,I,172. Angus: Arbroath.

    13 Gregor, *North-East*, p.110. Aberdeenshire.

    14 George Watson, 'Annual Border Ball-games', *Trans. Hawick Archaeological Soc.* (1922), p.7. Roxburghshire.

    15 Trotter, p.60. Kirkcudbrightshire.

    16 Chambers, *PRS*, p.382.

    17 Cheviot, p.292.

    18 *MRC*,I,89. East Lothian.

    19 From an entry in the Broughton House Museum Register, kindly supplied by Mr T.R. Collin, Hon. Curator, Broughton House, Kirkcudbright.

    20 *MRC*, I,238. Angus: Forfar.

21 *MRC*,I.168. Midlothian: Edinburgh.
22 Recorded from E.L., a former ploughman, aged 85, Middlebank, by Dunfermline, 8 July 1976. A rhyme similar to the first four lines occurs in a version of AT 500 from the west of England (Briggs, *Dictionary* AI,219).
23 Beveridge, p.71.
24 Simpson, p.169.
25 Jean C. Rodger, *Lang Strang* (Forfar, n.d.), p.33.
26 M.M. Banks, *British Calendar Customs: Scotland*, II (London, 1939), 46-7, quoting D. MacRitchie, *Scottish Review* (21 December 1905).
27 Marwick, p.96, quoting from J. Jakobsen, *An Etymological Dictionary of the Norn Language in Shetland* (1928-32), I,cxvi-cxvii.
28 Trotter, p.442. Kirkcudbrightshire.
B 1 *MRC*, I,122. Lanarkshire: Crawford.
  2 Recorded from E.L., a former ploughman, aged 85, Middlebank, by Dunfermline, 8 July 1976.
  3 Lowson, p.145. Angus.
  4 Cheviot, pp.317-18.
  5 Cheviot, p.287.
  6 Simpkins, p.348. Clackmannanshire.
  7 *MRC*, II,44. Midlothian: the Pentland Hills district beyond Balerno.
  8 MacEdward Leach, 'Superstitions of South Scotland from a Manuscript of Thomas Wilkie', *Folklore International*, ed. D.K. Wilgus (Hatboro, Penn., 1967), pp.122-3.
  9 *MRC*, I,174.
IV Riddles. All the riddles come from the Southwest. Most derive from John Corrie, 'Folk Riddles' and 'Glencairn Folk Riddles', *TDGS*, 8(1891-2), 81-5 and 13 (1896-7), 115-22, but nos 40 and 42 are from Frank Miller, 'The Macmath Song and Ballad MS' in the same journal (1925), 108-9, and nos 7,8,16 are from Joseph Laing Waugh, 'Dumfriesshire Rhymes', *TRC*, III, 102-3, and nos 15,34,38 from J. Matthewson, 'Rhyming Riddles from Kirkcudbrightshire', *MRC*,II,90.

4 FOLK DRAMA

## Bibliography

An account of the basic British material is to be found in E.C.Cawte, A. Helm, and N. Peacock, *English Ritual Drama. A Geographical Index* (London, 1967), while E.C. Cawte *et al.*, 'A Geographical Index of the Ceremonial Dance in Great Britain', *Journal of the English Folk Dance and Song Society*, 9(1960), 1-41, and E.C.Cawte, *Ritual Animal Disguise* (Cambridge, 1978) provide comparable services for related areas of traditional custom.

Books on folk drama include Herbert Halpert and G.M. Story, eds, *Christmas Mumming in Newfoundland* (Toronto, 1969), Alan Brody, *The English Mummers and their Plays* (London, 1971), E.K. Chambers, *The English Folk-Play* (Oxford, 1933), which develops his much earlier treatment of the subject in *The Mediaeval Stage* (2 vols; Oxford, 1903), and R.J.E. Tiddy, *The Mummers' Play* (Oxford, 1923). Related dramatic traditions are discussed by Alan Gailey, *Irish Folk Drama* (Cork, 1969), and Leopold Schmidt, *Le Théâtre populaire Européen* (Paris, 1965). Relevant articles are Margaret Dean-Smith, 'The Life-Cycle Play or Folk Play', *Folklore*, 69(1958), 237-53 (the first advancing of the Life-Cycle Theory), Roger Abrahams, 'British West Indian Folk Drama and the "Life-Cycle" Problem', *Folklore*, 81(1970), 241-65, and Susan Pattison, 'The Antrobus Soulcaking Play: An Alternative Approach to the Mummers' Play', *Folk Life*, 15(1977), 5-11 (see also Sue Pattison and Tony Green, *Soulcaking at Antrobus*, Leeds, 1976, a booklet accompanying the University of Leeds film of the same name). A comprehensive investigation of traditional drama in chapbooks undertaken by M.J. Preston, M.G. Smith, and P.S. Smith has resulted in *An Interim Checklist of Chapbooks Containing Traditional Play Texts* (Newcastle, 1976), and *Chapbooks and Traditional Drama . . . Part I: Alexander and the King of Egypt Chapbooks* (Sheffield, 1977).

The Scottish texts are listed in Cawte, Helm, and Peacock, pp.66-7, and the most accessible are to be found in Chambers, *PRS*, pp.169-81 (Peebles text, fragments from Falkirk and the West of Scotland, and the Papa Stour Sword Dance ceremony), Simpkins, pp.142-6 (Fife text), and Andrew Cheviot, *Proverbs . . . of Scotland* (Paisley, 1896), pp.169-73 (Borders text). The subject has received rather thin coverage. Anna J. Mill's *Mediaeval Plays in Scotland* (Edinburgh, 1927), pp.9-35, though written fifty years ago, still provides the starting point; F.M. McNeill, *The Silver Bough*, III(Glasgow, 1961), 81-8, has a brief discussion, while A.L. Taylor correlates memories and fragments entertainingly in 'Galatians, Goloshen, and the Inkerman Pace-Eggers', *Saltire Review*, 5(1958), 42-6. More recent writings are J. Braidwood's review of Cawte, Helm, and Peacock in *SS*, 14 (1970), 94-6, David Buchan, 'The Folk Play, Guising, and Northern Scotland', *Lore and Language*, 1:10(1974), 10-14, and M.J. Preston, M.G. Smith, and P.S. Smith, 'The Peace Egg Chapbooks in Scotland', *The Bibliotheck*, 8:3(1976), 71-90. M.M. Banks, *British Calendar Customs: Scotland* (3 vols; London, 1937-41) provides the background of related folk custom.

# Notes

1 The Roxburghshire play is from Thomas Wilkie, 'Old Rites, Cerimonies and Customs of the Inhabitants of the Southern Counties of Scotland' (c. 1815) NLS MS 123, printed by kind permission of the Trustees of the

National Library of Scotland. I have regularized the punctuation and capitalization in the commentary and silently expanded the contraction '&' throughout. The Wilkie MSS came into the possession of James Hardy, secretary of the Berwickshire Naturalists' Club, and after his death two unpublished versions of the folk play found among his papers were used by James Fleming Leishman in compiling his composite text (*A Son of Knox*, Glasgow, 1909, pp.103-16), but he took very few lines from the text printed here. The peculiar first line of the commander's speech probably relates to a line in a Fermanagh text, 'We'll act the young, we'll act the age' (Gailey, p.54).

2 The Stirling play is from James Maidment, ed., *Galations, An Ancient Mystery* (Edinburgh, 1835), reprinted as 'The Guisers in Stirling', *Stirling Antiquary*, I(1893), 67-9; it was taken from 'the manuscript of the late James Lucas' and was recorded c. 1815. A.L. Taylor notes that 'an elderly gentleman recalled for me a performance of the play in which he took part sixty years ago in Stirling [i.e. c. 1898, five years after the local printing of the text]. It was Hogmanay and nearly twelve o'clock. As it was a fine moonlight night, the proceedings took place outside and the population of a large tenement building came out to see them. The players were drawn up in a semi-circle with the open end towards the spectators, rather like a formation of the Salvation Army. As each character spoke his entry lines, he marched round in a circle. The combat was a stately exchange of sword-blows, rather than an exhibition of fencing and there was no horse-play. The line spoken by the Doctor, 'Rise up, Jack, and sing!' and the song which followed were the only words actually recalled by this witness, who was very young at the time and had not been honoured by a speaking part' (p.44).

3 The Sword Dance Ceremonial. Sir Walter Scott in his diary for 7 August 1814 records an account he heard in Scalloway of the sword dance 'still practised in the Island of Papa' (J.G. Lockhart, *The Life of Sir Walter Scott*, 1837, III, 162), though the first published version occurs in Samuel Hibbert, *A Description of the Shetland Isles* (Edinburgh, 1822). Folk drama scholars habitually refer to 'the 1821 text' as if Scott's version appeared in the first edition of *The Pirate*, but in fact it was not published until Scott composed the Notes for the *Magnum Opus* edition (1831). This version (the one printed here) was transcribed from a MS copied from 'a very old one' by William Henderson jun., of Papa Stour, about 1788. The ceremony consists, first, of individual dances from the Seven Champions of Christendom (St James, St Dennis, St David, St Patrick, St Anthony, St Andrew) led and introduced by St George of England who delivers all the lines in monologue, and then of the 'Figuir', the collective dance. Brody summarizes succinctly (p.160) the relationship of the ceremony to the Sword Dance Play: 'The Papa Stour Ceremony contains the Calling-on Song, the circle of linked dancers and the formation of the Lock as features

in common with other sword ceremonies. It lacks the death, the resurrection, the accompanying clowns and we can infer no mimetic action at all from the text.' Brody discusses the problems raised by the Scott text (to which can be added that of the status of its very literary English language in this Norn-speaking 'remote island') and concludes that it is 'a curious mixture of folk ceremony and imposed literary explanations. It seems likely that the "Words" of the Papa Stour text as we have them from William Henderson's version were literary creations.' The ceremony is discussed in detail by Alfred W. Johnson, 'The Sword-Dance. Papa Stour, Shetland', *Old-Lore Miscellany*, 5(1912), 175-85, and Ivor Allsop, 'The Sword Dance of Papa Stour – Shetland', *Folk Music Journal*, 3:4 (1978), 324-42.

An interesting 1633 account of a sword dance (but not a sword dance play) appears in the records of the Perth Glovers, a craft which performed for Charles I on 15 June in the garden of Gowrie House: 'his Majestie's chair being sett upon the wall next to the Tay, whereupon was ane flatt stage of timber, clead about with birks, upon the which, for his Majestie's welcome and entry; thirtein of our brethren of this our calling of Glovers, with green caps, silver strings, reid ribbons, white shoes, with bells about their leigs, schering rapers in their hands, and all other abulziment, danced our sword dance, with many difficult knotts and allafallajessa, five being under and five above upon their shoulders; three of them dancing through their feet; drink of wine and breaking of glasses about them (which, God be prased,) wis acted and did without hurt or skaith to any, – which drew us to great charges and expences, amounting to the sum of three hundred and fifty merks (yet not to be remembered), because wee was graciouslie accepted be our Sovereign and both estates, to our honour and great commendation' (George Penny, *Traditions of Perth*, Perth, 1836, p.322).

# GLOSSARY

Where there exists only a minor difference in sound and spelling between the Scots and the English no gloss has been thought necessary; for example, doon/down, lang/long, muir/moor, mune/meen/moon, wha/who.

a, aa, aw *all*
a *have*
aafae, affa *very, awfully*
a'body *everybody*
abulziment *garments*
abune, aboon, abeen *above*
adee *to be done*
ae *one; only; of*
afore *before*
agley *off the straight; unsuccessfully*
ahint, ahin *behind*
aiblins *perhaps*
aik *oak*
ail *trouble, afflict*
ain *own*
aince *once*
airn, ern *iron*
airt(s) *direction, parts*
ajee *awry*
aleen, alane *alone*
allafallajessa *? footwork*
amaist *almost*
an *and; if; one*
aneath *beneath*
anent *concerning*
ankyr *anchor*
aperit *appeared*
ark *large wooden chest (for meal, etc.)*
ase *ash*

athegither *altogether*
a'thing *everything*
atower *across, outside*
atweel *indeed, truly*
atween *between*
auchteen *eighteen*
aught (for – I ken) *all*
auld, aald, aal, aul *old*
auld-farrant *old-fashioned*
ava *of all, at all*
Averile *April*
awyte *assuredly*
aye *always; one; yes*
ayont *beyond*

back end *the close of the year, or of a season; autumn, winter*
baggit *with a big belly; pregnant*
bairn, n., v. *child; get with child*
bairn-time (a good – ) *a numerous litter*
bane *bone*
bannock, bannick *girdle-cake*
barm *yeast*
bawbee *halfpenny*
bead *both*
beadle *church officer*
begood *began*
begunk *cheat, disappoint*

bellises  *bellows*
ben  *within; through*
ben-end  *the better room of a two-room house*
bente  *coarse grass that grows near the sea*
bere  *coarse barley*
besom  *broom*
bicker  *wooden beaker*
bide (bade, baid, bidden)  *stay, wait; reside; suffer*
big  *build*
bike  *nest of wild bees*
billie  *fellow*
bin  *bind;curse*
bing  *heap*
binna  *be not*
birk  *birch*
birr  *whir*
birse  *bristle*
birse (set up someone's –)  *rouse someone's anger*
blackfit  *lovers' go-between*
blae  *bluish*
blaen  *sore, pustule*
blaes  *marks left on the skin by illness or wounds*
blashy  *rainy, gusty*
blaw  *blow;boast*
bleed, blude, bluid  *blood*
bleert  *bleared*
bock  *retch*
bode  *foretell*
body, buddy  *person*
bogle  *supernatural creature*
boll  *an old dry measure*
bookin  *getting larger*
boor  *bower, parlour*
bore  *crevice, hole*
boun, boon  *bound (for), ready to start*
boustresslie  *boisterously, roughly*
boutree, bourtree  *elder-tree*
box-bed  *enclosed bed*

brace  *chimney-piece*
brae  *hillside*
braid  *broad*
bran  *husks of grain separated from the flour after grinding*
brander  *gridiron*
braw  *handsome, handsomely dressed*
bree, broo  *brow*
breeks  *trousers, breeches*
breet  *brute*
bress  *brass*
brig  *bridge*
brokit  *with black and white stripes*
broo  *broth; brow*
brose  *oatmeal dish, variously prepared*
browst  *brewing*
browster-wife  *ale-wife, brewer*
bud  *had to*
buffit-stool  *stool with sides*
bun  *bound*
burn  *stream*
bus, buss  *bush*
bushel  *vessel (used as bushel measure)*
busk  *dress*
but an, but than  *and also*
butt, ben  *the two rooms of a two-roomed cottage*
butter-saps  *oatcake or wheaten bread soaked in melted butter and sugar*
byre  *cattle shed*

ca  *call; keep in motion; work; drive*
caa  *movement*
cadger  *travelling hawker (esp. of fish); lowly person*
callant  *lad, stripling*
canel  *candle*
cannie  *cautious*
cantrips  *tricks; frolics*
cap, cappy  *(drinking-) cup*
carle, carl  *fellow*
carline  *old woman*

carriet ('Can dee' is easy –) *a skill is easily carried about with you*

caudron *cauldron*

cauf *calf*

caul, cauld *cold*

chack *clack*

chamber day *master bedroom, parlour*

channer *scold fretfully*

chap *knock*

chattle *rattle; ? gnaw*

chaumer *ploughman's bedding place*

cheild, chiel *man*

chess *cut portion of apple or pear*

claes *clothes*

claith *cloth*

clap *stroke*

clashes *tales*

clatter *chatter loudly*

claw *scratch*

cleadin *clothing*

cleekit *clutched*

clekit, cleckin *hatched, hatching*

clink *strike, jingle*

cloots *clothes, rags*

close *narrow alley; farmyard*

cock *prick up; wear jauntily*

cock-a-leekie *soup made of a fowl boiled with leeks*

contramawcious *obstinate, perverse*

coo, koo *cow*

coorie, cour *crouch, cower*

corbie *crow, raven*

cote *cottage*

couthy, coothy *kind, agreeable; comfortable*

cow down *surpass*

crabbit *cross-grained, peevish*

crack, n., v. *conversation; converse*

craig *throat, neck*

cramasie *crimson*

crap *crop; stomach*

crater *creature*

creel *basket*

creesh *grease*

crook *twist*

crooks *chain and hook from which pots, etc. hung over the fire*

croon *low*

crouse *proud; brisk*

crowdie *thick oatmeal gruel, used for food in general; a kind of soft cheese*

cruik-saikle *saddle for supporting panniers*

cruisie *lamp using animal oil and rushes*

cruket *crooked*

cruse *proud; conceited; brisk*

cry *call, summons*

cuddy *donkey*

curchie *curtsy*

cushie doo *wood-pigeon*

cuttie *short*

cutty-stool *stool of repentance in church*


da *the*

dae *do*

daes't *dazed*

daff *sport*

daft *foolish, giddy*

dambrod *draught-board*

dane, deen, dune *done*

daunder *stroll, saunter*

daunted *discouraged*

dauntingly *courageously*

daw *dawn*

dawtie *pet, darling*

de *the*

deave *deafen*

dee, de *die; do*

deid *dead; death*

deil, deel *devil*

deil-drum *melancholy*

dener *dinner*

deuds *deeds*

dicht *wipe*

251

ding, pa, p. dang *beat*; (neut. pass.)
  *be shifted*
dinnae *don't*
dirket *stabbed with a dagger*
dis *this*
div, dis *do, does*
dochter *daughter*
docken *dock plant*
docket *with tail cut short*
doo *dove, pigeon*
door-cheeks *door-posts*
doot *doubt*
dottled *in dotage*
doun-lyin *birth-time*
doup *bottom or end of anything*
downa *am unable*
dron brat *apron worn behind*
drookit *drenched*
drooth, drouth *drought*
dross *coal-dust*
drucken *drunken*
drummelt *stupefied*
du *thou*
duds *(shabby) clothes*
dulefu' *doleful*
dumfoondered *dumbfounded*
dunt, n., v. *blow; strike*
dwain *faint*
dwine *waste away*
dyke *wall*

echty *eighty*
ee, een, eyne, ees *eye(s)*
een, en *end*
een, ene *one*
e'en *evening, eve*
eese *use*
eident *steady, continual*
eilton *? Eildon*
ell *old measure of length*
Elleree *person of preternatural insight*
eneuch *enough*
enoo *just now*
ewe-bught *sheep-pen*

ey *aye, always*

fa *fall; who*
fack *fact*
fae *from; foe*
faelie *made of turf sods*
faid *feud, quarrel*
fan, fen, fin, whin *when*
fan, faun *found*
far *where*
farer, farrer *further*
farra *bring forth pigs*
fashes *troubles*
fashious *troublesome*
Fasternseen *Shrove Tuesday*
fat *(used of soil) rich, fertile*
fatt, fat *what*
fauld *(sheep-) fold; shelter*
fecht *fight*
fee, v. *engage as servant, esp. for*
  *half-yearly terms*
feel *fool*
feere *draw the first furrow in*
  *ploughing*
feid *enmity*
fell *keen*
fen *when*
fendin *means of subsistence*
fentlins *faintly, imperceptibly*
ferlie *marvel, wonder*
fess, fesh *fetch*
file *foul*
fin *when; find*
fit *foot*
fit, fat, whit *what*
flech *flea*
flee *fly*
fleeching *cajolery, flattery*
fleyed *afraid*
flig *scare*
flinder *splinter*
flit *shift a tethered animal from one*
  *place to another; remove from one*
  *house to another*

flobbery  *slipshod*
fluff  *puff, slight explosion*
flyte  *scold, quarrel*
fog  *moss*
foggy bee  *small yellow humble-bee*
follow  *fellow*
foo  *how; drunk*
fool  *foul*
forbye  *as well*
forenicht  *earlier evening; between twilight and bedtime*
forlorn  *destroyed*
fornent  *opposite, facing*
forren  *foreign*
forret, forrit  *forward*
foslin  *wheezing*
fosser  *mat of rushes placed on a horse to prevent the skin being fretted*
fou  *drunk*
fouks, fowk, fock  *people*
four-oories  *light meal*
fozie  *stupid*
frae, fae  *from*
freen  *friend; relative*
freit  *superstitious belief, saying, or rite*
fremit  *unrelated by blood; foreign*
fricht  *fright*
fu  *full; drunk*
fun  *whin, furze*
further, v.  *prosper*
fush  *fetched*
fushionless  *powerless*
fyle  *soil*

gaber reel  *a sprightly dance-air*
gad  *goad*
gae  *go, gave*
gaed, gaid  *went*
gaet  *way*
gaire, gare  *triangular piece of cloth inserted in a garment; gusset*
galland  *young fellow*
gallimaufry  *hotch-potch*

gan  *began*
gane  *gone, went*
gang, gyang, gan, ging  *go*
gar, gaur  *make*
gaun (-ie)  *going (to)*
geer, gear  *goods, cattle*
geet  *child*
gentie  *genteel*
gerse  *grass*
gett  *child*
gey  *as in 'gey roch', pretty rough*
gie, gee (gien, gine, gied)  *give*
gif  *if*
gin  *if; by*
girdle  *circular iron plate for baking*
girsy  *interspersed with grass*
give (Folksong 55)  *grant, and/or if*
glaiket  *giddy, senseless, silly*
glaur  *mud*
glebys  *lands*
gless  *glass*
glint  *glimpse*
glowes  *gloves*
glowr  *intent scowl*
glunchy  *bad-tempered*
gnap  *snatch at*
goud, gowd  *gold*
gowk, gouk  *cuckoo*
gran, grane, grain  *groan*
gree  *agree*
greet, grat  *cry, cried*
grozit buss  *gooseberry bush*
grumph  *grunt, grumble*
grun  *ground*
gryse  *pig*
guesses  *riddles*
guid, gude, guide  *good*
guide  *treat*
guiser, gysart  *mummer*
gully-knife  *large knife*
gumption  *common sense*
gut  *rheumatism*
gutcher  *grandfather*
gweed, gueede  *good*

gyaun  *going*

ha  *hall; have*
had, haud  *hold*
hae  *have*
hafflins  *half, partially*
hail  *haul*
hail  *whole; hale*
hailt (hairt, hilt) or hair  *any particle*
hain  *preserve, save*
hairen  *made of hair*
hale  *whole*
haly  *holy*
hamely  *familiar, friendly*
hantle  *a large quantity, a number*
hap  *cover*
happity  *lame*
hash  *work at speed and under strain*
haud  *hold; keep*
haudin  *holding*
haveless  *slovenly*
heather-bleat  *snipe*
hecklepins  *steel teeth of a comb for dressing flax and hemp*
heely  *slowly and steadily*
heich  *high*
heid  *head*
hem, hame  *home*
hempie  *wild girl; rogue*
henchbane  *haunch-bone*
herry  *plunder*
hert-fricht  *'heart-fright'*
hesp  *hank of yarn*
het  *hot*
heuch  *deep glen*
heugh  *cry — in dancing*
hie  *high*
High Drumayes  *ref. perhaps to a stallion*
hin  *hind*
hinch  *haunch*
hinna  *have not*
hinner en (i the –)  *in the end*
hireman  *hired servant, farm labourer*

hirple  *limp*
hissel  *himself*
hizzie  *housewife, hussy, lass*
hoast  *cough*
hodden  *coarse homespun*
hoor  *hour*
horse-couper  *horse-dealer*
hou  *hollow*
houlet  *owl*
howe  *hollow, dale*
howket, howcked  *dug*
hugger  *purse*
hunner  *hundred*
hurdies  *buttocks*
hus  *us*

ilka; ilkane:  *each, every; each one*
ill  *evil; unkind; hard; difficult*
ill-gaeted  *having bad habits*
ill-willy  *bad-tempered, disobliging*
in  *an; and; if*
ingin  *onion*
ingle-cheek  *fireside*
ingle neuk  *chimney corner*

jad, jaud  *jade, lass*
jaw  *wave; chattering talk*
jeely jars  *jam jars*
jimp  *slender, neat*
jinker  *a wag*
jo  *sweetheart*
jokus  *fond of a joke*
jouk  *jink, swerve*

kail, kale  *borecole; cabbage; vegetable soup*
kail-yard  *vegetable plot*
kaim, kemb, kame, keam  *comb*
kebbick  *a whole cheese*
keek  *peep*
kelpie  *supernatural water-horse*
kemp  *strive*
ken  *know*
kenel, ken'le  *kindle*

kent   *long pole*
kep, keep   *catch*
kerryin   *carrying*
kettle   *large pot*
kick   *show off*
kinna   *kinds of*
kintra   *country*
kirking   *ceremonial kirk attendance for, e.g., the first time after a wedding, birth, or funeral*
kirkyaird   *churchyard*
kirn   *churn*
kirn   *meal-and-ale; harvest home*
kist   *chest*
kitchie   *relish; something spread on oatcake or bread*
kitlen   *kitten*
knockin'-stane   *large flat stone where linen was beaten*
kye   *cattle*

lad-bairn   *boy*
lae   *leave*
laif   *rest*
lailly, layle   *loathly*
laird   *lord; heritor*
lairdship   *lordship, property*
lane   *alone*
lang-nebbed   *'long-nosed', difficult to understand*
langsyne   *long ago*
lassock   *young girl*
lap   *jumped*
lat   *let*
lat ower   *swallow, tolerate*
lauch, leugh, leuch   *laugh*
lav'rock, laverock, laverick   *lark*
least   *laced*
leather   *ladder*
lee   *lie; grass-land*
leed   *song, language*
lee-lang   *livelong*
Leerie   *cock*
leesin   *falsehood*

leevin   *living*
leil   *true*
lesse   *lace*
lest   *pleased*
leugh   *low; laugh*
ley, lee   *grass-land*
ley-rigg   *ridge of unploughed grass between arable ridges*
licht   *light*
lichtsome   *pleasant, trifling*
lick   *beat*
lift   *sky*
lilt   *sing softly; sing briskly*
limmer   *malevolent person, scoundrel*
lintie   *linnet*
lint-swinglings   *beatings by which flax is separated*
lint-wheel   *spinning-wheel*
lippen   *trust*
lock   *a small quantity*
loe, loo   *love*
loffie   *small loaf*
loon   *boy; rascal; loose woman*
loose   *louse*
loot, lute   *let*
loup   *jump*
lout, loot   *bend down, bow*
lug   *ear*
lugged like   *with ears like*
luggie   *wooden pail*
lum   *chimney*
lunder   *heavy blow*
lyne, lyin   *lain*

machrel   *mackerel*
made up at   *annoyed at*
maen   *moan*
mair, may   *more*
maligrumph   *fit of spleen*
malysone   *curse*
mane, maun, man   *must*
mary   *maid (of honour)*
marynalis   *sailors*
masel   *myself*

255

maut  *malt*
mawkin  *hare*
meat  *food*
meat-heal  *having a healthy appetite*
meddle  *hurt; assault*
meer  *mare*
meikle  *greatly; large*
mend  *alter*
men't  *mended*
merk  *a money of account with value, originally, of 13s. 4d. Scots*
merls  *measles*
merrit  *married*
mess  *dish, meal*
mickle, mikle, muckle  *much; great*
midden  *dunghill*
mider, mither  *mother*
millband  *belting for wheels*
mim-mou'ed  *affectedly proper*
mind (on)  *remember*
mirk  *dark*
misca  *speak ill of*
missel pin  *pin which fits into the iron loop at the front of the plough's beam to which the draught is attached*
mister  *need, requirement*
molligrumphs  *stomach-ache*
morrne, morn  *morrow, morning*
moss  *peat-bog*
mou, moo  *mouth*
muck  *clean out an animal's quarters*
muckle  *much; large*
muckle-mou'ed  *large-mouthed*
muskin  *mutchkin (¼ pint Scots)*
mutch  *woman's cap*
myre-snipe  *snipe*

nae  *no; not*
naebody  *nobody*
naig  *stallion*
neb  *nose*
ne'rday  *New Year's Day*
nerels  *chicken-pox*
newsed  *talked over the news*

nicht, nycht  *night*
niest, neist  *next*
nieve  *fist*
nocht  *nothing; not*
nor  *than*
nowt  *cattle*
noy  *grief*

ocht  *aught, anything*
onbekent  *unknown*
ongauns  *goings-on*
oniewey  *anyway*
'oo  *wool*
or  *before*
ousen  *oxen*
owre, ower  *over; too*
owreladen  *weighed down*

pa, pall  *fine cloth*
paich  *groan*
paily  *feeble*
pairt  *part; divide*
partricks  *partridges*
pat  *pot; put*
patten  *overshoe*
pawky  *shrewd, roguish*
pech  *pant*
peck  *a large quantity*
peck  *find fault with*
peeck  *'notorious' (Hecht)*
peer, puir  *poor*
peerie  *little*
peeseweep  *lapwing*
penny waddin  *wedding at which the guests contributed for their own entertainment*
pent  *paint*
pey  *pay*
pick  *find fault with; pilfer; gouge*
pick  *pitch*
pickle  *handful; particle*
pike, pyke  *pick (bare)*
pillar  *platform in church where sinners stood on Sundays for penance*

pin  *fill; stop a hole; fasten*
pinch  *belly*
pine  *pain*
pintle  *penis*
pip  *term used for various diseases*
pirm  *pirn; amount of yarn wound on a pirn*
plaet  *plaited*
play  *boil with force*
plenish  *furnish*
pleuch, plew  *plough*
pliskie  *prank, trick*
pock, poke  *sack, bag*
poor  *power*
pooshion  *poison*
poother  *powder*
porte  *lively tune on the bagpipe*
pou, pu  *pull*
pouch  *pocket*
pow  *head*
pownie  *pony*
prat wi  *meddle with*
preef  *proof, testing*
preein  *tasting*
preen  *pin*
pu  *pull*
puddock  *frog*
puttit  *knocked over, butted*
pyoke  *sack, bag*

quater  *quieter*
queel  *cool*
queen  *lass*
queets (oot o the –)  *with ankles harmed by fashionable footwear*
quhen  *when*
quin  *queen*

raches  *scenting dogs*
raip  *rope; rope of straw or hay made on the farm*
ramfeezl'd  *confused*
ram-stam  *headstrong*
randy  *reckless person, loose woman*

range  *heather scrubber for cleaning pots*
ranting  *roistering, romping, revelling*
raper  *small sword used in sword dances*
rashes  *rushes*
ravel  *wind; tangle*
rax  *reach*
redd up  *clear up*
red lan  *ploughed land*
reek  *smoke*
reel  *spinning-wheel*
reid  *red*
reipit  *searched thoroughly*
reive  *rob, pillage*
richt, rycht  *right; (v. heal)*
rig  *raised strip of ploughed land*
riggin  *rafters of a house*
roan  *illness of some kind*
roch  *rough*
rock  *distaff*
room ye roun  *make room by moving round*
roon  *round*
roostie  *rusty*
rotten  *rat*
rout  *belching*
rout  *make a loud noise*
row  *wrap; roll*
rowan  *mountain ash*
ruit  *root*
rumble  *knock about*
rung  *cudgel; staff*
ryve  *burst*

sa, sau  *salve*
sacran bell  *small bell rung to summon parishioners or to mark points in the service*
sae  *so*
saelins  *silence*
sain  *bless; shield from evil influences*
sair  *sore, sorely*
sal, sall  *shall*

257

sald  *sold*
samyn  *same*
sane, sin  *since*
san pock  *sand-bag*
sant  *saint*
sark  *shirt*
saugh-bush  *willow*
saut  *salt*
scaith  *harm*
scale  *disperse*
scaud  *scabbed*
schering  *shearing*
sclate  *slate*
scoor  *scour*
scorn  *shame, humiliation*
scraich, schreech  *screech*
scrythe  *crowd, large number*
scunner  *dislike, disgust*
seed  *saw*
seen  *soon*
ser's  *serves*
session  *the elders of a Presbyterian congregation in session*
set  *suit*
shank  *handle, shaft*
shank  *travel on foot*
sharger  *smallest of the litter; weakly child; person of stunted growth*
shead  *sheath*
sheen, shoon  *shoes*
sheugh  *ditch; ravine*
shill  *shrill*
shillin  *grain freed from the husk*
shouther  *shoulder*
shuin, sune, seen  *soon*
sib  *blood-kin, intimate*
sicken, sick  *such*
sicker  *firm; (of bargain) hard; sure, reliable*
side  *wide, long*
siller, sillert, sillar  *silver; money*
simple  *poor*
sin  *since; son*
sinon  *sinew*

skaeth (gien the –)  *done a wrong*
skail  *leak; let out; spill*
skaith  *harm*
skeely woman  *a 'wise woman'*
skeer'd  *scared*
skep  *hive*
skirl  *shriek*
skraigh o' day  *dawn*
skug  *shade*
skule, schule  *school*
slash  *rush*
sma  *small, subtle*
smeddum  *good sense*
smoor, smore  *smother*
sna'ba  *snowball*
snapper  *stumble*
sneck  *door-latch*
sned  *lop, prune*
snirt  *laugh in a suppressed way, sneer*
snod  *make neat and tidy*
snüddin'  *winding*
sober  *in poor condition*
socht  *asked for; sought*
sodger  *soldier*
soo  *sow*
soom  *swim*
soon  *sound*
soor  *sour*
sorn  *sworn*
souing  *sounding*
souter  *shoemaker*
spang  *speed; spring*
speed  *give success to*
speen  *spoon*
speer  *ask*
spill, spilt  *spoil, spoiled*
splaes  *having splay feet*
spotch  *seek*
spulzie  *plunder*
spunk  *splinter, match*
spurtle  *stirring-rod; a spattle for turning bread*
sta  *stole; stall*
staibler  *man appointed by hunters to*

*keep a station*

stang *pole*

stannin *standing*

stappit *stepped*

stark *strong*

steen, stane *stone*

steer, steir *rudder*

stell *put in a stell (sheep-shelter)*

stey *steep*

stick *butcher, kill*

stid *steed*

stirk *steer; yearling calf*

stock *the non-wheel part of a spinning wheel*

stoiter *stagger*

stoond *throbbing ache*

stoot *stout, well-built*

stour, stoor *dust*

stour *robust*

stra'd *strewn*

strae, stray *straw*

stripe *small stream*

strucking 'oor *a whole hour by the clock*

succer-bread *sugared bread*

sud *should*

suit *sweet*

sun'er *separate*

sweer, sweere *lazy; reluctant*

sweerie *box or basket for holding bobbins of yarn*

sweerty *sloth*

swerf *swoon*

swope *struck rhythmically, as in using a scythe*

syke *ditch, trench*

syne *then*

tackets *hobnails*

tae *to; toe*

tae, tane . . . tither *the one . . . the other*

taen, tain *taken, taking*

taid *toad*

takin' ta them (Folk wi' lang noses are aye – ) *assuming anything critical said refers to them*

tane *taken; one*

tangs *tongs*

tap *top*

tass *? conflation of tate (lock of hair) and chess (strap, jess)*

tate *lock of hair*

tattie *potato*

teem *empty*

teended *troubled*

tell *till, to*

telt, tell't, tauld *told*

tentlins *gently, carefully*

tesment *last will; testament*

teuch *tough*

thacket *thatched*

thae, they *pl. of that*

than *then*

thees *thighs*

thig *beg; borrow; solicit gifts on certain occasions*

think lang *grow weary*

thocht *thought*

thon *that*

thraw *twist; throw; shape*

thrawn *stubborn, ill-humoured, perverse*

thrawn sang *nonsense song*

tick *dot*

tilt *(till it) to it*

timber-stairs *steps leading up to the pillory or stool of repentance in a church*

time till't (an –) *not before time*

timmer *wooden*

tine *lose*

tint (tak – o) *take care of*

tinte *loss*

tirl (at the pin) *rattle (at door-fastening or early form of knocker)*

tither *the other; tether*

259

to *toe*
tocher *dowry*
tod *fox*
tod and the lambs, the *game played with wooden pins on a perforated board*
toom *empty*
toun, toon, town *hamlet, farm*
tow *let down with a rope*
trapse *assert positively*
treed *thread*
trig *spruce, neat*
troo *through*
trow *believe; assure you*
tryst, n. *rendezvous; betrothal; journey undertaken by those pledged to travel together*
tryst, v. *betroth*
twal *twelve*
twine *twist; spin*
tyke *dog; (playfully) child*
tyne *lose*

ugsome *horrible*
unco, adj., adv. *uncommon, extraordinary; very*
unshemly *unseemly*

vaguing *wandering*
vance *prob. vaunt*
vattir *water*
veynd *wind*
vitht *with*
vogie *cheerful*
vrang *wrong*

wa, waa *wall*
waas *ways*
wad, wid *would*
wad *wager; forfeit*
wae *woe*
wal, wall *well*
waly *exclamation of sorrow*
wame *belly, stomach*

wan *one; won; wand*
wan *dark-coloured; colourless*
wance *once*
wap-tow *cord connecting the treadle and the axle of a spinning wheel*
war, waur *worse*
war *were*
wardly *worldly*
wardle, warl *world*
wark *work*
wasie *way*
wat *know; assure*
wat thooms *wet thumbs (to seal a bargain)*
we, wi *with*
wean *child*
webster *weaver*
weed *clothing*
weel-faured *handsome, well-favoured*
weird *prophesy, predict*
wer *our*
werrocks *bunions*
wey *way*
whang *slice, large piece*
wheen *quantity*
whiles *sometimes*
whilk *which*
whim-whams *fancy trifles*
whin *furze; when*
whip *run quickly*
whit, whut *what*
whorl aff *strip off*
whummle *upset*
wid *mad; wood; would*
widen *wooden*
wiffie *wife*
wight *strong, lively*
wile *desire*
while awa *while away pleasantly*
win *when*
win *wind*
win, won, in, up *get in, up*

winna  *will not*

wir  *our*

wist  *know, known*

wony  *windy*

worry o  *balk at; choke over*

wraith  *spectral apparition of a living person*

wud  *mad; wood*

wun  *win*

wuss  *wish*

wut  *know*

wyte  *blame; fault*

yeard-fast  *fixed firmly in the earth*

yeel  *Christmas, Yule*

yese  *you*

yestreen  *last night*

yett  *gate*

yill  *ale*

yin  *one*

yird  *earth*

yitt  *gate*

yon  *that, those*

yowe  *ewe*

yt  *that*

# AFTERWORD AND ACKNOWLEDGMENTS

Between the completion of the manuscript and its going to press a number of useful books have been published. Among the more outstanding are: in general, Edward J. Cowan, ed., *The People's Past* (Edinburgh, 1980), Billy Kay, ed., *Odyssey* I and II (Edinburgh, 1980 and 1982), and John MacTaggart, *The Scottish Gallovidian Encyclopaedia* (1824; Old Ballechin, Perthshire, 1981); in Folk Narrative, Alan Bruford, ed., *The Green Man of Knowledge* (Aberdeen, 1982), and Herbert Halpert, ed., *A Folklore Sampler from the Maritimes* (St John's, 1982) (for 'A Bibliographical Essay on the Folktale in English', pp. 36–106); in Folksong, Patrick Shuldham-Shaw and Emily Lyle, eds, *The Greig-Duncan Manuscripts*, vol. I (Aberdeen, 1981); in Folksay, David Murison, *Scots Saws* (Edinburgh, 1981); and in Folk Drama, Alex Helm, *The English Mummers' Play* (Woodbridge, Suffolk, 1981).

The manuscript of the book was compiled on two continents and I pay tribute to the willing professionalism of typists on both sides of the Atlantic, to Miss Margaret Prentice and Mrs Kathy McLintock in Stirling, and to Mrs Cindy Turpin in St John's. For their good offices in connection with the book I thank Ms Julia Bishop, Dr Ian Campbell, Mr Murray Charters and Dr Donald Cook. To Memorial University of Newfoundland I am indebted for a Vice-President's Research Grant for July 1980. For the boons and benefits of unstinted friendship I owe much to Emeritus Professor Herbert Halpert of St John's, Mr Andrew Noble of Fraserburgh, and Drs Douglas and Diana Wilson of Denver.

For permission to reprint or print material I am grateful to a number of people and institutions: to Sheila Douglas (Folksong no.20); Jill Goldy (Folksong no.42); Dr Helena Mennie Shire (Folksong no.55); Aberdeen University Library (Folksong no.62); the Houghton Library, Harvard University (Folksong nos 10, 30, 36);

Jas Johnstone & Son (Folk Narrative no.56); the Trustees of the National Library of Scotland (Folksong nos 23, 28, 41, 55; Folk Drama no.1); the University of Oklahoma Press (Folksong no.63); the Council of the Scottish Text Society (Folksong nos 32, 64); the School of Scottish Studies (Folk Narrative nos 7, 12, 15, 19, 21, 23, 57, 62; Folksong nos 1, 18, 38, 43, 44, 51, 59); and the Shetland Folk Society (Folksong nos 11, 13).

# INDEXES

## TYPE-INDEX: NARRATIVE

## TYPE-INDEX: NARRATIVE SONGS

| Type no. | No. in Folk Narrative section | Type no. | No. in Folksong section |
|---|---|---|---|
| CH 3 | 63 | CH 79 | 52 |
| CH 14 | 54 | CH 163 | 59 |
| CH 15/16 | 55 | CH 178 | 61 |
| CH 19 | 53 | CH 184 | 60 |
| CH 21 | 62 | CH 281 | 64 |
| CH 36 | 50 | | |
| CH 37 | 51 | | |
| CH 58 | 58 | Laws K21 | 43 |
| CH 63 | 56 | Laws L18 | 39 |
| CH 64 | 57 | Laws N11 | 38 |